The Washington Cookbook

"A Tasteful Tour of the Nation's Capital"

The Herb Cottage at The Washington Cathedral

Cover design and illustrations
by Lily Spandorf

The Washington Opera
John F. Kennedy Center for the Performing Arts
Washington, D.C.

A new cookbook to benefit The Washington Opera—what a happy combination of delicious gastronomy and euphonious harmony! My congratulations to the Women's Committee for conceiving and bringing this concept to fruition. There is a genuine affinity between haute cuisine and The Washington Opera which, under the direction of Chef Martin Feinstein and his extraordinary staff, has mixed exceptional talent with carefully selected ingredients of music, drama, scenery and costume, simmered the melange to a turn on the grill of painstaking rehearsals, and produced incomparable feasts for eyes and ears.

This may sound like extravagant praise, but in fact it is well merited. What other opera company has within the past two years joined the top half dozen of American companies in critical acclaim, audience response and length of season?

To turn to the delights of the palate, which I am sure await those who test the recipes in this book, I express my grateful appreciation to the Women's Committee for compiling these culinary treasures for the benefit of The Washington Opera. And when next we present La Bohème I will urge our General Director to use a recipe from this cookbook in the last act—to help cheer Mimi in her final hour.

David Lloyd Kreeger
President
The Washington Opera

To our generous friends who shared their favorite recipes with us, go our sincere thanks and gratitude. Without their support, this book would not have been possible. We regret that we could not use all the delicious recipes we received, due to similarity and lack of space. Some adjustments have been made in order to standardize and simplify—we hope they meet with your approval. We hope, also, that you will receive as much pleasure and have as many mouth watering moments as we have had putting this book together.

CHAIRMAN
Jeananne Petrus

COMMITTEE

Marnell Bruce   Paula Jeffries
Sally Davidson   Renee Kraft
Evelyn DiBona   Ellen Lewis
Anne Green   Sarah T. Minikes
Pauline Innis   Terry Stone

The Women's Committee of The Washington Opera
and the supportive staff of The Washington Opera

Our grateful appreciation to
U.S. News and World Report for their invaluable assistance.

CONTENTS

The Washington Opera is unique in the United States in that it presents grand opera in one of the world's finest lyric opera houses, the John F. Kennedy Center Opera House. Additionally, it presents traditional operatic repertory within the intimate ambiance of the Kennedy Center Terrace Theater. This unusual two-theater situation prompted the Washington Post to comment that " . . . The Washington Opera is paralleling the operation of La Scala in Milan".

The Washington Opera is dedicated to the ultimate performance goal of the balance of musical, dramatic and visual elements. To achieve this, it is committed to featuring outstanding, emerging American singers, as well as international stars, in principal roles.

There can now be no doubt that The Washington Opera is a company in which not only the nation's capital, but also the entire country can take pride.

APPETIZERS

Ling-Ling and Hsing-Hsing

MOUSSE DE FOIES DE VOLAILLE   Serves 12

"An absolutely delicious, light pâté from the Belgians"

2 tablespoons oil	½ teaspoon salt
1 tablespoon butter	¼ teaspoon pepper
2 pounds fresh chicken livers	½ cup Cognac
or pheasant or duck	½ cup port wine
1 onion, sliced	1 cup chicken bouillon
1 bay leaf	12 gelatine leaves
½ teaspooon thyme	1 cup heavy cream, whipped

In a heavy skillet, heat the oil and butter. When very hot, brown the livers on both sides. Add the onion, bay leaf, thyme, salt and pepper. Simmer for a few minutes then flame with Cognac and port wine. When the flame subsides, add the chicken bouillon. Simmer a few minutes more. • Place the gelatine leaves in cold water to soak for a while. • Remove the livers and onions from the skillet and bring the cooking liquid to a boil. Add the softened gelatine leaves, stir and remove from heat. Allow to cool. • Put livers and onion through a meat grinder and add to cooled gelatine. Beat with an electric mixer until very smooth then put through a fine sieve. Let cool until partially set, not too thick. Fold in the whipped cream and additional salt and pepper as needed. You may also wish to add some more Cognac and port. Place in a serving dish and chill.

Embassy of Belgium
For cooking classes to benefit
The Washington Opera

CHOPPED CHICKEN LIVERS   Serves 12

2 tablespoons butter	Salt
2 pounds chicken livers	Pepper
3 large onions, chopped	Paprika
1½ teaspoons oil	Parsley for garnish
6 hard-boiled eggs, chopped	

Melt the butter and sauté the chicken livers for 20 minutes, turning once. When cooled, chop by hand. • Sauté the onions in oil. • Combine chopped liver, onions and chopped egg (save a small amount of egg for garnish). Season with salt, pepper and paprika. • Garnish with chopped egg and parsley. Serve with crackers or small bread rounds.

Mrs. Martin Feinstein

TERRINE DE RIS DE VEAU "AGNES"   Serves 10–12

*"Sweetbread Paté from this Watergate
restaurant deserves high praise indeed."*

2¼ pounds veal or
  lamb sweetbreads
Salt
2–3 carrots, chopped
2 onions, chopped
2 stalks celery, chopped
1½ ounces butter
2–3 sprigs fresh parsley
1 bay leaf
1 sprig fresh thyme
Dash nutmeg
Freshly ground black pepper

⅔ cup white wine
2 cups ground lean veal
2 cups ground lean pork
½ pound cooked tongue,
  diced
6 ounces paté de fois gras
3 cups sliced mushrooms
½ cup sliced truffles
  (optional)
2 ounces brandy
Slices of fatback for lining
  terrine

Soak the sweetbreads in cold water for 2 hours, rinse thoroughly and blanch in boiling salted water for 4 minutes. • Sauté the carrots, onions and celery in butter until soft. Add the herbs, nutmeg, salt and pepper and place the sweetbreads on top. Pour in the wine and braise for 20–30 minutes. • Drain the sweetbreads, trim and cut into pieces. • Combine the veal, tongue and pork. Mix in the sweetbreads, mushrooms and truffles and moisten the forcemeat with brandy.

• Line a large rectangular terrine with the fatback and fill with the forcemeat, pressing down well. Cover with fatback. Place terrine in a roasting pan, half-filled with boiling water and bake in preheated 325° oven for 1½–2 hours. • Serve with Waldorf or cucumber dill salad and cumberland sauce.

*Chef Klaus Helmin
Jean Louis Restaurant
The Watergate*

A dinner plate from the White House china

BILL'S PATE   Serves 8–12

1 pound ground pork shoulder
½ pound ground pork liver
¼ pound ground fatback
1 egg, beaten
1 tablespoon green pepper corns
2 tablespoons minced onion
1 teaspoon thyme
¼ teaspooon allspice
½ teaspoon nutmeg
3 tablespoons Cognac
1 teaspoon seasoning salt
½ teaspoon garlic powder
Bacon or thinly sliced fatback
½–¾ pound chicken breast strips
½–¾ pound ham strips
2 bay leaves

Mix the ground pork, liver, fatback, beaten egg and seasonings well.
• Line a terrine with bacon or thinly sliced fatback. Pour ⅓ of pork mixture into the terrine, spreading evenly. Add a layer of ½ the chicken and ham strips. Add another ⅓ of the pork mixture, top with the remaining chicken and ham strips and cover all with the last ⅓ of the pork mixture. Lay the bay leaves on the top and cover with bacon or fatback. Cook the pâté, uncovered, in a pan of water at 375° for 1¾–2 hours. Remove from the oven, cover with foil and weight with a brick or other 3–4 pound weight. Let cool to room temperature then refrigerate overnight, still weighted, before serving.

William J Kerns, Jr.

HOT CRAB MEAT DIP   Makes 3 cups

"A hearty cold weather favorite"

3 8-ounce packages cream cheese
½ cup mayonnaise
2 teaspoons dry mustard
⅔ cup dry white wine or vermouth
1 teaspoon onion juice
18 ounces crab meat (shrimp or lobster)
1 teaspoon chopped chives
Cayenne pepper to taste
Salt to taste

Soften the cream cheese and combine with the mayonnaise, mustard, wine and onion juice. • Pick over crab meat to remove all bits of shell and add to cream cheese mixture with the chives, cayenne and salt to taste. Heat slowly in a double boiler. • Serve hot in a chafing dish with melba toast rounds.

Mrs. W. Walker Lewis III

HORSERADISH DIP
Makes 1½ cups

1 clove garlic, crushed
8 ounces cream cheese
1 cup sour cream
5 drops Tabasco sauce
½ teaspoon salt

¼ teaspoon freshly ground
  pepper
2 tablespoons dehydrated
  horseradish
1 tablespoon minced parsley

Thoroughly blend the garlic, cream cheese and sour cream. This may be done in a blender or food processor. Add the Tabasco sauce, salt, pepper, horseradish and parsley. • Place in glass or earthenware bowl and refrigerate for 12 hours or more. Serve as a dip with crudités.

Mrs H M Pasewalk

CHIPPED BEEF DIP
Serves 10–20

8 ounces cream cheese
2 tablespoons milk
2½ ounces dried beef,
  chopped
1 teaspoon onion powder
½ teaspoon garlic salt

¼ teaspoon pepper
1 cup sour cream
2 tablespoons butter
½ teaspoon salt
½ cup coarsely chopped
  pecans

Combine the cream cheese and milk and blend well. Stir in the dried beef, onion powder, garlic salt, pepper, and sour cream. Mix well and turn into a casserole. • Melt the butter in a skillet, add the salt and pecans and "toast" them lightly. Sprinkle the nuts over the casserole and bake at 350° for 20 minutes. Serve hot.

Anne Shultz

HOT "A LIZ" SAUCE
Makes 4½ cups

1 16-ounce jar apple jelly
1 16-ounce jar pineapple preserves

3 ounces dry mustard
5 ounces horseradish

Blend ingredients in a blender or food processor. Store in a jar in the refrigerator 1–2 weeks before serving to let the flavors blend. Serve over cream cheese on crackers. (Note: Sauce keeps indefinitely in the refrigerator.)

Helen Coe

SALMON LOAF HORS D'OEUVRE   Makes 1½–2 cups

7½-ounce can sockeye salmon,
    drained
Juice of 1 lemon
Salt
1 teaspoon horseradish

1 medium onion, minced
1 teaspoon liquid smoke
8 ounces cream cheese
½ cup chopped parsley
3–4 ounces chopped pecans

Combine salmon, lemon juice, salt to taste, horseradish, onion, liquid smoke and cream cheese. Blend thoroughly and refrigerate until firm. Roll in chopped parsley and pecans and place on a serving dish surrounded with toast rounds.

Jen Holcombe

HADDOCK PATE   Serves 4

¼ pound smoked haddock,
    cooked, boned, and flaked
¼ pound butter
Pepper
1¼ teaspoons lemon juice

¼ teaspoon curry powder
Pinch chili powder
1 tablespoon grated onion
Chives, chopped

Place fish, butter, and pepper in a bowl and blend well. Stir in lemon juice, curry powder, chili powder and onion. • Blend this mixture in a blender or food processor until smooth. Chill, covered, in a small bowl for at least 2 hours. • Garnish with chopped chives and serve with toast triangles or fresh whole wheat bread. (Note: Add a little cream if mixture seems too dry. This freezes well, but thaw in refrigerator before serving.)

Mrs. Donald Bell Sole
Wife of the Ambassador of South Africa

ARTICHOKE SPREAD   Serves 6–8

"A delicious and different warm dip or spread"

14-ounce can artichoke
    hearts
1 cup mayonnaise

1 cup freshly grated Parmesan
    cheese
3–6 drops Tabasco sauce

Drain the artichoke hearts in a colander, pressing gently to remove excess liquid. Combine with remaining ingredients in a mixer or food processor. Blend well and pour into a small, unbuttered baking dish or ovenproof serving dish. Bake, uncovered, at 350° for 20 minutes. Serve with French bread, toast points or melba toast.

Gail Milner

DILLED SALMON
Serves 18

"An adaptation of a Scandinavian favorite"

3 pounds center cut fresh salmon, cut in 2 large filets, scaled, but with skin left on
4 teaspoons crushed peppercorns
4 tablespoons coarse salt

4 tablespoons sugar
Large bunch fresh dill, coarsely chopped
Bricks or heavy rocks
Vegetable oil

Crush peppercorns in a blender and measure. Combine them with the coarse salt and sugar. Rub the cut side of each salmon filet with ½ this mixture. • Place ½ the dill in the bottom of a glass or Pyrex dish large enough to hold the filets. Spread remaining dill on the cut side of one of the filets and cover with the other, cut sides together. Place them on the bed of dill. Cover the dish with foil and weight with bricks or rocks. This weight creates a brine which marinates and "cooks" the salmon. Refrigerate for 48–72 hours, turning salmon every 12 hours. • To serve, scrape away the dill and seasonings, brush lightly with oil and slice crosswise away from the skin, cutting diagonally as for smoked salmon. Serve with mustard sauce. (Note. Dilled salmon makes an excellent main course for a light luncheon.)

Mustard Sauce:

¼ cup Dijon mustard
3 tablespoons sugar
2 tablespoons wine vinegar
1 teaspoon dry mustard

⅓ cup French olive oil or salad oil
3 tablespoons chopped fresh dill

Combine mustard, sugar, vinegar, and dry mustard. Slowly beat in the oil and add the fresh chopped dill. Chill.

Mary Lynn Kotz

LANGOSTINO SPREAD
Makes about 2 cups

8 ounces frozen langostinos, thawed
8 ounces cream cheese
3 tablespoons mayonnaise

2 tablespoons minced onion
½ tablespoon curry powder
2–3 hard-boiled eggs, sieved

Pat langostinos dry and combine well with cream cheese, mayonnaise, onion, and curry powder. Pat into desired shape and cover with a coating of sieved hard-boiled eggs. Chill. Serve on crackers or toast rounds.

Mrs. Stephan M. Minikes

SHRIMP DIJON   Serves 20

2 pounds shrimp, cleaned
  and deveined
2 tablespoons shrimp and crab
  pickling spice
½ cup red wine vinegar
¼ cup salad oil
3 tablespoons finely minced
  chives

2 tablespoons Dijon mustard
1 tablespoon horseradish
  or to taste
3 tablespoons finely chopped
  dill pickle
1½ teaspoon salt
Parsley to garnish

Bring to boil enough salted water with the pickling spice to cover the shrimp. Add them and boil 5 minutes. Drain well. • Combine the remaining ingredients except the parsley garnish and toss well with the cooled shrimp. • Cover and refrigerate in the marinade for several hours or up to 2–3 days. Turn occasionally. • Before serving, drain excess marinade, arrange in a chilled serving bowl and garnish with parsley.

Mrs. James R. Patton, Jr.

SPICED SHRIMP   Serves 6–8

1 tablespoon pickling spices
1 teaspoon salt
Freshly ground black pepper
1 bay leaf, crushed
2 slices onion
2 tablespoons chopped
  parsley
¾ pound cleaned and shelled
  fresh shrimp
2–3 tablespoons olive oil

2 tablespoons white wine
  vinegar
1 large clove garlic, crushed
Oregano
Basil
Marjoram
Thyme
Rosemary
Sage
Dash of Tabasco

Fill a large pot with water and stir in the first 6 ingredients. Bring to a rapid boil. Immerse the cleaned shrimp in the boiling water. When it returns to boiling, cook shrimp for 1 or 2 minutes. Do not overcook.
  • Remove shrimp from heat, drain (retaining spices with the shrimp) and transfer to a bowl. While still hot, coat the shrimp with olive oil. Stir in the vinegar and mix well. Add the garlic, some additional freshly ground pepper and a generous pinch of the remaining herbs. If desired, finish with a dash of Tabasco. • Toss thoroughly, cover and refrigerate 12–48 hours, stirring occasionally.

Judith Patterson

SHRIMP ORIENTAL   Serves 6

"This Washington Opera soprano cooks as well as she sings"

½ cup oil
½ cup soy sauce
½ cup dry sherry

4 cloves garlic, crushed
3 tablespoons ground ginger
1 pound raw shrimp

Make a marinade of the oil, soy sauce, sherry, garlic and ginger.
• Peel and devein the shrimp and add to marinade. Let stand in the
mixture at least 5 hours. • Barbeque or broil in the oven about 3
minutes on each side. (Note: It is easier to turn the shrimp if you use a
double-sided mesh grill.)

Ashley Putnam

CRAB MOLD   Serves 10–20

1 can cream of mushroom soup
1 package unflavored gelatine
1 2-ounce can mushroom pieces
1 tablespoon sliced scallions,
  white part only
½ cup celery, thinly sliced

1 cup mayonnaise
16 ounces crab meat
2 tablespoons lemon juice
5 drops Tabasco
Parsley for garnish

Heat soup, undiluted, until lukewarm. • Mix gelatine with 3 tablespoons cold water. Add to soup and stir over very low heat for 1
minute. Stir in drained mushroom pieces, sliced scallions and celery.
Remove from heat and blend in mayonnaise. Fold crab meat into
mixture, adding lemon juice and Tabasco. • Correct seasoning and
pour into greased 1-quart mold. Refrigerate overnight. • To unmold, set in warm water for 30 seconds and invert onto a plate.
Garnish with parsley and serve with crackers.

Mrs. John Milward Buck

CRAB MEAT MELTAWAYS   Serves 12

"Great to have in the freezer for emergencies"

2 5-ounce jars Old English
  cheese
4 tablespoons mayonnaise
1 teaspoon seasoning salt

1 teaspoon garlic salt
2 teaspoons softened butter
1 pound backfin crab meat
12 English muffins

Blend first 5 ingredients with electric mixer or food processor. Stir in
the crab meat. Cut muffins in half and spread with the mixture. Put in
freezer. • When ready to serve, take from freezer and place immediately under the broiler 3–5 minutes, or until golden brown. Serve hot.

Mrs. H. B. Helfrich

CLAM ROLLS

2 dozen

7½-ounce can minced clams
3 tablespoons butter
2 tablespoons minced onion
1½ tablespoons flour

¼ teaspoon garlic powder
¼ teaspoon Worcestershire
  sauce
12 slices white bread

Drain the clams. Reserve the liquid. • Sauté the onion in 1 table-spoon of the butter. Blend in the flour, gradually add the reserved clam liquid and seasonings, stir in the clams and cook until thick. Cool. • Remove the crusts from the bread and flatten each slice with a rolling pin. • Melt the remaining 2 tablespoons butter. • Brush each bread slice with some of the melted butter and spread with 1 tablespoon of the clam mixture. Roll up, brush each roll with remaining butter and cut in half. • Arrange rolls on a cookie sheet and bake in a preheated 425° oven for 8 minutes.

Frances Bush

Scene from "The Barber of Seville"

CEVICHE

Serves 2–3

½ pound fresh, firm-fleshed fish
  such as cod or halibut,
  or use scallops
1 scallion, minced
½ small clove garlic
½ teaspoon minced fresh
  green chili

½ teaspoon thyme, or
  1 teaspoon fresh cilantro
  and/or parsley
Dash Tabasco
⅓ cup lemon or lime juice
1 tablespoon olive oil

Cut fish into bite-sized pieces. Combine remaining ingredients in a bowl, add the fish or scallops and refrigerate 4–5 hours to "cook." Serve as a first course or as an appetizer with melba toast or rye rounds.

Mrs. Tom Page

CLAM PIE   Serves 12

2   6½-ounce cans minced clams   ¼ cup minced parsley
2 tablespoons lemon juice   1 tablespoon oregano
1 onion   ¼ pound butter
1 clove garlic   ¾ cup bread crumbs
1 small green pepper   Parmesan cheese

In a saucepan combine clams and juice with lemon juice. Simmer 15
minutes. • In blender or food processor blend the onion, garlic,
green pepper and herbs until mushy. • Melt the butter and sauté
the blended vegetables and herbs. Add clams, their juice and bread
crumbs and stir. • Press into 9 inch glass pie dish, sprinkle with
Parmesan cheese and bake at 350° for 15 minutes. • Serve hot with
crackers or party rye, or bake clam pie in individual scallop shells and
serve as an appetizer.

Irene M. King

TUNA APPETIZERS   Serves 10–12

12½–13 ounce can tuna,   2 eggs
   well drained   ½ cup minced onion
¾ cup bread crumbs   Salt and pepper

Combine all ingredients and form into bite-sized balls. Place them on a
greased cookie sheet and bake at 350° for 15 minutes. Arrange on a
platter with toothpicks for serving and dip in mustard sauce.

Mustard Sauce:

¼ cup dry mustard   ⅛ teaspoon salt
¼ cup cider vinegar   1 egg
2 tablespoons sugar   1 cup mayonnaise

Combine all ingredients except the mayonnaise in the top of a double
boiler. Cook, stirring constantly, over hot water until thickened. Refrigerate and when cool, stir in the mayonnaise. Pass with the tuna
appetizers.

Dr. James L. Olson

CAVIAR ROULADE   Serves 10

4 tablespoons unsalted butter
½ cup sifted flour
2 cups milk, scalded
4 large eggs, separated, at
  room termperature
Pinch salt
¼ teaspoon cream of tartar
6 ounces cream cheese
1 cup sour cream

4 ounces red salmon caviar or
  substitute lumpfish caviar
2 tablespoons chopped fresh
  dill
2 tablespoons chopped fresh
  parsley
1½ tablespoons lemon juice
  or to taste
Watercress or parsley to
  garnish

Melt butter in a 2–3 quart saucepan and whisk in the flour. Add the
scalded milk and cook 1 minute, stirring constantly. Beat the egg yolks
lightly and add. Set aside. • Beat the egg whites at low speed with
an electric mixer until foamy. Add the cream of tartar and salt and
beat at high speed until stiff and shiny. Stir ¼ of the whites into the
yolk mixture, then fold in the rest. • Grease and line a 10 x 15 inch
jelly roll pan with waxed paper. Grease the paper, sprinkle with flour
and shake out excess. Spread prepared batter into the pan and bake at
325° for 1 hour and 20 minutes or until cake springs back when
touched. Let rest 1 minute and then turn out onto wax paper on a
damp towel. Trim crusty edges. • While cake is baking, cream the
cream chese and sour cream. Stir in the caviar, dill, parsley and lemon
juice. • Spread ¾ of the caviar filling on the still warm and pliable
cake leaving a ½–inch border on all edges. Carefully roll cake into a
cylinder and refrigerate or freeze if not ready to serve. To serve, warm
the cake gently or leave cold. Cover with the remaining caviar filling
and garnish the dish with greens. Slice as you would a jelly roll.

Shelly P. Levi

CAVIAR-NOVA SCOTIA PIE   Serves 8–10

9 hard-boiled eggs
2 tablespoons butter, softened
2 cups sour cream
3½-ounce jar caviar

¼ pound Nova Scotia salmon,
  thinly sliced
½ bunch parsley, chopped
1 small onion, minced

Sieve eggs, combine with softened butter and press firmly into a 9-
inch pie plate. Freeze 20 minutes. Remove from freezer and fill with
sour cream. Arrange caviar and salmon in alternating wedge-shaped
sections over the sour cream. Arrange a rim of chopped parsley
around the outer edge of the pie. Within the parsley ring, arrange a
smaller ring of chopped onion. Make a center parsley "flower."

Dorothy Stone

BABA GHANNOUJ   Serves 16

"An eggplant hors d'oeuvre"

3 large eggplants	1 teaspoon salt
1 cup tahini	Olive oil
1¼ cups lemon juice	Chopped parsley
3 cloves garlic, chopped	Pomegranate seeds, optional

Bake the eggplants on a cookie sheet at 350° until very soft, up to 1 hour. Peel them, place them in a bowl and mash the meat. • In a blender or food processor, combine and whirl ½ the mashed eggplant, the lemon juice, garlic and salt. Mix this with the remaining mashed eggplant and transfer to a serving dish. Film the top of the eggplant mixture with a thin layer of olive oil and garnish with parsley and pomegranate seeds if desired. Spread on wedges of pita bread.

Dorothy B. Wexler

CHEESE BISCUITS   Makes several dozen

"Zing!"

3 cups sifted flour	½ pound butter
½ teaspoon salt	4 cups grated sharp cheddar
2 teaspoons baking powder	cheese
1 heaping teaspoon cayenne or to taste	Pecan halves

Sift together all the dry ingredients. • Cream the butter and grated cheese and add to the dry mixture to form a dough. Roll out dough ¼ inch thick, cut into rounds with a small biscuit cutter and press a pecan half into center of each biscuit. Transfer to cookie sheets and bake at 375° for 10–12 minutes until light brown. (Note: Biscuits may be stored in an airtight tin for several weeks.)

Mrs. Edward M. Geltman

EGG SALAD MOUSSE WITH CAVIAR   Serves 6–8

1 tablespoon lemon juice
1 tablespoon sherry
1 envelope gelatine
½ cup mayonnaise

½ cup minced onion
5 hard-boiled eggs, coarsely
    chopped
1 small jar black caviar

Mix the lemon juice, sherry and gelatine. Stir in the mayonaise. When well blended, add the onion and eggs. Gently fold in the caviar and place in an oiled mold. Chill for several hours or overnight. Serve with toast points or crackers.

Mrs. John R. Lindsay

MEATBALL HORS D'OEUVRES   Serves 12–16

4 pounds ground beef
1 cup red wine
1 cup chopped onion
2 garlic cloves, minced

4 eggs, lightly beaten
2 teaspoons salt
Freshly ground black pepper

Combine all ingredients. Mix well and form into balls about 1–1½ inches in diameter. Sauté for 10 minutes or until done.

Sauce:

2 garlic cloves
1 teaspoon salt
½ cup tomato juice
½ cup oil
½ cup red wine vinegar
½ cup beef bouillon
2 tablespoons minced onion

¼ cup finely chopped
    green pepper
½ teaspoon cumin seed
¼ teaspoon crushed chili
    peppers
Dash of Tabasco sauce
Dash of cayenne

Crush the garlic with the salt and combine in a saucepan with remaining ingredients. Bring to a boil, reduce heat and simmer for 15 minutes, stirring occasionally. Pour over meatballs and serve warm. (Note: Best if kept warm in a chafing dish.)

Mrs. Robert L. Anschuetz

KATHLEEN'S HAM ROLL-UPS

Makes 3 dozen

"Easily doubled and designed for 'do-ahead' cooks."

8 ounces cream cheese
1 tablespoon chopped
  blanched almonds
3 dashes Tabasco sauce
½ teaspoon Worcestershire
  sauce
¼ teaspoon dry mustard
¼ teaspoon Pickapeppa sauce

¼ teaspoon soy sauce
¼ teaspoon paprika
⅛ teaspoon each salt and
  pepper
2 tablespoons mayonnaise
2 teaspoons chives, minced
4-ounce package imported
  ham, precut into 4 slices

Soften cream cheese and mash well with a fork. Add remaining ingredients, except the ham, and blend well. • Spread ¼ of the mixture evenly on each ham slice. Roll ham lengthwise and place, fold side down, on a cookie sheet. • Freeze the ham rolls for 45 minutes before slicing each into nine or ten pieces. If desired, refreeze until solid and store in a plastic bag or container for up to six weeks. Allow one half hour to thaw.

Mrs. John C. Camp

HAWAIIAN COCKTAIL MEATBALLS

Serves 50

4 pounds ground chuck
2 cups bread crumbs
2 cups minced onions
1 cup water
¼ cup soy sauce
2 eggs

4 teaspoons salt
½ teaspoon pepper
1 teaspoon nutmeg
1½ teaspoons coriander
1 teaspoon cinnamon

Combine all ingredients and blend well. Mold into 1-inch balls and sauté or bake at 300° until done. Arrange the meatballs on a platter with toothpicks or tiny skewers. Serve, if desired, with a sweet and sour dipping sauce.

Jane Roberts DeGraff

OYSTERS IN OYSTER SAUCE   Serves 2

"A happy alternative to horseradish and ketchup"

16 oysters on the half shell
1 clove garlic, crushed
½ teaspoon grated lemon peel
Juice of 1 lemon
¼ teaspoon mustard

4 smoked oysters
4 tablespoons oil
Salt and freshly ground
   black pepper
1 tablespoon minced parsley

Arrange 7 oysters on the half shell on each plate. • Combine remaining 2 oysters, grated lemon peel, lemon juice, mustard, smoked oysters and oil in a blender or food processor and purée. Season to taste with salt and pepper. Either top each oyster with some of the sauce, and garnish with parsley, or serve sauce in a separate bowl as a dip.

Anne Crutcher

CARPACCIO   Serves 4–6 as a first course

2 cups julienne strips cold
   raw beef, top round or
   eye of round
6 fresh white mushrooms,
   sliced
2 tablespoons capers, drained
1 tablespoon pine nuts
¼ cup fine olive oil

¼ cup salad oil
2 tablespoons tarragon
   vinegar
½ clove garlic, crushed
1 teaspoon salt
⅛ teaspoon pepper
⅛ teaspoon dry mustard
2 tablespoons chopped
   parsley

Prepare and combine the meat, mushrooms, capers and pine nuts. Whisk together the remaining ingredients until well blended. Toss it all together and chill. • Serve very cold on chilled plates as a first course.

Mrs. Hugh Newell Jacobsen

EMPANADAS   Makes about a dozen

"A treat from Chile"

4 cups sifted flour
1 teaspoon baking powder
1 teaspoon salt
1 pound lard
1 cup scalded milk
2 large onions, coarsely
  chopped
1 pound chopped or ground
  beef
3 tablespoons oil

Bay leaf
Pinch of oregano
Pinch of cumin
6 drops Tabasco
Salt and pepper to taste
3–4 hard-boiled eggs
1 cup raisins
Pitted black olives
2 egg whites, lightly beaten
2 egg yolks, lightly beaten

Sift together the flour, baking powder and salt. Combine with the lard. Gradually add the hot milk and knead the dough until it is no longer sticky. Let stand for 10 minutes, covered with a cloth • Prepare the meat filling. Sauté the onions and meat in oil. Add the seasonings, simmer until browned and set aside to cool. • When the meat mixture is completely cool (so the empanadas will not burst), prepare the dough. Roll it out, very thin, and cut into circles approximately 5 inches in diameter. Place a spoonful of the meal mixture on lower left of dough circle. Add a black olive, some raisins and a slice or wedge of hard-boiled egg. Close top half of circle over all and join the edges with egg white. Brush the top with beaten egg yolks. Place on a greased cookie sheet and bake at 425° for ½ hour or until browned.

Embassy of Chile
For cooking classes to benefit
The Washington Opera

MISSOURI CHEESE ROLL   Serves 12

½ pound Velveeta cheese
½ pound cream cheese
2 cloves garlic, crushed

½ pound pecans
Chili powder
Ritz crackers

Thoroughly mix Velveeta and cream cheese. Put through a meat grinder with crushed garlic. Put pecans through the grinder, mix with cheese and put it all through the grinder once again. Roll the mixture into a cylinder. • Spread chili powder on a sheet of waxed paper. Roll cheese log over chili powder until well coated. Chill. • Slice and serve on Ritz crackers.

The Honorable James W. Symington

"PLAINS SPECIAL" CHEESE RING   Serves 6–8

1 pound sharp cheese, grated
1 cup finely chopped nuts
1 cup mayonnaise
1 small onion, finely grated

Black pepper
Dash of cayenne
Strawberry preserves, optional

Combine all ingredients except preserves. Season to taste with pepper.
Mix well and place in a lightly greased 5–6 cup ring mold. Refrigerate
several hours or overnight. • To serve, unmold and, if desired, fill
center with strawberry preserves or serve plain with crackers.

Mrs. Jimmy Carter

SPICED PINEAPPLE PICKUPS   Serves 12

"These spicy fruit chunks are a nice
diversion from normal cocktail fare."

20-ounce can unsweetened
  pineapple chunks,
  packed in own juice
¾ cup cider vinegar

1¼ cups sugar
Dash of salt
6–8 whole cloves
1 cinnamon stick

Drain pineapple chunks, reserving ¾ cup of the juice. • In a saucepan combine pineapple juice, vinegar, sugar, salt, cloves and cinnamon. Heat 10 minutes. Add the pineapple chunks and bring to a
boil. • Refrigerate overnight in a covered bowl. To serve, drain
pineapple and serve cold with toothpicks.

Vera C. Davis

BAKED POTATO SKINS   Serves 6

"Here's how to duplicate a popular
restaurant treat at home"

8 large baking potatoes
½ cup melted butter

Salt and pepper

Bake potatoes in a pre-heated 400° oven for 1 hour. • Remove
potatoes from the oven, cut them in half lengthwise, and scoop out the
insides. • Cut the skins in 1-inch strips with sharp scissors and
arrange them on cookie sheets. • Brush the skins lavishly with
melted butter, and sprinkle with salt and pepper. • Bake at
475° for 6–8 minutes or until very crisp. Serve hot.

Merrilyn J. Slack

The Washington Monument

SHORT SNAILS   Makes 2 dozen

"The cook was short of snails one day!"

8-ounce jar mushroom caps
6 tablespoons butter
½ cup chopped parsley
3 tablespoons Parmesan cheese

4–6 cloves garlic, pressed
½ cup minced onion
24 snail shells

Cut 12 whole mushrooms in half and set aside. • Drain and mince the remaining mushrooms and blend throughly with the butter, parsley, Parmesan, garlic and onion. • Place a mushroom half in each snail shell. Fill with the mixture. Bake at 400° for 15 minutes. Serve immediately.

Nancy Marcello

ITALIAN PICKLED MUSHROOMS   Serves 10–12

"A spicy relish to serve with cocktails"

1 pound mushroom caps	2 teaspoons salt
White vinegar	2 teaspoons peppercorns
Hot water	2 cloves garlic, minced
¼ cup olive oil	1 teaspoon ground mace

Wash mushrooms and cut tips off stems. Place in a saucepan with equal amounts of vinegar and hot water to cover. Bring to a boil and cook 5 minutes. Drain and cool. • Pack mushrooms in 1 pint jars. Mix remaining ingredients and add to jars in equal amounts. Add enough additional vinegar to cover. Refrigerate 48 hours before serving. (Note: This recipe can be doubled easily. May be stored in the refrigerator for up to 1 month.)

Mrs. Joseph W. Henderson, III

SPINACH SQUARES   Makes 20 pieces

"A nice spinach quiche hors d'oeuvre"

1 package frozen chopped spinach	1 teaspoon salt
4 tablespoons butter	1 teaspoon baking powder
3 eggs	1 cup milk
1 cup flour	1 pound sharp cheddar cheese, grated

Defrost the spinach, but do not drain. Set aside. • Place the butter in a 9 x 13 inch baking dish and melt it in the oven. • In a mixing bowl, beat the eggs. Add the dry ingredients and milk and blend thoroughly. Add the grated cheese and spinach. Mix well and pour into the baking dish over the melted butter. Bake at 350° for 35 minutes. Cool at least 30 minutes before serving. Cut into squares. (Note: To freeze, place baked squares on a cookie sheet until firm. Then freeze. When ready to serve, spread on cookie sheet and heat 10–12 minutes at 300°.)

Martha Benedict

The entrance to the Naval Observatory, now the home of the Vice President of the United States

SPINACH BALLS

Makes about 5 dozen

2   10-ounce packages frozen chopped spinach
2 cups herb seasoned stuffing mix
2 medium onions, minced
6 eggs, beaten
6 ounces melted butter

½ teaspoon thyme
½ cup grated Parmesan cheese
1 tablespoon garlic salt
½ teaspoon pepper

Cook the spinach and drain it thoroughly. • Combine all the ingredients, blending well. Let stand in the refrigerator several hours or overnight. Form the mixture into balls, arrange on baking sheets and bake at 350° for 20 minutes. Serve hot. (Note: Spinach balls may be frozen and reheated.)

Mrs. Murray L. Weidenbaum

CURRY-CHUTNEY SPREAD

About 1 cup

8 ounces cream cheese
1 teaspoon curry powder

2 ounces slivered almonds
Major Grey's Chutney

Combine cream cheese and curry powder. Refrigerate for 2 hours. Pat into desired shape (such as a circle, square or a pine cone at Christmas) and cover with slivered almonds and chutney. Serve with crackers.

Barbara Hillcoat

PETITS CHOUX AU GRUYERE   Makes 4–5 dozen

1 cup water
8 tablespoons butter
1 teaspoon salt
⅛ teaspoon pepper
Dash nutmeg

1 cup flour, sifted
4 eggs
1 cup grated Gruyere
cheese

Bring the water to a boil in a saucepan with the butter and seasonings and boil slowly until the butter has melted. Off heat, add the flour all at once, beating vigorously with a wooden spoon until well blended. Return pan to moderately high heat and continue beating 1–2 minutes until mixture leaves the sides of the pan and forms a mass. Off heat again, make a well in the center of the paste and break 1 egg into the well. Beat the egg into the paste until it has been absorbed and repeat this procedure for each of the remaining 3 eggs. Add the cheese and blend well. • Mound by heaping teaspoonfuls 1–2 inches apart on buttered baking sheets. Bake at 425° for 20 minutes. The choux should be golden brown on top.

Mrs. Carter Cafritz

BEGGAR'S BOURSIN   Serves 6

8 ounces cream cheese,
  softened
1 tablespoon plain yogurt
2 shallots, crushed
1 small clove garlic, crushed
1½ teaspoons grated lemon
  rind

1 tablespoon chives or
  scallions, minced
Freshly ground black pepper
  to taste

Blend cream cheese and yogurt with a fork until very smooth. Add shallots, garlic, grated lemon rind, and chives or scallions and blend well. • Place mixture in a small crock and top with freshly ground black pepper. • May be refrigerated or frozen at this point, but bring to room temperature before serving with melba toast rounds.

Anne Denton Blair

YALANKI DOLMA

Serves 10–12

"Stuffed vine leaves"

16-ounce jar vine leaves
2 large onions, chopped
1 cup cooked rice
¼ cup currants
¼ cup pine nuts
¼ cup chopped fresh mint
¼ cup chopped fresh parsley,
  save stems

¼ cup chopped fresh dill,
  save stems
2 tablespoons lemon juice
⅔ cup olive oil
1 teaspoon sugar
½ teaspoon allspice
½ teaspoon salt
2 cups chicken broth
2 lemons, cut in wedges

Unroll leaves and place in 2 quarts boiling water for 2 minutes. Drain. • In a bowl, combine the onions, rice, currants, pine nuts, mint, parsley, dill, lemon juice, oil, sugar, allspice and salt. • Put parsley and dill stems at the bottom of a heavy saucepan or 2-quart casserole. On each vine leaf, shiny side down, place 1 teaspoon stuffing. Fold the sides of the leaf over and roll securely. • Fit the dolmas snugly in the pan and cover with chicken broth. Place a piece of wax paper and then a plate on top of the dolmas to weight them down and keep them in place. Bring to a boil and cook over medium heat for about 1 hour, until all liquid is absorbed. Serve with lemon wedges, hot or cold. (Note: These will keep in the refrigerator up to 2 weeks.)

Sally Boasberg

SHRIMP BISQUE MOLD

Serves 6

1 package lemon jello
1 package unflavored gelatine
½ cup boiling water
2 tablespoons vinegar
2 teaspoons Tabasco sauce
Salt and pepper to taste
1 tablespoon lemon juice

1 teaspoon Worcestershire
  sauce
1 tablespoon horseradish
1 can tomato soup
1–1¼ pounds cooked shrimp,
  broken into small pieces

Dissolve the lemon juice and gelatine in the boiling water. • In a separate bowl combine the remaining ingredients then add the gelatine mixture. Taste, adding more Tabasco sauce, horseradish and Worcestershire sauce if needed. Turn into a greased mold and chill thoroughly to set.

Nicole d'Amecourt

PISSALADIERE   Serves 8–10

*"This Italian version of quiche can also be made
as individual tarts for a different cocktail appetizer."*

Pastry:

2 cups flour	6 ounces unsalted butter
¼ teaspoon salt	Cold water, about 5 tablespoons

Mix flour and salt. • Cut butter in bits. Work butter and flour together with fingertips. Add just enough cold water to make pastry hold together. • Refrigerate 30 minutes. Roll out chilled pastry and line a 9-inch pie plate or small tart molds.

Filling:

2 pounds onions, chopped	2–3 medium tomatoes, thinly sliced
½ cup olive oil	1 tin flat anchovy filets (reserve oil)
1 teaspoon basil	24 pitted black olives, sliced

Cook onions slowly in the olive oil with the basil until tender, but not brown, about 45 minutes. • Spread the onions in the pastry shell. Top with a layer of thinly sliced tomatoes and make a decorative pattern with the anchovy filets and sliced black olives. Drizzle on a tablespoon of the oil from the anchovy tin. • Bake at 425° for 40 minutes for a large pie or 30 minutes for small tarts.

Pat Boeke

VELVET CHICKEN HUNAN   Serves 8–10

1 quart chicken broth	Toasted sesame seeds or finely
5 pieces star anise	chopped peanuts
3 thin slices peeled fresh	½ cup soy sauce
ginger	2 scallions, sliced
1 2½-pound broiling chicken	Pinch red pepper flakes
Sesame seed oil	

Bring broth, star anise and ginger to a boil in a large pot. Lower the chicken into the broth. When the broth returns to a boil, cover, reduce heat to simmer and cook 20–30 minutes. Turn off heat and allow to cool in broth, covered. • Remove chicken from broth, cut into bite-sized pieces, coat with sesame oil and sprinkle with sesame seeds or peanuts. • Serve at room temperature with a dip of soy sauce, scallions and red pepper flakes.

Dorothy Stone

SOUPS

The Smithsonian Castle on the Mall

AVOCADO SOUP BENGAL   Serves 4–6

2 ripe avocados, peeled
  and pits removed
2 cups cold chicken broth
1½ cups light cream
2 tablespoons white rum

2 teaspoons curry powder
Pinch salt
White pepper
4–6 tablespoons sour cream
Fresh dill or chives, chopped

Purée first 7 ingredients in a blender or food processor until smooth. Chill the soup mixture 12–24 hours. Serve in chilled soup cups garnishing each serving with 1 tablespoon sour cream and chopped dill or chives.

Mrs. Warwick M. Carter

COLD CREAM OF ARTICHOKE SOUP   Serves 8

2 9-ounce packages frozen
   artichoke hearts
1½ cans cream of mushroom
   soup
1 cup light cream

¼ cup chicken broth
¼ cup white wine
Salt and white pepper
   to taste
8 lemon slices

Cook artichokes according to package directions. • Combine all ingredients except lemon slices in a blender or food processor and purée. Correct the seasoning and chill well. Serve in chilled soup cups and garnish each with a thin slice of lemon.

Mrs. Warwick M. Carter

CUCUMBER SOUP   Serves 6

5 chicken bouillon cubes
4 cups water
2 cups peeled, seeded, and
  chopped cucumber
2 tablespoons butter

Salt to taste
½ teaspoon white pepper
1 slice onion
1 cup sour cream

In a saucepan, heat water and dissolve bouillon cubes. Add cucumbers, butter, salt, pepper and onion and heat together, but do not boil. Purée this mixture in a blender or food processor and refrigerate until very cold. Just before serving, whisk in the sour cream.

Mrs. E. Edward Bruce

VERY BEST GAZPACHO

Serves 8–10

46 ounces tomato juice
5 beef bouillon cubes
3 medium tomatoes, coarsely
  chopped
1 cup chopped, unpeeled
  cucumber
¾ cup chopped green pepper
½ cup chopped scallions

8 tablespoons red wine vinegar
4 tablespoons oil
1 tablespoon Worcestershire
  sauce
½ teaspoon hot pepper sauce
1 large clove garlic, crushed
Seasoned croutons
Fresh lime slices

Heat bouillon cubes in the tomato juice until they are dissolved. Stir in all remaining ingredients except croutons and lime slices. Chill at least 12 hours. Turn into serving bowls and garnish each with seasoned croutons and a thin slice of fresh lime.

Mrs. Patrick Hayes

Fort Washington, as seen from the Potomac

ARDSHEAL HOUSE CHEESE SOUP

Serves 8

2 tablespoons butter
¾ cup chopped onions
½ pound Stilton cheese,
  crumbled
½ pound cheddar cheese,
  crumbled
⅓ cup flour

3 cups chicken broth
1 cup heavy cream
⅓ cup dry white wine
1 bay leaf
Salt and pepper to taste
Milk for thinning, if desired

Heat the butter in a saucepan and sauté onions until wilted. Add the crumbled cheeses, sprinkle on the flour and cook, stirring, about 2 minutes. Remove from stove and gradually add the liquids and seasonings. Return to heat and bring the soup to a boil, then simmer 5–10 minutes. Remove the bay leaf and thin the soup with a little milk if desired.

Elizabeth Beach Rea

VICHYSSOISE A LA BRASILEIRA   Serves 10–12

3 medium leeks, chopped fine
2 celery stalks, chopped fine
1 medium onion, chopped fine
2 tablespoons butter
4 medium potatoes, peeled and
  thinly sliced
4 cups chicken consommé or
  stock

1 tablespoon Worcestershire
  sauce
1 pint cream
Salt and pepper
Scallions, chopped fine

Add leeks, celery and onion to melted butter in saucepan. Cook approximately 15 minutes over low heat so as not to darken. Add the potatoes, consommé and Worcestershire sauce, and cook covered, about 20 minutes until the potatoes are done. Pour into blender and purée until smooth. Stir in cream and add salt and pepper to taste. Chill thoroughly and garnish with the scallions.

Susan FitzGerald

CREAM OF MUSHROOM SOUP   Serves 8

2 pounds mushrooms
6 tablespoons butter
2 medium onions, sliced
½–¾ cup chopped celery
  leaves
1 cup heavy cream
1 cup chicken broth

1 teaspoon salt
2 teaspoons Worcestershire
  sauce
2 tablespoons sherry
Dash of pepper
1 cup sour cream for garnish
Chopped chives for garnish

Clean the mushrooms. Make sure they are dry and then quarter them. In a large skillet, melt the butter and sauté the mushrooms, onions and celery leaves until golden.   •   In a blender or food processor, combine ½ the mushroom mixture, ½ cup cream, ½ cup chicken broth and ½ the seasonings. Mix at high speed for 30 seconds, or until well blended.   •   Repeat procedure for second portion.   •   Reheat without boiling before serving. Pour into individual bowls and garnish with sour cream and chives.

Betty Beale

LEMON SOUP   Serves 8

8 cups rich chicken stock
6 medium cucumbers, peeled
   seeded and sliced
Salt and pepper

8 thin slivers lemon rind
Sour cream or plain yogurt
   for garnish

Simmer the sliced cucumbers in the chicken stock until tender. Cool.
Whirl the cooled mixture in a blender or food processor slowly adding
the lemon rind. Chill the soup thoroughly. Garnish each serving with a
generous spoonful of sour cream or plain yogurt.

Evelyn Lambert

U.S. HOUSE OF REPRESENTATIVES BEAN SOUP   Serves 6

*"Straight from the House Restaurant
kitchen . . . hearty, zesty and filling"*

2 pounds No. 1 white
   Michigan beans

1 smoked ham hock
Salt and pepper to taste

Place the dried beans in a mixing bowl, cover them with water and let
soak overnight. Drain, turn into a large soup pot and re-cover with
water. Add the smoked ham hock and simmer slowly for about 4 hours
until beans are cooked tender. Add salt and pepper to taste. Just
before serving, bruise the beans with a large spoon or ladle, enough to
cloud the soup.

House of Representatives Restaurant

CURRIED TOMATO SOUP   Serves 10

4 tablespoons butter
¾ cup chopped onions
2 tablespoons curry powder
3   14-ounce cans Italian tomatoes

3 cups chicken broth
1 bay leaf
½ cup sour cream

Heat the butter in a saucepan, add the onions and cook slowly, stirring,
until they are tender but not browned. Stir in the curry powder. Cook
5 minutes. Add the tomatoes, chicken broth and bay leaf. Bring to a
boil and simmer, uncovered, for 20 minutes. Remove the bay leaf.
•   Purée the soup in a blender or food processor, turn into a soup
tureen and stir in the sour cream.

Elizabeth Beach Rea

CARROT SOUP

Serves 6

2 tablespoons butter
1 clove garlic, minced
2 scallions, sliced
3 cups chicken broth
1 bay leaf
½ teaspoon pepper
1 pound carrots, peeled and
   sliced

½ teaspoon tarragon
1 tablespoon chopped parsley
2 cups milk
1 tablespoon flour
½ teaspoon caraway seeds
½ cup heavy cream
½ cup slivered almonds,
   toasted

Heat the butter in a saucepan and sauté garlic and scallions 1–2 minutes. Add the chicken broth, bay leaf, pepper, and carrots and simmer until carrots are tender. Cool. • Remove bay leaf and purée in a blender or food processor. • Return the purée to the saucepan, adding the tarragon, parsley, milk, flour and caraway seeds. Bring to a boil and simmer, stirring, for 3 minutes. Just before serving, stir in the cream. Pour into serving bowls and garnish each with toasted, slivered almonds.

Dorothy Leavitt

GARLIC SOUP

Serves 4–5

9 cloves garlic, finely
   chopped
¼ cup olive oil
3 slices French bread, cubed
6 cups rich chicken broth

3 eggs, beaten
Salt
Pepper
Lime wedges

Sauté chopped garlic in oil until golden brown. Carefully remove and discard garlic. Then sauté the bread in the same oil until golden. Add the bread to heated chicken broth and simmer, covered, for 10 minutes. • Remove 2 cups of chicken broth and place in an earthenware bowl. This will cool it a bit. Slowly add eggs to the broth, trying not to curdle them. Return this mixture to the soup pot. Season to taste and serve with lime wedges.

Sonia Henderson Curtis

EASY BORSCHT   Serves 12

5½–6 cups sour cream
Juice of ½ lemon
1 teaspoon salt
1 medium onion, chopped

3 cups sliced canned beets
3 cups cracked ice
Dill sprigs

Whirl 5 cups of the sour cream, the lemon juice, salt, onion and beets in a blender or food processor until smooth. Add the cracked ice and blend again. Chill thoroughly. Turn the soup into individual dishes and garnish each serving with a generous spoonful of sour cream and a sprig of dill or a sprinkling of dried dill.

Jamie Craft

BLACK BEAN SOUP   Serves 6–8

"A hearty main dish soup"

1 cup dried black beans
4 cups water
¼ teaspoon dried hot red
  pepper flakes
4 tablespoons butter
2 medium onions, coarsely
  chopped
1 clove garlic, chopped
½ teaspoon curry powder
¼ teaspoon turmeric

2 medium potatoes, peeled
  and quartered
2 medium carrots, peeled
  and quartered
2 medium parsnips, peeled
  and quartered
1-pound can stewed tomatoes
10½-ounce can beef broth
10½-ounce can chicken broth
Salt to taste

Pick over the beans, rinse and place them in a 3-quart saucepan with 3 cups water. Soak them 6–8 hours or overnight. Bring beans to a boil, cover, reduce heat and simmer 1½ hours. Add the red pepper flakes, continue cooking 30 minutes longer. Beans should be very tender.
• While the beans are cooking, heat the butter in a large saucepan and add the onions, garlic, curry powder and turmeric. Cook, stirring, until the onion is wilted. Add 1 cup water, all the vegetables and the undrained stewed tomatoes. Bring to a boil, cover and simmer about 25 minutes or until vegetables are tender. • Put the cooked beans, including their cooking liquid and the vegetable mixture through a food mill into a large saucepan. Stir in the undiluted beef and chicken broth. Salt the soup to taste. Bring to a boil and serve.

Marlene Tanzer

ONION WINE SOUP   Serves 6–8

¼ cup butter
5 large onions, chopped
5 cups beef broth
½ cup celery leaves
1 large potato, sliced
1 cup dry white wine

1 tablespoon vinegar
2 teaspoons sugar
1 cup light cream
1 tablespoon minced parsley
Salt and pepper

Melt butter in large saucepan. Add chopped onion and mix well. Add beef broth, celery leaves and potato. Bring to boiling. Cover and simmer for 30 minutes. • Purée mixture in a blender. • Return to saucepan and blend in wine, vinegar and sugar. Bring to boiling and simmer five minutes. Stir in cream, parsley and salt and pepper to taste. Heat thoroughly but do not boil.

Mrs. Ronald W. Reagan

MAIN-DISH TOMATO AND VEGETABLE SOUP   Serves 8

Base:

3 tablespoons oil
½ cup chopped parsley
2 cloves garlic, minced
1 large onion, chopped
2 ounces ham, diced
½ teaspoon basil
½ teaspoon thyme

1   28-ounce and 1   15-ounce
    can Italian plum tomatoes,
    drained
3 tablespoons tomato paste
4 cups chicken (or beef) broth
1 teaspoon sugar

Sauté parsley, onion, and garlic in the oil. Add remaining ingredients and simmer, uncovered, about 30 minutes. Purée. (Note: Base may be frozen.)

Finishing:

2 celery stalks, chopped
2 carrots, sliced
1 potato, chopped
1   10-ounce package frozen
    snowpeas
1 cup cauliflower florets

1½ cups lima or kidney beans
1 cup shredded cabbage
1 pound small meatballs,
    cooked and drained
Grated Parmesan cheese

Add any or all of the above to hot soup base. Cook until vegetables are tender. Serve with a sprinkling of grated Parmesan cheese.

Mrs. William Martindill

The spire of the old Post Office building

CHICKEN, RICE AND
EGG-LEMON SOUP A LA GRECQUE

Serves 10

1–2 pound chicken or 1 pound
   chicken wings and bones
   and 10 cups water or
   substitute 10 cups chicken
   bouillon plus
   1 tablespoon butter
Salt and white pepper to taste

2 carrots
1 stalk celery
2 onions
1 small zucchini, optional
⅓ cup rice
3 egg yolks
Juice of 3 lemons

Bring the chicken and water or the substitute chicken bouillon to a
boil, skim off the foam and add the vegetables and seasonings. Simmer
for 1 hour, strain, pressing juices from the vegetables. • Return the
liquid to the stove and add the rice. Boil 20 minutes. Meanwhile, chop
the cooked vegetables and add them to the soup when the rice is done.
• Just before serving, beat the egg yolks with lemon juice and gradually add them to the hot, but not boiling soup. (Note: The boiled
chicken meat may be cooled and reserved for another use.)

Mrs. John A. Tzounis
Wife of the Ambassador of Greece

MEATBALL SOUP

Serves 6

1½ pounds ground chuck
2 cups grated Parmesan cheese
2 eggs
1 cup seasoned bread crumbs
1 tablespoon chopped parsley
1 tablespoon Dijon mustard

Salt and pepper to taste
2½ quarts water
1 large onion, chopped
3 large carrots, sliced thin
2 stalks celery, chopped
1½ pounds escarole, chopped

Combine the ground chuck, 1 cup of the Parmesan cheese, eggs, bread crumbs, parsley, mustard and salt and pepper and mix well. Form into tiny meatballs. • In a soup pot, bring the water, onion, carrots, and celery to a boil. Add the escarole and simmer for 10 minutes. Add the meatballs, stirring as you do so. Season with salt and pepper to taste. Cook 30–40 minutes longer. Serve in bowls sprinkled with the remaining 1 cup Parmesan cheese to form a light melted veil over the hot soup.

Debra Silimeo

HEARTY BURGERSHIRE SOUP

Serves 4

1 pound ground beef
½ cup chopped celery
½ cup chopped carrots
½ cup chopped onion
1 green pepper, chopped
1 can beef bouillon
1 tablespoon flour

1   16-ounce can stewed
    tomatoes
Dash of sugar
Salt and pepper to taste
2 tablespoons barley
¾ teaspoon Kitchen Bouquet

Brown the ground beef in a large saucepan. Add the remaining ingredients and simmer 1 hour or so. Soup may be expanded or thinned by adding tomato juice or beef bouillon or both.

Mrs. William Webster

LEFTOVER ROAST CHICKEN SOUP   Serves 8

"You'll make roast chicken just to have the soup!"

1 roast chicken carcass
½–¾ cup chopped onions,
   carrots and celery
½ cup vermouth
3 tablespoons soy sauce
3 teaspoons salt or to taste
Pepper

12 fresh spinach leaves,
   shredded
10 fresh mushrooms, sliced
6 water chestnuts, sliced
Handful fresh bean sprouts
Paper thin slices of carrot
White or wild rice

Pick any remaining meat from chicken carcass and reserve. Place all bones in a large pot, add onions, carrots, celery and water to cover. Boil 3–5 hours. Add some water during cooking time as it evaporates.
• Sieve carcass and vegetables, reserving only the broth. Cool and refrigerate overnight. • Skim fat off chilled broth and reheat to boiling, adding the vermouth. Boil 5 minutes. Add soy sauce, seasoning and all vegetables. Add reserved chicken meat. Reduce heat and cook until vegetables are just tender. Correct seasoning.

Chris Hunter

HEARTY CLAM CHOWDER   Serves 6

6 slices bacon
5–6 scallions with tops, minced
6–7 medium potatoes, peeled
   and chopped
½ green pepper, chopped
2–3 stalks celery, chopped
2–3 carrots, chopped
1 clove garlic, minced
3 cups water
2–3 teaspoons salt
1 teaspoon pepper

2 teaspoons Worcestershire
   sauce
4–6 drops Tabasco
3–4 cups raw clams, chopped
2 cups half and half
1 cup heavy cream
2 tablespoons flour in
   2 tablespoons milk
Pinch–1 teaspoon curry
   powder

Fry bacon in a large pot, add next 6 ingredients and cook 5 minutes. Add remaining ingredients, correct seasoning and simmer covered until done, about 45 minutes.

Jackie Goldman

HELEN'S FISH CHOWDER Serves 6

1½ cups water
2 medium potatoes, peeled
    and diced
1½ pounds halibut or
    haddock filets
4 tablespoons butter
1 large onion, chopped
2 stalks celery, sliced

4 tablespoons flour
5 cups milk or 4 cups milk
    and 1 cup heavy cream
Salt and pepper to taste
1 green pepper, diced
2 tomatoes, seeded and diced
1½–2 teaspoons dill

Bring water and potatoes to a boil in a saucepan. Simmer 5–8 minutes until potatoes are almost tender. Add the fish and simmer 5 minutes. Remove fish and potatoes from liquid and cut fish into 1½-inch pieces. Reserve liquid, potatoes and fish. • Melt the butter in a clean saucepan and sauté the onion and celery until the onion is transparent. Add the flour and cook for 2 minutes. Add the fish liquid, stirring to blend well. Add milk or milk and cream and season to taste with salt and pepper. Bring to a boil and simmer for 5 minutes. • Parboil the chopped pepper for 1 minute, rinse under cold water and add to the chowder with the tomatoes and dill. Serve hot.

Mrs. Malcolm Price

Key Bridge and the Georgetown University spires

CHEF BELL'S FROSTED CRAB SOUP   Serves 6

4 tablespoons butter
1 large chopped onion
1 bay leaf
Small clove garlic, minced
1 teaspoon mild curry powder
¾ cup flour
1 quart chicken stock
6 tablespoons white wine

1½ cups light cream
½ teaspoon salt
Dash white pepper
¼ teaspoon MSG
½ pound crab meat, all bits
   of shell removed
Chopped chives or parsley for
   garnish

Melt the butter in a large saucepan and sauté the onions, bay leaf and garlic until tender but not brown. Add the curry powder and flour. Mix well and cook 1–2 minutes. Add the chicken stock, simmer, covered, 30 minutes, stirring occasionally. Strain and cool slightly. Add the wine and cream, return to the stove and heat slowly. Season to taste. If too thick, dilute with a little milk. Chill. To serve, put crab meat in the bottom of the serving bowl, then add soup. Garnish with chives or parsley.

Chef Forest Bell
Congressional Country Club

CRAB BISQUE
Serves 6–8

"This has superb flavor"

4 tablespoons butter	⅓ cup sherry or Cognac
1 pound lump crab meat	¼ teaspoon chopped chives
2 tablespoons flour	Pinch cayenne
2 cups heavy cream	1 teaspoon anchovy paste
3 cups milk	Salt and pepper

Melt the butter in a saucepan over low heat. Stir in crab meat from which all bits of shell have been removed. Add the flour and cook slowly for 10 minutes, stirring frequently. • In a clean saucepan, heat the cream and milk. Stir in the sherry or Cognac, chives, cayenne and anchovy paste. Pour into the crab mixture, season with salt and pepper, and heat thoroughly, being careful not to allow the bisque to boil.

Mrs. W. Walker Lewis III

OYSTER STEW
Serves 6–8

"Rich and warming, right down to your toes"

4 potatoes, diced	4 cups milk
2 carrots, chopped	2 pints shucked oysters
4 stalks celery, chopped	Pinch cayenne
2 tablespoons chopped onion	Salt and pepper
6 tablespoons butter	2 cups light cream
2 tablespoons flour	Chopped parsley, to garnish

Boil potatoes, carrots and celery together in salted water until tender. Drain and set aside. • Sauté the onions slowly in the butter until transparent. Stir in the flour until it forms a paste. Add the milk and cooked vegetables and heat, stirring constantly, until thickened. • In a clean saucepan, cook the oysters in their own juices until their edges curl, about 3 minutes. Add them to the milk mixture. Add seasonings and cream and heat, being careful not to let the soup boil. Garnish each serving with chopped parsley.

Mrs. W. Walker Lewis III

FISH AND SEAFOOD

Jefferson Memorial

THE KING'S FAVORITE FISH   Serves 6

"A royal treat"

2 sea bass or rockfish,
  1½ pounds each, cleaned,
  backbone removed, but head
  and skin on
¼ pound butter, melted
1 egg yolk

½ cup plus 2–3 tablespoons
  fresh white bread crumbs
1–2 shallots, minced
2 bunches parsley, minced
Salt and pepper to taste
1¼ cups white wine

Place the fish in a buttered baking dish, spread open so that skin side is down and flesh side is up, looking like a flounder. • Mix the butter, egg yolk, ½ cup bread crumbs, shallots, parsley, salt and pepper. Spread this on the fish. Sprinkle the additional 2–3 tablespoons bread crumbs over all and pour the wine around the fish. Bake at 350° for about 20 minutes or until fish has a golden surface. Serve surrounded by small boiled potatoes garnished with dill.

Countess Wachtmeister
Wife of the Ambassador of Sweden

POACHED ROCKFISH   Serves 4

1½ pounds rockfish, cut
  into 2 filets
2 dozen small cherrystone
  clams
1–3 cloves garlic
1 tablespoon olive oil

1 tablespoon minced celery or
  celery leaves
12 small shrimp, uncooked
Salt and pepper
2 tablespoons butter
White wine for poaching

Place the fish filets, skin side down, on each side of a baking dish, preferably copper. • Scrub the clams well and arrange them between the filets. Sprinkle them with the garlic, celery, and olive oil. • Place the shrimp on the fish, season with salt and pepper and dot with butter. Add enough white wine to half cover the fish. Cover tightly with aluminum foil, bring the wine to a boil and poach about 10 minutes until clams are steamed and fish is done.

Mrs. Tom Page

GRILLED FISH KEBAB   Serves 4

4 fish steaks, 1 inch thick,
  cut into 2-inch squares
  (rockfish, red snapper, etc.)
Juice of 2 lemons
Juice of 1 large onion
3–4 tablespoons olive oil

1 teaspoon ground cumin
  or thyme
2 green peppers
3 medium tomatoes
1/3 teaspoon salt
1/4 teaspoon pepper

Rinse fish pieces in cold water and pat dry. • Marinate the fish in a mixture of the lemon juice, onion juice, oil, and cumin or thyme for one to two hours in the refrigerator. • Cut the green pepper in thick strips. • Quarter the tomatoes. • Thread pieces of fish on skewers alternately with green pepper strips and tomatoes. Brush well with marinade. • Grill fish 5–6 inches from coals for about 20 minutes, turning occasionally and brushing with marinade. • Serve with rice.

Mrs. Ashraf Ghorbal
Wife of the Ambassador
of Egypt

FISH WITH CARROTS AND PRUNES   Serves 4–6

2–3 pounds fish, red snapper
  or grouper cut into
  serving pieces
Flour, to coat fish
Salt and pepper
Lemon juice
6 tablespoons oil
1 large onion, coarsely
  chopped

4 large carrots, thinly sliced
  or grated
1   28-ounce can stewed
  tomatoes
2 tablespoons ketchup
1½ tablespoons sugar, white
  or brown
15 pitted prunes

Coat fish pieces in flour, salt and pepper. Fry on both sides in 3 tablespoons oil. Sprinkle with lemon juice. • In a saucepan, sauté the onions in remaining oil until soft. Add carrots and cook for 5 minutes. Stir in tomatoes, ketchup, sugar, salt and pepper to taste and cook for 15 minutes. • Put half of the tomato and carrot sauce into a large casserole. Lay fish on top in one layer. Dot with prunes and pour on the rest of the tomato and carrot sauce. Cover with aluminum foil and cook at 350° for 30 minutes.

Mrs. G. William Miller

PICKLED FISH   Serves 6

"An excellent appetizer as well, serving many. Very spicy!"

4 medium-sized white fish
  filets
1 tablespoon flour
½ cup olive oil
2 large onions, sliced
3–4 cloves garlic, sliced

1 tablespoon grated fresh
  ginger
½ teaspoon salt
1½–2 tablespoons curry
  powder
1 tablespoon chutney

Flour the skinned and deboned fish and sauté until browned in 2–3 tablespoons olive oil. Remove. • Add remaining oil and sauté onions, garlic and ginger. When softened, add the salt and curry powder. Cook 3 minutes longer. Remove from heat and add chutney • Place fish in a serving dish or crock and cover with onion chutney mixture. Pour sauce (recipe below) over all and stir well. Chill. • Serve as a cold entreé or spread on toast. (Note: Keeps 2–3 weeks in refrigerator.)

Sauce:

½ cup vinegar
2 tablespoons flour

2 large onions, sliced

In a saucepan, combine the vinegar and flour. Add sliced onions and boil gently until onions are soft. Pour over fish.

Anne Green

CATHERINE'S FISH STEW   Serves 8

"Ah, memories of supper at the shore."

2 pounds any fresh fish filets
4 potatoes, peeled and cubed
A few celery leaves
1 bay leaf
1 clove garlic
4 whole cloves
3 onions, sliced

½ cup butter
1 cup white wine
2½ teaspoons salt
½ teaspoon white pepper
2 cups boiling water
2 cups cream
¼ cup chopped dill or parsley

Place all ingredients except the cream and dill in a casserole dish with the potatoes on the bottom and the fish on top. • Cover and bake at 375° for 1 hour. • Heat cream to scalding and add to the casserole, stirring to break up the fish. Garnish with dill or parsley and serve.

David P. Fogle

FISH FILETS With JULIENNED VEGETABLES IN LETTUCE

*"Use this single serving recipe as a guide
to serve as many people as desired."*

⅓ carrot
⅓ leek
⅓ zucchini
1 tablespoon butter
Lemon juice to taste
Salt and pepper to taste

1 fish filet, such as sole,
   flounder or other white fish
Large leaf romaine
Court bouillon or
   ½ wine and ½ water
Beurre blanc, see
   instructions below

Cut the carrot, leek and zucchini into julienne strips. Heat the butter and cook the vegetables slowly in a covered pan until tender, about 5 minutes. Cool. • Season the fish with lemon juice, salt and pepper and spread ½ the vegetables on it. Fold the filet over the vegetables, tucking the ends under to form a packet. • Blanch the lettuce leaf for several seconds in boiling water. Place the filet packet on the lettuce leaf, top with remaining vegetables, and fold the lettuce leaf around all. Place packet(s) in a skillet with enough court bouillon or white wine and water to cover. Poach the fish for 7–8 minutes. Serve immediately with beurre blanc.

Beurre blanc: *Serves 4*

1 teaspoon minced shallots
¼ cup wine vinegar
¼ cup fish poaching liquid
¼ cup butter, softened

2 tablespoons mixed fresh
   parsley, chives, basil and
   tarragon, or 1 tablespoon
   of dried herbs

Simmer the shallots, vinegar and fish poaching liquid together until reduced to about ¼ of its original volume. Beat in butter, a little at a time, using a wire whisk, until creamy and whitened. Add the herbs.

Joan Davidson

The Fountain at Dupont Circle

BAHAMIAN GINGER GROUPER   Serves 6

3 pounds grouper filets or
  substitute cod, sea bass
  or snapper
1 medium onion, thinly sliced
¼ green pepper, thinly sliced
¼ cup oil

4 cups stewed tomatoes
½ cup ginger preserves
¼ teaspoon marjoram
¼ teaspoon thyme
1 bay leaf
1 teaspoon salt

Place fish in a shallow casserole dish and set aside. • Sauté the onion and green pepper in the oil until lightly browned. Add tomatoes, ginger preserves and seasonings. Bring sauce to a boil, then pour over the fish. • Bake at 350° for 15 minutes (fish should flake when tested with a fork). Serve with rice.

Mrs. John W. Nairn

MUSSELS WITH EGG YOLK SAUCE   Serves 6–8

4 pounds mussels
¼ pound butter
2 medium onions, thinly
  sliced
½ cup dry white wine
Juice of ½ lemon

1 tablespoon cornstarch
  or arrowroot, dissolved
  in ¼ cup water
2 egg yolks, well beaten
1 tablespoon chopped parsley
Salt and pepper to taste

Have the fishmonger give the mussels a preliminary cleaning, then scrub and debeard them thoroughly. Put them in a large pot (preferably in one layer) and put the pot in a hot oven (400°) for up to 5 minutes until the mussels are opened. Discard any that did not open and remove the rest from the shell, reserving all the mussel liquid. Keep warm while you prepare the sauce. • Melt ½ the butter in a saucepan and sauté the onions until golden. Add the wine, dissolved cornstarch or arrowroot, lemon juice, remaining butter and the mussel liquid. Simmer for a few minutes, whisking constantly. Strain through a fine sieve pressing well on the onions. Return to pan, add the yolks, and cook over low heat for a minute or two being careful that the yolks do not curdle. Add the parsley and the mussels and warm them slowly. • Serve immediately with sautéed potatoes or toast points. (Note: With the addition of ½ cup heavy cream, this can be used as a sauce with any kind of thin spaghetti.)

Mrs. Vasco Futscher Pereira
Wife of the Ambassador of Portugal

MARTHA'S VINEYARD SWORDFISH BAKED IN CREAM

Serves 4

4 thick slices fresh swordfish
2 tablespoons Coleman's hot
  mustard

Salt and pepper
1 cup light cream
1 cup sour cream

Lightly spread each slice of swordfish with mustard and season with salt and pepper. Place in Pyrex dish and pour light cream around the fish. Cover the slices of fish with sour cream. Bake at 325° for 20 minutes.

Mrs. J. M. Colton Hand

RED SNAPPER FLAKES IN MUSTARD SAUCE   Serves 6–8

"Invite your guests to a real White House dinner"

1½ cups water
½ teaspoon salt
A spice bag consisting of a
  pinch thyme and marjoram,
  12 peppercorns and a small
  bay leaf
1 cup mixture of chopped
  onions, celery and carrots
Juice of ½ lemon

1 cup Chablis wine
1½ pounds red snapper filet
2 tablespoons butter
1½ tablespoons flour
1 teaspoon dry mustard
½–1 cup heavy cream
½ teaspoon Worcestershire
  sauce

In a wide but shallow saucepan bring water, salt, spice bag and chopped onions, celery and carrots to a boil. Simmer 5 minutes. Add the lemon juice and wine and bring to a boil. Add the red snapper and boil slowly 5–6 minutes. Remove pan from heat and let the fish cool in the liquid 1 hour or overnight. • When ready to continue, remove fish and strain liquid reserving 2 cups. Melt the butter in a 2-quart saucepan, add the flour, stirring well to make a roux. Mix in the dry mustard. Reheat the 2 cups reserved fish stock and whisk into the mustard roux. Simmer the sauce, stirring often, and gradually add the cream. Add the Worcestershire sauce and continue cooking to reduce the mustard sauce to a velvety consistency. • Flake the red snapper into small pieces, removing any bones. Add to the mustard sauce, bring to a boil and serve. (Note: Cheese or spinach soufflé and home-made noodles or steamed rice are suggested accompaniments.)

Chef Henry Haller
The White House

SUPREME OF RED SNAPPER DUGLERE   Serves 8

12 shallots
8 6-ounce filets of
    red snapper
1 quart fish fumet
1 cup white wine
2 quarts heavy cream

2 pounds canned whole
    tomatoes
1 tablespoon butter
Salt and pepper
2 bay leaves
½ teaspoon thyme

Finely chop 6 of the shallots and spread them in the bottom of a buttered baking dish. Lay the snapper filets on top and sprinkle them with salt and white pepper. • Reduce the fish fumet to a syrup or until it coats the bottom of the pan. • In a separate pan, reduce the white wine. • In still another pan, reduce the heavy cream until it coats the back of a spoon. Mix the fish fumet reduction and the wine reduction into the cream pan to make a white wine sauce. • Drain the tomatoes, remove the seeds and chop them roughly. • Chop the remaining 6 shallots. • Heat the butter in a saucepan, add the tomatoes, shallots, salt, pepper and the bay leaves and thyme which have been tied in a cheesecloth bag. Sauté until dry. Blend into the white wine sauce. • Add lightly salted water to barely cover the snapper filets and poach them gently 10–15 minutes. Drain the filets and arrange them on a serving dish. Coat them with the sauce.

The Jockey Club

SIMPLE SALMON   Serves 6

"Renee's family likes it without the pie crust too!"

¼ cup chopped onion
2 tablespoons butter
3 eggs, lightly beaten
½ cup milk
2 tablespoons minced parsley

½ teaspoon basil
½ teaspoon salt
1-pound can salmon, flaked
1 small can asparagus spears
1 unbaked 9-inch pie shell

Sauté onion in the butter. • Combine eggs, milk, herbs, salt and onion. Fold in flaked salmon. • Reserving 6 asparagus spears, place remainder in pie shell. Pour in the salmon mixture and arrange the 6 asparagus spears like spokes on the top. • Bake at 425° for 35–40 minutes or until set.

Renee Subrin

SALMON EN CROUTE MADISON

Serves 10

4 cups coarsely chopped onion
½ cup coarsely chopped celery
1 cup peeled and chopped
 carrots
10 whole black peppercorns
4½ teaspoons salt
2 cups dry white wine
3 pounds fresh salmon, in one
 piece
6 tablespoons butter
2 pounds fresh mushrooms,
 sliced

3 tablespoons fresh lemon
 juice
½ teaspoon white pepper
¼ cup minced fresh dill
2 tablespoons minced parsley
1 teaspoon nutmeg
¼ cup brandy
10 cups cooked rice
3 eggs, hard-boiled and finely
 chopped

Bring 3 quarts of water to boil in a large pot with 2 cups of onions, the celery, carrots, peppercorns, 3 teaspoons salt and the wine. Add the salmon, reduce the heat and simmer 10 minutes. Remove the salmon, discard the skin and bones and separate the meat into small flakes.
• Sauté the mushrooms in 2 tablespoons butter for 5 minutes. Transfer them to a bowl and pour the lemon juice over them.
• Sauté 2 cups onions in 4 tablespoons of butter until soft but not brown. Stir in 1 teaspoon salt and the white pepper. Add them to the mushrooms. • Combine the flaked salmon and the mushroom mixture with all remaining ingredients in a large bowl. Correct the seasoning and refrigerate while preparing the pastry.

Pastry:

4 cups flour
½ pound unsalted butter
6 tablespoons vegetable oil
1 teaspoon salt

12 tablespoons ice water
1 egg yolk beaten with
 2–3 tablespoons cream

Combine the flour, butter, oil and salt. Work the flour and fats together with your fingertips until they resemble coarse meal. Add the ice water, toss together and gather into a ball. Divide the dough in ½, wrap each piece in wax paper and refrigerate until firm. • Roll out ½ the dough into a rectangle and lay it on a large buttered cookie sheet. Spread salmon filling on the pastry, leaving a 1-inch border on all the edges. Brush the pastry border with the egg yolk and cream mixture. Roll out remaining dough and lay it over the filling. Seal edges of the pastry together by pressing down firmly with a wooden spoon. Brush the entire surface of the pastry with the remaining egg yolk and cream mixture.
• Bake the salmon en croûte on the center rack of a 400° oven for 1 hour or until golden brown. Serve immediately.

Marshall Coyne
Madison Hotel

SALMON STEAKS WITH GOLDEN CAVIAR AND PARSLEY SAUCE

Serves 4

2 bunches parsley,
  stems removed
4 shallots, minced
3 ounces dry vermouth
¼ teaspoon thyme
4 cups fish stock

2 cups cream
4 salmon steaks
Salt and pepper
Olive oil
8 ounces golden caviar

Poach the parsley in highly salted boiling water, drain, and mince in a blender or food processor. • Heat the vermouth in a saucepan, add the shallots and thyme and reduce by ½. Add the fish stock and reduce again. Add the cream and reduce the mixture by ½ one more time. At this point the sauce should be creamy in consistency. Set aside. • Season the salmon steaks lightly with salt and pepper. Sauté them in the olive oil, not more than 2 minutes on each side. Remove the salmon steaks to a heated platter. • Add the puréed parsley to the vermouth sauce, beating to blend well. Reheat the sauce but do not let it boil. Stir in the caviar. Surround the fish with the sauce and serve.

Chef Jean Louis Palladin
Jean Louis Restaurant
The Watergate Hotel

CURRIED SEA SCALLOPS

Serves 3

1 pound scallops, rinsed
1¼ cups dry white wine or
  dry vermouth
3 tablespoons butter

3 tablespoons flour
½ teaspoon curry
¼ cup heavy cream
Buttered bread crumbs

Boil the scallops for 3 minutes in the wine or vermouth. Drain them, reserving the liquid, and turn them into a well buttered baking dish. • Melt the butter in a saucepan and add the flour and curry powder. Add 1 cup of the cooking liquid and heat, stirring constantly, until thickened. Remove from heat and stir in the cream. Pour the sauce over the scallops, cover with buttered bread crumbs and brown quickly under the broiler.

Mrs. Garrison Norton

SCALLOPS FLORENTINE   Serves 6

"Not a recipe for purists, but great for cooks with no time."

2 tablespoons butter
2   10-ounce packages frozen
   leaf spinach, cooked
   and drained
Onion salt

1½ pounds scallops
1 can cheddar cheese soup
¼ cup white wine
1 large or 2 small tomatoes
Pinch oregano

Grease a 2-quart casserole and place spinach in a layer on the bottom.
Season with onion salt and add scallops. • Combine soup and wine
until smooth and pour over scallops. Slice tomatoes and arrange on the
top. Sprinkle with oregano and onion salt. Bake at 350° for 25
minutes.

Mrs. Robert H. Craft, Jr.

Entrance to the National Zoo

COQUILLES SAINT-JACQUES   Serves 6

1½ pounds scallops
1 cup boiling salted water
6 shallots, minced
1 tablespoon minced parsley
¼ pound mushrooms, sliced
6 tablespoons butter

3 tablespoons flour
½ cup white wine
Salt and pepper to taste
1 egg yolk, beaten
⅓ cup bread crumbs

Wash scallops, then immerse them in boiling salted water for 3 minutes. Drain them, reserving the water. • Brown the shallots, parsley
and mushrooms in 2 tablespoons of butter. Set aside. • Melt 2
tablespoons butter in a saucepan, whisk in the flour and add the wine,
½ cup of scallop water, salt and pepper. Cook, stirring with the whisk,
about 2 minutes. Add the beaten egg yolk and blend well. Stir in the
mushroom mixture and scallops and turn into 6 scallop shells. Sprinkle
each shell with bread crumbs and dot with the remaining butter. Broil
them until hot and browned.

Janine Bowie

SCALLOP-STUFFED ARTICHOKES WITH GREEN MAYONNAISE

Serves 8

"A very festive first course"

8 artichokes
¾ cup vermouth
1 small onion, minced
1 sprig parsley

1 bay leaf
1 pound bay scallops, whole
  or sea scallops, quartered

Trim stems and prickly points of leaves off artichokes. Boil in salted water for 18 minutes or until bottoms test tender. Drain the artichokes bottoms up. When cool, remove tender inside leaves to make a hollow and reserve. Remove the chokes with a spoon. Refrigerate until ready to assemble. • Combine the vermouth, onion, parsley and bay leaf in a sauté pan. Bring to a boil, add scallops and simmer 2 minutes, shaking the pan as they cook. Off heat, cover and let stand 2 minutes more. Drain the scallops, reserving the cooking liquid with the onions. Discard parsley and bay leaf. Cool scallops and liquid.

Sauce:

3 egg yolks
1½ teaspoons Dijon mustard
2–3 tablespoons lemon juice
½ teaspoon salt
½ teaspoon ground
  white pepper
1 cup peanut oil
1 cup olive oil
1 cup spinach, blanched in
  boiling water, squeezed dry
  and minced

¾ cup minced parsley
¼ cup minced chives
¼ cup minced scallions
  with tops
1 tablespoon fresh tarragon or
  ½ teaspoon dried
1 tablespoon minced fresh
  dill
1 lemon
Parsley to garnish

Using a food processor with steel blade or a blender, process the egg yolks, mustard, lemon juice and seasonings for 2 minutes. With motor running, add peanut oil in a thin stream. Add olive oil in the same way, producing 2¼ cups very thick mayonnaise. Add remaining ingredients, except lemon and parsley garnish to the mayonnaise, thinning with some of the reserve scallop liquid to the consisency of a commercial mayonnaise. • Mix 1 cup mayonnaise with the scallops, adding more, if necessary, to thoroughly coat them. Fill each hollowed artichoke with some of the scallop mixture. • Cut narrow strips of peel from the lemon, working from top to bottom. Slice the lemon thin. The slices will be decoratively scalloped. Top each artichoke with a lemon slice and garnish with minced parsley. Place on individual plates, pressing down bottom 2 rows of leaves to make a flower. Pass

Continued

remaining sauce separately. (Note: Reserved inner leaves and any leftover sauce can be combined with some minced chicken and chopped celery for a light luncheon salad.)

Mrs. Matthew Huxley

EASY AND ELEGANT SHAD ROE   Serves 2

1 large pair shad roe
2 tablespoons butter
2 tablespoons chopped shallots

Salt and pepper
Chopped parsley for
    garnish

Place shad roe on a piece of foil large enough to enclose. Dot with butter, scatter shallots on top and fold foil into a package. Bake at 400° for 20 minutes. • When cooked, salt and pepper to taste and garnish with parsley. Crisp bacon is a very nice accompaniment.

Mrs. Robert H. Craft, Jr.

BAKED SOLE WITH CRAB MEAT   Serves 4–6

3 cups white wine
2 leeks, chopped
Salt and pepper
5 white peppercorns
8 filets of sole
1 pound crab meat,
    drained

1   15-ounce can asparagus
    spears
2 tablespoons butter
1 tablespoon flour
1 egg yolk

Heat 3 cups water, the white wine, leeks, salt, pepper and peppercorns in a poaching pan or large skillet and simmer for 5 minutes. Carefully add fish filets and poach for 5 minutes. Remove filets and drain, reserving liquid. • Place filets in a single layer in a large, oiled baking dish. Arrange crab meat and asparagus on top of fish. • In a saucepan, melt butter and add flour. Stir and make sauce using ½–1 cup of the poaching liquid. Sauce should be of coating consistency. Remove from heat and beat in egg yolk. • Pour sauce over the fish, dot with butter and bake at 350° for 10 minutes or until golden brown.

Mrs. Charles J. DiBona

CLAM AND CHEESE PIE

Serves 6

1 8-ounce package cream
cheese
4 eggs, separated
2 7-ounce cans minced
clams, drained

1 teaspoon grated onion
¼ teaspoon Tabasco sauce
1 9-inch pastry shell, partly
baked

Work the cream cheese until very soft. Beat in the egg yolks. Add the clams, onion and Tabasco sauce. Check the seasoning and add a little salt if needed. • Beat egg whites until stiff and fold into cheese mixture. • Pour into the partially baked pastry shell. Bake at 400° for 30–35 minutes until crust is golden and center is just set. Remove from oven and let stand 5 minutes before cutting into wedges to serve.

Manuel E. Ramirez

TUNA PIE WITH CHEESE CRUST

Serves 8

1½ cups flour
1 cup grated sharp cheese
1 teaspoon salt

1 teaspoon paprika
½ cup butter

Mix all crust ingredients with a fork until blended. Pat ½ the mixture into a 9 or 10-inch Pyrex pie plate. Save other ½ for topping.

Filling:

2 7½-ounce cans
water packed tuna
3 eggs
1 cup sour cream
½ cup grated cheese

¼ cup mayonnaise
1–2 tablespoons diced
pimento
1–2 pinches dill weed
1 teaspoon grated onion

Thoroughly drain the tuna, crumble it and put into pie crust. Mix together the rest of the filling ingredients. Pour on top of the tuna. Sprinkle with remaining crust mixture. Bake at 400° for 35 minutes.

Mrs. J. Edward Day

The Swan Boat on the Tidal Basin

AEGEAN SHRIMP WITH OUZO   Serves 6–8

"Unusual appetizer with a Greek flavor"

½ cup olive oil
1 medium onion, thinly sliced
2 cloves garlic, crushed
8 whole canned tomatoes,
  chopped
1 small bay leaf
1 teaspoon oregano
½ teaspoon fresh basil
½ cup finely chopped fresh
  parsley
½ teaspoon Chinese hot oil
A few red pepper flakes
¼ teaspoon sugar

Salt and pepper to taste
2 tablespoons butter
¾ pound or more large
  shrimp, shelled and
  deveined
2 tablespoons ouzo
2 tablespoons brandy
½ pound feta cheese,
  crumbled
2 tablespoons capers
Lemon juice
8 black calamata olives,
  halved and pitted

Heat the oil and sauté the onion and garlic. Add tomatoes, bay leaf, oregano, basil, ½ of the chopped parsley, hot oil, red pepper flakes, sugar, salt and pepper. Cook over moderate heat for 20 minutes. • In a skillet, melt the butter and sauté the shrimp over high heat until they turn pink. Add the ouzo and brandy, heat for a moment and flame the shrimp. • To the tomato sauce, add the crumbled feta cheese and the capers. • Place the shrimp in individual serving dishes (see note), sprinkle with lemon juice and top with a generous amount of sauce. Garnish with olives and the rest of the parsley. • Place under the broiler for a few minutes until bubbly. (Note: May be served in ramekins or pastry shells.)

Anastasia Shaw

SHRIMP A LA BORDELAISE

Serves 3–4

1 pound fresh shrimp
1 medium carrot, diced fine
1 medium onion, diced fine
2 tablespoons shallots, minced
1 sprig parsley
1 clove garlic, crushed
Pinch of thyme

1 small bay leaf, pulverized
5 tablespoons butter
1 teaspoon salt
2 tablespoons Cognac
¾ cup dry white wine
1 teaspoon flour
Chopped parsley

Clean and devein the raw shrimp. • Put carrot, onion, shallots, parsley, garlic, thyme, bay leaf and 2 tablespoons butter in a saucepan. Cook very slowly until the vegetables are soft, about 15 minutes. Add the shrimp and salt, and cook over a moderately hot flame, shaking the pan gently all the time, until the shrimp turn pink. Remove shrimp to a warm, deep serving dish. Add Cognac and wine to the saucepan and continue cooking for about 15 minutes, reducing the quantity somewhat. Cream together the flour and remaining butter, and add to the sauce to thicken. Do not allow the sauce to boil after it thickens. Correct seasoning if necessary, and pour over the shrimp. Sprinkle with the chopped parsley and serve immediately.

Harry Torno

SHRIMP IN COINTREAU CREAM

Serves 3

½ cup chopped parsley
1 cup chopped scallions
   or ¼ cup shallots, diced
1 pound medium shrimp,
   shelled and deveined
2–3 tablespoons butter

3 tablespoons Cointreau
3 tablespoons grated cheddar
   cheese
½ cup sour cream
Salt and pepper to taste

Heat the butter in a skillet and sauté the onions or shallots with the parsley for 2 minutes. Add the shrimp and cook 3 minutes more, turning them once. Slowly add the Cointreau and cheese, stirring. When cheese is melted, cool slightly and add the sour cream, salt and pepper. • Reheat gently and turn into a serving dish or individual shells or ramekins. • Serve with rice.

Jenne W. Jones

BEER BATTER SHRIMP   Serves 8

40 jumbo shrimp
6 eggs
5 tablespoons horseradish
8-ounce jar Grey Poupon
   mustard

4 cups beer
5 cups flour
½ teaspoon yellow food
   coloring

Clean, peel and devein the shrimp, leaving tails intact. • Mix the remaining ingredients until well blended. • Dip the shrimp into the batter, coating thoroughly, and fry in very hot oil (350°) until golden brown. Allow oil to reheat between batches. • Serve with mustard marmalade sauce on the side.

Mustard Marmalade Sauce:

3 cups orange marmalade
3 tablespoons horseradish

4 tablespoons Grey Poupon
   mustard

Chef Jacob Gravitt
Clyde's of Georgetown

CAJUN SPICED SHRIMP   Serves 6

"Finger licking good!"

¾ pound butter
4 cloves garlic, minced
4 tablespoons chili sauce
2 teaspoons Worcestershire
   sauce
1 tablespoon pickling spices
6 ounces beer
½ teaspoon paprika

Dash oregano
Dash Tabasco
Salt to taste
5 lemons
Cayenne pepper
Cracked black pepper
2 pounds jumbo shrimp,
   raw in shells

Melt butter in saucepan over low heat adding next nine ingredients. • Slice lemons in rounds and remove seeds. Line the bottom of a 9 x 12 inch baking dish with lemon slices. Sprinkle lemon slices generously with cayenne pepper and black pepper. Lay shrimp, still in shells, tightly in one layer on top of lemon slices. Pour heated butter mixture over shrimp. • Bake for 10 minutes in 350° oven, turn and bake 10 minutes more.

Gwen A. Holden

SHRIMP CURRY   Serves 4

3 tablespoons butter
6 tablespoons finely chopped,
   peeled apple
¼ cup finely chopped onion
¼ teaspoon minced garlic
2–3 teaspoons curry powder
⅓ cup finely chopped banana
½ cup chicken broth
¼ cup tomato sauce

⅔ cup heavy cream
Salt and pepper
1 tablespoon flour
1 pound medium shrimp,
   shelled and deveined
Chutney, coconut, chopped
   peanuts and yellow raisins
   as condiments

Heat 1 tablespoon of butter in a skillet. Add the apples, onion and garlic and cook 5 minutes. Add the curry powder and stir to blend well. Add the banana, chicken broth and tomato sauce. Simmer 2 minutes. Add the cream, salt and pepper. Simmer 2 minutes again and add 1 tablespoon of butter and sprinkle on the flour. Stir to blend and correct seasoning, adding more curry powder if desired. Remove from heat. • In another skillet, heat 1 tablespoon butter, add the shrimp and cook over high heat for 3 minutes. Add the sauce and stir. Serve the curry over rice and pass the condiments in individual bowls.

Mrs. Martin Feinstein

SHRIMP MADAGASCAR   Serves 4

2 tablespoons butter
¾ cup chopped scallions
2 tablespoons flour
½ cup dry white wine
1 cup plain yogurt
2 tablespoons chopped parsley
½ teaspoon salt

1–2 tablespoons green
   peppercorns crushed
   (available in gourmet shops)
1 pound raw shrimp, peeled
   and deveined
1 pound fresh mushrooms,
   quartered

In a large skillet melt butter. Add scallions and sauté 3 minutes. Stir in flour. Gradually stir in wine; cook 1 minute, or until mixture is thick. Stir in yogurt, parsley, green peppercorns and salt; blend well. Add shrimp and mushrooms. Cook, covered, over low heat, stirring occasionally, for 8–10 minutes, or until the shrimp turn pink.

Belinda D. McKenzie

SHRIMP WITH EGGS   Serves 4–6

"A meringue topping hides a delicious surprise"

2 medium onions, chopped
¼ cup chopped parsley
2 tablespoons butter
1 pound shrimp, shelled
   and deveined
1 pound canned tomatoes,
   drained and chopped

4 teaspoons cornstarch
¼ cup milk
¾ teaspoon salt
Dash Tabasco sauce
4 egg whites
4 egg yolks
4–6 fresh onion rings

Sauté the onion and parsley in the butter until tender but not brown.
Add the shrimp and tomatoes. Cover and cook over medium heat
about 10 minutes. • Blend the cornstarch with the milk and stir
into the shrimp mixture. Add ½ teaspoon salt and the Tabasco sauce.
Cook, stirring, until thick and bubbly. Keep warm. • Beat the egg
whites with ¼ teaspoon salt until stiff. • In a separate bowl beat the
egg yolks, then fold them into the whites. • Turn the hot shrimp
mixture into a 8 x 8 x 2 inch casserole dish. Spread the meringue over
the top and arrange the onion rings on the meringue. Bake at 375° for
20–25 minutes. Serve immediately.

Karen Petrus

SHRIMP REMOULADE   Serves 6

1 clove garlic
½ cup olive oil
¼ cup vinegar
1 teaspoon salt
¼ teaspoon pepper
1 teaspoon paprika
4 tablespoons mayonnaise

8 tablespoons creole mustard
3 tablespoons finely chopped
   parsley
½ cup chopped celery
½ white onion, chopped
1 pound cooked shrimp

Rub a serving bowl with garlic. • Combine all remaining ingredients, adding the shrimp last, and marinate overnight in the refrigerator. Taste and correct seasoning before serving on a bed of lettuce.
(Note: Creole mustard such as Zapatrane's is available in specialty food
stores).

Gerson Nordlinger, Jr.

WOK-FRIED SHRIMP AND WALNUTS   Serves 2

"Last minute delicacy with rice, salad and fruit"

2 tablespoons oil
½–¾ cup walnuts
½ pound shrimp, shelled
  and deveined
3 scallions cut into
  ½-inch lengths

4 carrots cut into julienne
  strips
½-inch piece fresh ginger,
  minced
½ teaspoon white pepper
Salt to taste

Heat 1 tablespoon oil in a wok or skillet and stir fry the walnuts for 2 minutes. Add the remaining oil and the shrimp. Cook over medium heat for 3 minutes. Add the scallions, carrots and ginger and season with salt and white pepper. Stir fry for 2–3 additional minutes. Serve with rice.

Mrs. Parker T. Hart

LA TIMBALE DE SCAMPIS MADRAS   Serves 8

3 pounds jumbo raw shrimp,
  about 54 pieces
Salt
1 tablespoon curry powder
5 tablespoons butter
1 tablespoon flour
1 cup clam juice

2 tablespoons chopped
  shallots
⅓ cup brandy
2 cups heavy cream
½ cup raisins
½ cup sliced toasted almonds
1 tablespoon chopped parsley

Shell and devein the shrimp. Season them with salt and curry powder.
• Heat 1 tablespoon of butter in a saucepan, stir in the flour and add the clam juice. Heat, stirring, until thickened to form a fish velouté. Set aside. • Melt 4 tablespoons of butter in a large skillet and add the shallots and the seasoned shrimp. Sauté 3 minutes, remove grease from the pan, pour in the brandy and ignite. When the flame subsides, add the cream and fish velouté. Reduce until the sauce has thickened. Add the raisins. Transfer the shrimp to a serving dish, top with the sliced toasted almonds and garnish with chopped parsley. Serve this dish with wild rice.

Chef Michel Laudier
Rive Gauche Restaurant

ZINGY BUTTERED SHRIMP   Serves 1

*"Multiply the recipe times the number of
guests and then double the napkins."*

4 tablespoons butter	1 tablespoon minced green
Pinch chili powder	pepper
Minced garlic to taste	4–6 large shrimp, shelled
1 tablespoon minced celery	and deveined
1 tablespoon minced onion	

Place butter in an individual ovenproof ramekin or small bowl and add
a pinch of chili powder and garlic to taste. Heat in a 350° oven until
butter is hot and bubbling. Remove bowl and add remaining ingredients. Return to the oven and bake 10 minutes. Serve with French
bread.

Anne Green

Main Avenue wharf

ASPARAGUS AND CRAB   Serves 6

6 ounces crab meat
1 can cream of chicken soup
1⅓ cups half and half
⅛ teaspoon crushed tarragon
¼ teaspoon salt
Dash of white pepper
1½ pounds asparagus spears

1 tablespoon sherry
1 tablespoon lemon juice
Toast, English muffins or
  avocado halves
½ cup toasted shredded
  coconut

Place crab meat in top of double boiler. Add chicken soup, half and half, tarragon, salt and pepper. Stir, cover, and heat over boiling water for 20 minutes. • Snap off bases of asparagus spears and slice diagonally into bite-sized pieces, leaving tips whole. Cook in boiling, salted water 3–4 minutes until barely tender. Drain and add to creamed crab along with sherry and lemon juice. • Serve on toast slices, toasted English muffins or in avacado halves. Garnish with toasted coconut.

Pam Burge

CRAB FOO YUNG WITH SWEET-SOUR SAUCE   Serves 5–6

½ cup diced celery
¼ cup green diced pepper
¼ cup thinly sliced scallions
1 pound can bean sprouts,
  drained
½ cup Kelloggs Concentrate
  cereal

1 tablespoon unprocessed bran
6 eggs, lightly beaten
½ teaspoon salt
Dash pepper
6 ounces crab meat
3 tablespoons oil

Combine first 6 ingredients. • Combine the eggs and seasonings and add to the vegetables. Carefully mix in the crab meat. • Heat some of the oil in a skillet. Spoon crab mixture onto skillet to form 3 inch cakes and cook until brown on both sides, turning only once. Repeat until 10–12 cakes are formed. Keep them hot and serve with sweet-sour sauce.

Sweet-Sour Sauce:

1 cup sugar
½ cup distilled vinegar
½ cup water
1 tablespoon diced green
  pepper

1 tablespoon diced pimento
½ teaspoon salt
2 teaspoons cornstarch,
  dissolved in 1 tablespoon
  water

In a saucepan combine the first 6 ingredients. Add cornstarch and water mixture and heat. Serve over Crab Foo Yung. (Note: This sauce may be refrigerated for up to 3 months.)

Mrs. J. W. Fisher

CRAB MEAT CASSEROLE   Serves 8

1 14-ounce can artichoke
   hearts
1 pound crab meat
½ pound fresh mushrooms
4 tablespoons butter
2½ tablespoons flour
1 cup cream
½ teaspoon salt

1 teaspoon Worcestershire
   sauce
¼ cup medium dry sherry
Paprika to taste
Cayenne to taste
Pepper to taste
¼ cup grated Parmesan
   cheese

Place artichokes in bottom of baking dish. Spread a layer of crab meat.
Add a layer of sauteed mushrooms. • Melt butter in a saucepan and
add remaining ingredients except cheese, stirring well after each
addition to form a smooth sauce. • Pour sauce over artichoke-crab
layers and sprinkle cheese on top. • Bake 20 minutes at 375°.

Mrs. Ronald W. Reagan

CRAB AND SPINACH CASSEROLE   Serves 4

2 packages frozen chopped
   spinach
1 pint sour cream
2–3 cups toasted bread crumbs
1 pound lump crab meat
¼ pound butter

Chopped tops of 6–7 scallions
Dash of cayenne
Salt to taste
2–4 teaspoons chopped
   parsley

Thaw spinach in the top of a double boiler and barely cook it. Spread
½ in the bottom of a buttered casserole and top with ½ the sour
cream. Add a thick layer of toasted bread crumbs. Next, add a layer of
all the crab meat, then the remaining spinach. • Make a smooth
creamy paste of the butter and remaining sour cream. Stir in the
chopped scallion tops, cayenne, salt, parsley and more bread crumbs.
Spread this over all and heat at 300° just until mixture begins to
bubble. Do not cook it.

Elizabeth Beach Rea

CRAB IMPERIAL   Serves 4

"A Maryland favorite"

1 pound backfin crab meat
½ cup mayonnaise
½ cup sour cream
1 teaspoon lemon juice
1 teaspoon Worcestershire sauce

1 teaspoon Dijon mustard
⅛ teaspoon curry powder
1 tablespoon capers
Butter
Breadcrumbs

Clean crab meat thoroughly. • Combine mayonnaise, sour cream, lemon juice, Worcestershire sauce, Dijon mustard, and curry powder. Toss this mixture lightly with the capers and crab meat. • Line individual serving shells with butter and breadcrumbs and fill with crab meat. • Heat in a slow (250°– 300°) oven for 20 to 25 minutes, taking care that sauce does not curdle or separate. Do not freeze.

Mariana Fleming

DEVILED CRAB CAKES   Serves 4

"Strom's favorite seafood dish"

1 pound crab claw meat
2 eggs
2 tablespoons mayonnaise
1 tablespoon Kraft's
    horseradish mustard
¼ teaspoon salt

⅛ teaspoon pepper
Dash Tabasco
1 tablespoon chopped parsley
½ cup freshly rolled
    cracker crumbs
Oil for deep frying

Combine all above ingredients, except cracker crumbs and oil, and mix lightly together. • Form mixture into desired size cakes or croquettes. Do not pack firmly, but allow the cakes to be light and spongy. Pat the crumbs onto the crab cakes. • Fry in deep fat just until golden brown. Remove immediately and drain on absorbent paper. Serve hot with a smile.

Mrs. Strom Thurmond
Wife of the Senator from
South Carolina

MARYLAND CRAB CAKES   4 cakes
"A regional favorite"

1 cup crumbled bread (use day
  old close-grained bread such
  as Pepperidge Farm White)
¼ cup mayonnaise
2 teaspoons prepared mustard

Dash black pepper
Dash cayenne
½–1 teaspoon salt
8 ounces backfin crab meat
2 tablespoons butter

In a bowl combine the crumbled bread with the mayonnaise, mustard, pepper, and salt. Work crab meat in gently, being careful not to flake it. Shape mixture into 4 cakes and refrigerate until ready to serve.
• Heat a griddle or skillet with butter and sauté the cakes 3–5 minutes or until hot and golden on both sides. Serve immediately.

Mrs. E. Edward Bruce

SHRIMP AND CRAB MEAT AU GRATIN   Serves 8

1 pound shrimp
5 tablespoons butter
½ pound mushrooms, sliced
1 clove garlic, minced
2 tablespoons chopped shallots
2 tablespoons flour
½ teaspoon pepper
¾ cup milk

8 ounces cheddar cheese,
  grated
⅔ cup white wine
14 ounces crab meat
1   14-ounce can artichoke
  hearts
2 tablespoons bread crumbs

Peel and devein the shrimp. Boil until pink, drain and set aside.
• Melt 4 tablespoons butter in a saucepan and sauté the mushrooms. Remove the mushrooms and sauté the garlic and shallots for 5 minutes. Stir in flour, brown slightly and add pepper and milk. Bring to a boil and remove from heat. Stir in ½ the cheese and the wine.
• Carefully pick over the crab meat, removing any bits of shell.
• Cut the artichoke hearts in half. • Combine the shrimp, crab meat and artichokes with the sauce and place mixture in a buttered casserole. • Mix the remaining cheese and butter with the bread crumbs. Sprinkle over casserole. • Bake at 375° for 30 minutes.

Susan Koehler

SEAFOOD MOUSSE   Serves 8

1½ cups chopped seafood
(lobster, shrimp or tuna)
1 cup finely chopped celery
½ cup finely chopped green
pepper
2 tablespoons grated onion
3 tablespoons lemon juice
1 tablespoon Worcestershire
sauce

15 drops Tabasco
10 ounces condensed tomato
soup
8 ounces cream cheese
3 envelopes unflavored
gelatine
1 cup mayonnaise
1 teaspoon salt

Combine seafood, celery, green pepper, grated onion, salt, lemon juice, Worcestershire sauce and Tabasco. Mix well and let stand 1 hour. • Combine soup and cheese in the top of a double boiler. Heat over boiling water, stirring until cheese is melted. • Soften gelatine in 1 cup cold water and add to soup mixture, stirring until it has dissolved. Remove from heat and cool. • When soup mixture begins to thicken, blend in mayonnaise. Stir in fish mixture. Turn into greased 1½ quart mold and chill until set.

Garnish:

Watercress or other greens
Lemon slices

Paprika
Mayonnaise

Garnish with watercress or other greens and lemon slices dipped in paprika. Serve with mayonnaise. (Note: Stuffed olives and green pepper strips may be used for eyes and tail.)

Bob Waldron

SEAFOOD CASSEROLE   Serves 6–8

6½ ounces crab meat
1 pound cooked shrimp
6 ounces lobster meat
5 hard-boiled eggs, cut up
1½ cups mayonnaise
½ teaspoon salt

½ teaspoon pepper
2 tablespoons chopped fresh
parsley
½ cup chopped onions
6 ounces evaporated milk
1 cup mild grated cheese

Mix all ingredients and bake at 350° for 20–30 minutes. Serve with rice. This recipe can be doubled and may be frozen.

Mrs. Marvin L. Stone

CURRIED SEAFOOD CASSEROLE

Serves 6–8

2 cups mayonnaise
1 tablespoon Worcestershire sauce
1 tablespoon prepared mustard
4 teaspoons capers, optional
½ cup sherry
1 teaspoon curry powder
1 tablespoon minced parsley

1 cup finely chopped onion
1 cup finely chopped celery
1 cup shredded bread
1 cup water
1½ pounds lump crab meat
1 pound cooked shrimp

Mix ingredients in the order given. Bake in 350° oven for 30 minutes. Serve over rice.

Judy Hobart

CIOPPINO, SAN FRANCISCO STYLE

Serves 6–8

2 cups chopped onions
¼ cup chopped green pepper
6 garlic cloves, minced
½ cup olive oil
35-ounce can Italian
  tomatoes with basil
6-ounce can tomato paste
2 cups red wine
1 lemon, thinly sliced
1 cup chopped parsley
1 teaspoon oregano

1 teaspoon basil
1 teaspoon salt
Freshly ground black pepper
1½ pounds boned sea bass,
  cut into 2-inch slices
3½ pound lobster, cut into
  pieces
1 pound shrimp, shelled and
  cleaned
12 hardshell clams
24 mussels

In a large pot, combine onions, green pepper, garlic and olive oil. Cook over low heat for 10 minutes, stirring occasionally. • Add the tomatoes, paste, wine, lemon, ½ cup parsley and remaining seasonings. Bring to a boil. Reduce heat, cover and simmer for 20 minutes. • Add the bass, lobster and shrimp. Simmer for 20 minutes. • Add the clams and mussels and simmer, covered, for 10 minutes more or until the clams and mussels are open and the fish is done. • Pour into a large serving dish and sprinkle with remaining parsley.

Anna Maria Via

HOMARD SOUFFLE A L'ARMORICAINE   Serves 4

"A well-known Washington hostess shares her version of a classic."

4 live 1½ pound lobsters, female if possible
Melted butter

Split the lobsters in two lengthwise, beginning at the point where the head joins the body. Cut off claws and legs at the joints near the body. Reserve. Snip off antennae, remove stomach sac and intestine and discard. Reserve the roe (if present) and half the tomalley. • Place the lobster halves cut side up on a large broiling pan, brush with melted butter, and broil in a pre-heated oven 12–15 minutes. • When cool enough to handle, remove tail meat, cut into bite-sized pieces and reserve with the shells.

Sauce Armoricaine:

2 tablespoons olive oil	**3 cups dry white wine**
4 tablespoons unsalted butter	**2 cups chicken stock**
⅓ cup Cognac	**Salt and pepper**
2 tablespoons minced shallots	**Pinch cayenne**
3–4 tomatoes, peeled, seeded,	**Reserved roe and tomalley**
and chopped	**2 tablespoons flour**
1 teaspoon tarragon	**1 cup heavy cream**
1 tablespoon chopped parsley	

Heat oil and 2 tablespoons butter in a large skillet. Sear claws and legs until red. Flame with Cognac. Add shallots and cook briefly. Add tomatoes, tarragon and parsley and cook 2–3 minutes. Transfer to a large pot and add wine, stock and seasonings. Cover and simmer 15 minutes. Remove claws, cut up the meat and add it to the tail meat. Return shells to sauce and continue cooking, uncovered, until reduced by half. Strain. • Blend the roe, tomalley and 2 tablespoons butter in a blender or food processor. Add flour and blend again. • In a clean pan, simmer the reduced sauce briefly with the cream. Whisk a little of the sauce into the tomalley mixture, then whisk that into the rest of the sauce. Cook, stirring, until sauce thickens slightly. Do not boil. Remove from heat and add lobster meat. (Note: Recipe may be prepared ahead to this point. Reheat carefully when ready to proceed.)

Soufflé:

2 tablespoons butter	**3 egg yolks**
2 tablespoons plus 1 teaspoon	**4 eggs whites**
flour	**Pinch salt**
¾ cup milk, heated to simmer	**Pinch cream of tartar**
¼ teaspoon salt	**2½ ounces grated cheese**
Pepper	**(Emmenthaler with a**
Dash cayenne	**little Parmesan)**
¼ teaspoon Dijon mustard	

Continued

In a saucepan whisk butter and flour together and cook, stirring occasionally 2–3 minutes. Whisk in the hot milk and add seasonings and mustard. Cook until smooth and thick (2 minutes). Off heat, beat in the egg yolks one at a time. • Beat egg whites until frothy. Add salt and cream of tartar and continue beating until glossy and stiff but not dry. • Whisk ¼ of the whites into the yolk mixture, fold in the remaining whites and add 2 ounces of the cheese.

Final Assembly:

Place the half shells of the lobsters on a large flat pan and fill the entire cavity of each with hot lobster and sauce. (You will probably have more than you need.) Cover each with some of the soufflé mixture, sprinkle on remaining cheese and bake at 375° for 20 minutes. Soufflé should look puffed and lightly browned. Serve immediately. (Note: Recipe may also be used to serve 8 as a first course.)

Mrs. W. Averell Harriman

The Seaman's Memorial

LOBSTER AND SCALLOP NEWBURG   Serves 8

6 tablespoons butter
5–6 tablespoons flour
3 cups half and half
Salt to taste
Nutmeg to taste

1 teaspoon Worcestershire sauce
2 cups cooked and diced lobster
  meat
2 cups diced raw scallops
¼ cup sherry

In a large saucepan, melt the butter over low heat. Using a whisk, blend in flour, stirring constantly for 3–5 minutes. Slowly add half and half. Season with salt, nutmeg and Worcestershire sauce. Add lobster meat and raw scallops. Cook to just below boiling, about 1 minute. Add sherry, stirring well. Pour into the center of a rice ring on a heated platter and serve immediately.

Mrs. Albert E. Ernst

LOBSTER AND MUSHROOMS IN CREAM   Serves 8

2 pounds cooked lobster
2 pounds fresh mushrooms
¾ pound butter plus
  4 tablespoons
¾ cup flour
1½ quarts milk

1 pint half and half
2 teaspoons salt
Dash of cayenne
Dash of nutmeg
½ cup sherry

Slice the lobster meat and set aside. • Thinly slice the mushrooms and sauté in 4 tablespoons butter. Set aside. • Make a cream sauce of the remaining ingredients, beating in the sherry at the end when the sauce has thickened. • Combine lobster, mushrooms and sauce and serve in a chafing dish.

Mrs. W. H. Robinson, Jr.

ROCK LOBSTER A LA BORDELAISE, DUBERN STYLE

Serves 4

*"The brothers Dubern, who ran one of Bordeaux'
best known restaurants, cooked crayfish in this
marvelous sauce. Here it is, slightly modified."*

1 tablespoon olive oil
⅓ cup butter
4 rock lobster tails
½ teaspoon salt
Pinch of cayenne pepper
⅓ cup brandy
½ cup dry white wine
2 shallots, minced
2 medium carrots, finely diced
3 tablespoons tomato paste

¼ cup fish stock or bottled
  clam juice
Bouquet garni (sprig of
  parsley, thyme and bay leaf
  tied with a thread)
Beurre manié
  (1 tablespoon each butter
  and flour, blended)
Parsley, minced

In a large deep skillet, heat oil and butter. Sauté lobster tails over medium heat for 5 minutes. Add salt and cayenne, cover and cook 5 minutes more. Pour in brandy, heat briefly and flame. When flame subsides, add all remaining ingredients except beurre manié and parsley. Cover and simmer 10 minutes over very low heat. Remove lobster to heated serving dish and keep warm. • Reduce by half the liquid in the pan. Pour liquid through a sieve and return to pan. Add the beurre manié and simmer 5 minutes to thicken. • Correct seasoning. Pour sauce over the lobster and sprinkle with parsley.

Donna Shor

MUTTI'S HERRING SALAD

Serves 8

"Something different for the buffet table"

½ cup mayonnaise
¼ cup cider vinegar
2 teaspoons sugar
1 teaspoon salt
Pepper
½ pound canned, sliced,
  drained beets, plus two
  tablespoons beet juice

12-ounce jar herring in wine
  sauce, drained, and diced
½ onion, chopped
2 dill pickles, chopped
2 apples, pared and chopped
4 medium potatoes, peeled,
  boiled, cooled and diced

Combine first 5 ingredients in a serving bowl. Stir in beet juice. Add remaining ingredients, mix well and refrigerate until ready to serve.

Mrs. Stephan M. Minikes

FISH BOBOTIE   Serves 4

"A traditional South African dish"

¾ pound white fish,
  cooked, skinned and boned
5 tablespoons butter
1 large onion, chopped
2 tablespoons chopped
  almonds
2 tablespoons raisins
2 teaspoons curry powder

Juice of 1 lemon
1 teaspoon salt
¾ teaspoon pepper
1 slice white bread, crust
  removed
1¼ cups milk
2 large eggs
2 bay leaves

Flake the fish and place it in a bowl. • Sauté the onion in the butter until light brown and add it to the fish. Add the almonds, raisins, curry powder, lemon juice, salt and pepper and mix well. • Soak the bread in the milk. Squeeze the milk from the bread and reserve the milk. Stir the bread into the fish mixture. Turn the fish into a greased baking dish. • Beat the eggs, add the milk from the previous step and beat again. Pour over the fish. Place the bay leaves on top and bake at 375° for 35 minutes or until the egg and milk mixture has set. • Serve with rice and chutney.

Mrs. Donald Bell Sole
Wife of the Ambassador of
South Africa

SOFT-SHELL CRABS WITH OUZO   Serves 2

6 medium "prime" soft-shell
  crabs
¼ pound unsalted butter

⅓ cup ouzo
Chopped fresh parsley

Pat the crabs dry with paper towels. • Melt the butter in a skillet over medium heat, taking care that it does not brown. Add the crabs, back side down and cook, partially covered, for 3–4 minutes. Turn the crabs over and cook 3 minutes more. Butter will now be browning. Add the ouzo, ignite and let flame subside. Turn crabs out on a heated platter, pour the pan juices over them and garnish with the parsley.

Mrs. Sander Vanocur

POULTRY AND GAME

The White House

COLD CHICKEN WITH CURRY CREAM DRESSING

Serves 4–5

1 cold roasted chicken
1 tablespoon oil
1 small onion, minced
2 teaspoons curry powder
½ teaspoon curry paste
2 teaspoons tomato purée
4 tablespoons red wine

2 teaspoons lemon juice
2 tablespoons fresh apricot
  purée or sieved apricot jam
1 cup mayonnaise
3 tablespoons light cream
Salt and pepper to taste
Paprika to taste

Cut the cold roasted chicken into serving portions, remove skin and arrange on a platter. • In a skillet heat the oil, add the onion and cook over low heat until tender but not browned. Add the curry powder and paste, and cook 3 more minutes. Stir in tomato purée, red wine, lemon juice and apricot purée. Raise heat and cook 3–4 minutes. Cool the mixture and stir in mayonnaise and cream. Season to taste with salt, pepper and paprika and liberally coat the chicken with the dressing. (Note: Serve with "Grape and Almond Rice Salad".)

Lady Parkinson
Wife of the Ambassador of Australia

CHICKEN MOUSSE

Serves 8–10

1½ envelopes unflavored
  gelatine
3 egg yolks
1½ cups chicken broth
1 teaspoon salt

½ cup heavy cream
2½ cups diced cooked
  chicken
½ cup chopped almonds
¼ cup sweet pickles

Soak gelatine in 2 tablespoons cold water. • Beat the eggs slightly and add the chicken broth. Place in the top of a double boiler and cook until mixture coats the spoon. Be careful not to overcook. Stir in the gelatine and salt and remove from heat. • When mixture has cooled, add the cream, chicken, almonds and pickles. Blend thoroughly and pour into a well greased mold or individual molds and chill. • Unmold and serve with appealing garnish of your choice. (Note: A curry mayonnaise on the side is an excellent accompaniment. Blend ½–1 teaspoon curry powder to 1 cup mayonnaise.)

Mrs. Robert W. Oliver

CHICKEN BREASTS TONNATO   Serves 4

"Perfect for a hot summer night"

2 whole boned chicken breasts,
    split to make 4 pieces
White wine and water

Onion powder to taste
Celery salt to taste

Place chicken in a shallow pan and add wine and water in equal proportions to cover. Sprinkle with onion powder and celery salt. Poach until just done, 15–20 minutes, drain and cool.

Sauce and Assembly:

2 cups mayonnaise
1 can chunk light tuna
Juice of 1 lemon
½ small onion, chopped
Dash garlic powder

Salt and pepper
1 Bermuda onion
Capers
Parsley

Place first 6 ingredients in a blender or food processor and blend until smooth. Correct seasoning.   •   Cut cooked chicken breasts horizontally to make 8 pieces. Arrange in a shallow serving dish and pour sauce over. Garnish with paper thin rings of Bermuda onion, capers and parsley. Chill thoroughly.

Mrs. Robert H. Craft, Jr.

KIRI BOSHI   Serves 8

2   2-ounce packages sengiri
    daikon (dried radish in
    strips, available in Oriental
    grocery stores)
1 cup soy sauce

½ cup sugar
1 teaspoon oil
¼ teaspoon MSG
6 boneless, skinless chicken
    breasts

Soak the daikon in several changes of cold water for about 1 hour or until water runs almost clear.   •   Mix soy sauce, sugar, oil and MSG with 3 cups of water. Cook daikon in this mixture for about 20 minutes. Cut chicken into bite-sized pieces and cook with daikon for 40 minutes more.   •   Serve hot with rice or cold as a side dish.

Mrs. Marvin L. Stone

CIRCASSIAN CHICKEN   Serves 8

3–3½ pound chicken
Salt and pepper to taste
4 slices white bread,
  crusts removed
1 cup milk

1 pound ground walnuts
Cherry tomatoes for garnish
Parsley for garnish
Black olives for garnish
4 avocados, optional

Place the chicken in a large saucepan with water to cover and ½ teaspoon salt. Bring to a boil and simmer until chicken is tender and meat can easily be removed from the bones. • Remove the chicken to a plate to cool. Reserve broth. • Soak the bread in the milk until soft, then add the walnuts and 2 cups of the reserved broth. Whirl this mixture in a blender or food processor to form a creamy sauce. • Shred the cooled chicken meat and combine with ½ the sauce and salt and pepper to taste. Chill. • Stuff the chicken into peeled avocado halves if desired and garnish with tomatoes, parsley and black olives. Spoon a little remaining sauce over each serving.

Mrs. Sukru Elekdag
Wife of the Ambassador of Turkey

CHICKEN ADOBO   Serves 6

"From old Havana"

1 3-pound chicken
1 pound lean pork
1 teaspoon peppercorns,
  crushed or ground
4 tomatoes, peeled, seeded
  and chopped

3 cloves garlic, crushed
¼ cup cider vinegar
½ cup stuffed olives
2 teaspoons salt
1 small bay leaf
2 cups water

Cut the chicken into serving pieces and the pork into 1 x 2 inch strips. • Prepare the marinade by combining the remaining ingredients in a casserole dish. Stir until well blended. Add the chicken and pork and marinate for 1 hour. • Place the casserole in a 350° oven. Baste and stir occasionally until all liquid is absorbed. This should take 1–1½ hours, by which time the meat should be tender ... and delicious. Serve with rice.

Mrs. Harry L. Selden

CARIBBEAN COCONUT CHICKEN   Serves 6

6 skinned and boned
  chicken breasts
Salt
Freshly ground pepper
7 tablespoons butter
2 medium-large sweet onions,
  thinly sliced

1 tablespoon brown sugar
2-ounce jar sliced pimentos
3 tablespoons currants
1½ tablespoons fresh
  lemon juice

Season chicken generously with salt and pepper. In a large skillet, melt 4 tablespoons butter. When bubbling, add chicken breasts and sauté 10–12 minutes until golden on both sides. Remove and place in a single layer in a shallow baking dish. • Put remaining butter in skillet and sauté onions until tender. Stir in remaining ingredients and pour over chicken breasts. Cover and bake at 375° for 10 minutes. Sprinkle with coconut topping (recipe below) and continue baking, uncovered, 10 minutes longer.

Coconut Topping:

3 tablespoons melted butter
1½ tablespoons fresh
  lemon juice
3 tablespoons finely chopped
  fresh parsley

¼ teaspoon salt
¼ teaspoon freshly ground
  pepper
¾ cup flaked coconut

Thoroughly toss together all ingredients.

Mrs. David J. Taylor

CHICKEN APRICOT   Serves 4

1 package instant onion
  soup mix
2½ pound chicken, cut up

Salt and pepper
Apricot preserves
½ cup boiling water

Sprinkle ½ package of onion soup mix in bottom of well greased pan. Lay chicken pieces on top and season lightly. Spread apricot preserves over chicken (as spreading on bread). Pour remaining soup mix over chicken. Pour boiling water around chicken. Bake in 350° oven for 1 hour.

Renée Zlotnick Kraft

CURRY   Serves 6

Sauce:

1 medium onion, sliced
4 tablespoons butter
2 tablespoons flour
2 cups coconut milk or
  substitute (see below)
½ cup white wine
2 bananas, sliced
2 apples, peeled and sliced
½ cup raisins

1 teaspoon thyme
2 bay leaves
4–5 tablespoons curry powder
3 tablespoons preserved or
  crystallized ginger
Chicken broth (as needed)
Cooked meat or seafood
  (see below)
1 cup cream

Brown onion in butter. Add flour and coconut milk. (If no coconuts are available, soak 2 cups shredded coconut in 2 cups scalded milk for 30 minutes. Strain before using.) Add white wine, bananas, apples and raisins. Season with thyme, bay leaves and the curry powder which has been made into a paste with 1 tablespoon water. Add the ginger, cut into small pieces or grated, and simmer until apples and bananas are cooked through and make a soft mash. • If sauce is too thick at this point, thin with chicken broth. • Taste and correct seasoning with salt, pepper and curry. If you like the curry hot, add Tabasco sauce or cayenne pepper to taste. • Add the cooked meat or seafood and simmer for at least 10 minutes or until done. • Add a cup of cream at the last minute. Serve with rice and at least 5 condiments: chutney sauce, diced bananas, chopped apples, coconut, raisins, peanuts, finely chopped onion, sour cream, etc.

Meat or Seafood:

Chicken: Meat from 1 large or 2 small chickens, roasted or
  stewed
Lamb: 3–4 cups roast lamb, preferably rare
Lobster: Cooked meat from 1 or 2 lobsters and 24 cooked
  shrimp
Crab: 2 cups crab meat and 24 cooked shrimp

Mrs. Norbert L. Anschuetz

The easy way to see Washington

CHICKEN AND VERMOUTH

Serves 3–4

"An elegant chicken meal."

1½ tablespoons minced green
  onions
2 tablespoons butter
2–3 cups cooked chicken,
  roughly cut

⅓–⅔ cup dry vermouth
1 teaspoon fresh tarragon
  (or ½ teaspoon dried)

In a 2-quart saucepan cook the onions in butter for 1 or 2 minutes over low heat until clear. Add cut up chicken and cook for 2 minutes over low heat. Add vermouth, cover and simmer for one minute. • Remove cover, raise the heat and boil rapidly until the liquid is almost gone. Season to taste with salt and pepper and add tarragon.

Sauce:

2 tablespoons butter
2½ tablespoons flour
1 cup boiling milk
salt and pepper

1 egg yolk
¼ cup heavy cream
½ cup grated Swiss cheese

In a saucepan cook the butter and flour together slowly for 2 minutes. Do not allow color to change. Remove from heat and beat in the boiling milk. Add salt and pepper to taste. Return to heat and boil, stirring constantly for one minute. • Beat egg yolk and cream in a bowl. Remove sauce from heat and beat the yolk and cream mixture into it a spoonful at a time. Return to heat and simmer, stirring constantly for 1 minute. Sauce should be very thick. Correct seasoning. • In a serving dish, fold previously prepared chicken, then the cheese into the sauce. Check seasoning again. • If not served immediately, dot with butter to prevent a skin from forming.

Mary H.D. Swift

CHICKEN CURRY   Serves 12

"Very good for a low cholesterol diet"

4 medium green peppers,
  sliced
8 celery stalks, sliced ½ inch,
  diagonally
8 carrots, sliced
3 medium onions, quartered
  then sliced

2 packets instant chicken broth
8 chicken breasts, skinned and
  boned
1 box S&B Golden Curry
  Sauce Mix–mild
1 box S&B Golden Curry
  Sauce Mix–medium hot

In 3 cups boiling water cook vegetables for 15 minutes, or until almost done. • In a large skillet mix instant chicken broth with 6 ounces water and cook chicken until no longer pink, about 15 minutes. • Add chicken to vegetables and stir in the 2 curry mixes and more water if the sauce is too thick. Stir until smooth, about 5 minutes. • Serve over rice with condiments such as: chutney, raisins, slivered almonds, coconut, chopped pickles.

Mrs. Marvin L. Stone

CHICKEN CURRY CASSEROLE   Serves 12

"Contralto Maureen Forrester shares one of her favorites"

12 slices bacon
1 cup onion, chopped
Chicken thighs, drumsticks
  and/or breasts to serve 12
1 cup flour
1 teaspoon salt
½ teaspoon pepper
1 tablespoon powdered
  ginger
1 can beef bouillon, undiluted

1 can cream of mushroom
  soup
3–4 ounces sliced mushrooms
8 ounces applesauce
2 tablespoons curry powder
2 tablespoons shredded
  coconut
2 tablespoons lemon juice
2 tablespoons ketchup
½ teaspoon garlic powder

Fry bacon until crisp, crumble and set aside. • Sauté onion in bacon grease and combine with bacon. • Dredge chicken pieces with the flour seasoned with salt, pepper and ginger. Arrange chicken in a baking dish. • Add remaining ingredients to the bacon and onion mixture and pour over the chicken. Bake uncovered at 350° for 1 hour and 15 minutes.

Maureen Forrester

VIENNESE HEURIGER CHICKEN   Serves 4

"This is 'Brathendl', Vienna's famed deep fried
chicken, which accompanies the new 'heurige' wine."

2 small chickens (about 1½ pounds each)	Salt
⅓ cup lemon juice	12 ounces lard
5 egg yolks, lightly beaten	Melted butter to taste
2 cups fine bread crumbs	Lemon wedges
	Parsley for garnish

Quarter the chickens, cut off wing tips and remove skin from all pieces except wing joint. Place in bowl and marinate in lemon juce for at least 1 hour, turning several times. • Place flour, beaten egg yolks and bread crumbs in 3 separate soup plates. • Dry chicken pieces well and sprinkle with salt. With each piece: coat with flour, dip in beaten egg yolks and then in bread crumbs. Pat crumbs well into egg coating. Let stand for ½ hour before cooking so coating will adhere. • In a heavy, deep frying pan, heat lard to 350°. Fry chicken pieces without crowding. Turn and fry until golden brown on all sides. • Place fried chicken pieces in baking dish. Viennese cooks dribble melted butter over the pieces before baking to help insure the prized crispness and flavor. Heat in 300° oven for 10–12 minutes to cook thoroughly. • To serve, garnish with lemon wedges and parsley.

Donna Shor

TAGINE OF CHICKEN WITH ONIONS   Serves 8
AND ALMONDS

2 frying chickens, cut into serving pieces	½ teaspoon pepper
½ pound blanched almonds	1 stick cinnamon
¼ pound butter	½ packet saffron
1 onion, minced	4 cups water
2 cloves garlic, crushed	2 pounds small white onions
Salt to taste	1 bunch parsley, chopped

Combine all the ingredients except the 2 pounds of onions and the parsley in a large pot and cook, partially covered, over medium heat for one hour. • Add the onions and parsley, cover completely and simmer 20–25 minutes longer. • Remove chicken pieces and arrange them on a serving dish. Spoon onions and almonds over the chicken, add some of the cooking juices and serve hot.

Mrs. Ali Bengelloun
Wife of the Ambassador of Morocco

CHICKEN TETRAZZINI   Serves 6

8 ounces spaghetti
7 tablespoons butter
4½–5 tablespoons flour
2½ cups milk
Salt and pepper to taste
1 4-ounce can mushrooms,
   sliced

1 small onion, chopped
1 cup water chestnuts, sliced
2 cups cooked chicken, cut in
   bite-sized pieces
2 tablespoons sherry
Parmesan cheese

Boil spaghetti according to package instructions. Drain and set aside.
• In a large skillet, melt 5 tablespoons butter over low heat. Using a
whisk, blend in flour, stirring constantly for 3–5 minutes. Slowly add
milk and season to taste with salt and pepper. • In a saucepan, melt
2 tablespoons of butter and sauté the mushrooms and onion. • To
the cream sauce, add sautéed mushrooms and onion, the water chestnuts and the chicken pieces. Stir in sherry and correct seasoning.
• In a buttered baking dish arrange a layer of spaghetti, then a layer
of creamed chicken. Sprinkle with grated cheese. Repeat layering
procedure until dish is full. Bake in 400° oven 30–40 minutes.

Mrs. Dale Miller

PARMESAN CHICKEN   Serves 6
"Elegant and easy"

2 cups corn flakes
¾ cup grated Parmesan cheese
1 clove garlic, crushed
2 teaspoons salt
⅛ teaspoon pepper

Lawry's seasoned salt
   (optional)
½ pound butter
12 boned chicken breasts

Combine corn flakes, Parmesan cheese, garlic, salt and pepper in a
bowl. • Melt the butter. • Dip the chicken pieces in the butter,
then in the crumb mixture, and arrange them in a shallow roasting
pan. Dot with butter. • Bake at 350° for 1 hour.

Mrs. John S. Stump

TARRAGON CHICKEN   Serves 4

1 3½-pound chicken	2 tablespoons Marsala or
2 tablespoons unsalted butter,	Madeira wine
melted	1 medium onion
1 tablespoon fresh tarragon or	2 medium carrots
dry equivalent	Heavy cream

Remove excess fat from chicken cavity. Lightly salt it inside and out and truss it tightly. Brush chicken on all sides with the melted butter and sprinkle with the tarragon. • Dice the onion and carrots together and place in the bottom of a roasting pan. Place the chicken on the vegetables and arrange the giblets around it. Add 2 tablespoons hot water to the pan and bake chicken at 375° for 1 hour or until done. Carve into serving pieces, place on serving platter and keep warm. • Remove vegetables and giblets from roasting pan pressing out the juices and deglaze it using the Marsala or Madeira. Add any juices remaining after carving the chicken and heat. Thicken with heavy cream and season to taste. Spoon sauce over chicken pieces and serve.

Howard de Franceaux

EASY CHICKEN N' DUMPLINGS   Serves 6

8 chicken breasts	3 tablespoons flour
2 celery stalks	1 cup light cream
5 chicken bouillon cubes	1 small can buttermilk biscuits,
3 tablespoons butter	such as Hungry Jack

Salt the chicken breasts and place in a large skillet, overlapping the pieces. Add water with 2 chicken bouillon cubes to barely cover, lay broken-up celery stalks on top, cover and simmer until chicken is done, 20–30 minutes. • Remove chicken and slip the meat from the bones. • Strain the broth. • In the same pan, melt the butter, whisk in the flour and add the strained broth, stirring constantly with the whisk until thickened. Add the cream and the 3 remaining bouillon cubes. Return chicken to gravy. • Separate each biscuit into at least 3 thin layers and place layers on top of chicken and gravy. Cover and simmer 30 minutes or until biscuits are done.

Mrs. James H. Pipkin

CHICKEN TERIYAKI   Serves 4

2½–3 pounds frying chicken,
   cut into serving pieces
⅔ cup soy sauce
¼ cup vermouth
⅓ cup water

1 drop garlic juice or
   ⅛ teaspoon garlic powder
⅔ cup sugar
Dash powdered ginger

Preheat oven to 325°. • Wash chicken pieces, dry thoroughly and place in a roasting pan. • Combine remaining ingredients and pour over the chicken. Cook in the top level of the oven for 1½ hours, basting the chicken frequently with the sauce. The chicken should brown nicely. Serve with white rice. (Note: This recipe can be prepared ahead, allowing chicken to marinate in the sauce in the refrigerator.)

Chris Hunter

CHICKEN MARENGO   Serves 6

"Chicken in a lovely tomato, wine and mushroom sauce"

2 broiling chickens, cut up
   into serving pieces
Flour seasoned with salt
   and pepper
¼ cup plus 1 tablespoon
   olive oil
4 small white onions, chopped
1 small clove garlic, crushed

1½ cups sliced fresh
   mushrooms
2 tablespoons chopped parsley
4 tomatoes, peeled and sliced
1 cup white wine
1 tablespoon brandy
1 tablespoon tomato paste
1 tablespoon flour

Dust the chicken pieces with seasoned flour to coat lightly. • Heat ¼ cup olive oil in a large skillet and brown chicken evenly on all sides. Remove and keep warm. • In the same skillet, heat 1 tablespoon olive oil and add the onions, garlic, mushrooms and parsley. Cook until mushrooms are tender. Add the tomatoes, white wine, brandy, tomato paste and 1 tablespoon flour. Cook, stirring, about 10 minutes. Return chicken to the sauce, cover and cook 30 minutes more or until chicken is tender. Serve in the sauce.

Anna Maria Via

SUPREMES DE VOLAILLES VINAIGRE AUX FRAMBOISE

Serves 4

"Chicken breasts sauced with raspberries"

1½–2 pounds chicken breasts, boned and skinned
Salt and white pepper
¼ cup red wine vinegar
8 tablespoons butter
1 tablespoon oil

1⅔ cups rich chicken stock
¼ cup framboise liqueur or crème de cassis
½ pint raspberries, fresh or frozen
Chopped parsley

Pound chicken breasts in wax paper to achieve uniform thickness. Salt and pepper the underside of each, then rub a few drops of vinegar into the salt and pepper. Heat 5 tablespoons butter with the oil in a skillet and sauté the chicken breasts 2 minutes on each side. Remove and keep warm. • Pour out all but 1 tablespoon of fat, add ¼ cup vinegar and reduce until syrupy. Add stock and boil 1 minute. Add the liqueur and reduce to taste or about ½ cup. Add the raspberries (drain well if using frozen) and stir into sauce. Off heat, swirl in 2–3 tablespoons butter, a little at a time. Arrange chicken on a serving platter, pour the raspberry sauce over and garnish with chopped parsley.

Allen Thomas

CHICKEN PIQUANT

Serves 2

2 6-ounce chicken breasts, split, boned and skinned
Flour, seasoned with salt and pepper

4 tablespoons butter
¾ cup dry white wine
¼ cup capers
Salt and pepper

Dredge the 4 chicken pieces in the seasoned flour. • Melt the butter in a saucepan and sauté the chicken until brown on both sides. • Deglaze the pan with white wine. Add the capers and simmer until liquid is reduced by half. Sauce will thicken slightly. Season to taste with salt and pepper.

Rose Narva

CREAMED CHICKEN   Serves 4

2 cups cooked chicken,
  cubed
5 tablespoons butter
2 tablespoons dry Madeira
½ teaspoon thyme
3 tablespoons flour

1½ cups boiling liquid
  (chicken broth, milk, cream
  or a combination)
1 egg yolk
¼–½ cup grated Swiss cheese
Salt and pepper

Gently heat chicken in 2 tablespoons butter. Add Madeira, raise heat and reduce liquid. Add ½ teaspoon thyme and set aside. • Melt remaining 3 tablespoons of butter, whisk in flour, add boiling liquid and return to a boil. Cook for 2 minutes, stirring. Off heat, slowly beat hot liquid into the egg yolk. Return to heat, bring almost to boiling again and cook 2–3 minutes until the mixture is very thick. Stir in the cheese. • Add chicken to the sauce and correct seasoning. Serve with noodles or rice. (Note: You may substitute crab for the chicken. Use clam juice for liquid.)

Sally Boasberg

CHICKEN BREASTS BRAISED IN WHITE WINE   Serves 2

4 small chicken breasts
Salt and pepper
Flour for dredging
2 tablespoons butter
1 tablespoons oil

2 tablespoons lemon juice
1 tablespoon soy sauce
3 tablespoons water
½ cup dry white wine

Salt and pepper the chicken and sprinkle with flour to coat it lightly. Heat butter and oil in a skillet, add chicken, skin side down, and sauté until well browned. Turn the chicken over and reduce the heat. • Combine the remaining ingredients and add enough wine to measure ¾ cup. Pour over chicken. Cover and simmer slowly for 40 minutes basting occasionally with the wine mixture. Add 2 tablespoons wine and water if liquid seems to be cooking down too quickly. Sauce should equal only a few tablespoons, however, at the end of the cooking time.

Mrs. Edward M. Geltman

ARROZ CON POLLO

Serves 6–8

3 pounds chicken, cut into
  serving pieces
2 teaspoons salt
5 tablespoons olive oil
4 cloves garlic, crushed
1 large onion, sliced
6 small ripe tomatoes, skinned
  and chopped
5 chili peppers, sliced
1 green pepper, sliced

1 red pepper, sliced
  lengthwise
1 bay leaf
2 cups rice, uncooked
4½ cups chicken broth
¼ cup Madeira or sherry
⅛–¼ teaspoon saffron
½ cup black olives
2 tablespoons capers

Salt the chicken, place in a large skillet, and sauté in the olive oil until
well browned. Remove and keep warm. • In the same oil sauté the
garlic, onions, tomatoes, chili peppers and green pepper for 8 minutes.
Add the red pepper, bay leaf and rice and continue cooking, stirring,
for 6 minutes. Turn this mixture into a casserole dish or paella pan.
Arrange the chicken pieces on top and add 4 cups chicken broth and
the Madeira or sherry. Add the saffron, olives and capers. Cover, and
bake at 350° for 45–50 minutes. (After 30 minutes of baking, add
remaining ½ cup chicken broth if necessary.) Remove cover and bake
15 minutes more.

Mrs. Rafael Molina
Wife of the Ambassador of the
Dominican Republic

The courtyard in the Pan American Union

CHICKEN AND MEAT CASSEROLE

Serves 6

1 3½-pound frying chicken,
  cut into serving pieces
3 tablespoons flour
½ teaspoon pepper
1 teaspoon paprika
¼ cup oil
1 medium onion, sliced
½ pound mushrooms, sliced
1 cup water

8 ounces tomato sauce
¼ teaspoon caraway seeds
1 pound ground beef
2 slices bread, soaked in water
  and squeezed dry
½ teaspoon salt
¼ teaspoon marjoram
¼ teaspoon thyme
1 package frozen peas

Dust the chicken pieces with the flour that has been seasoned with the pepper and paprika. Brown them on all sides in a large skillet in ¼ cup oil. Set aside. • In the same pan, sauté the onion and mushrooms 3 minutes. Stir in any remaining flour from dusting. Return chicken to the skillet, add water, tomato sauce and caraway seeds and simmer, covered, for 20 minutes. • Combine ground beef, bread, salt, marjoram and thyme. Make about 40 tiny meat balls of the mixture, add to the chicken and continue cooking gently 20 minutes more. Add the peas and cook 5–10 minutes longer.

Dorothy Leavitt

EASY CHICKEN

Serves 4–6

6 boneless, skinless split
  chicken breasts
7 tablespoons unsalted butter
1 tablespoon vegetable oil
½ pound sliced mushrooms
1 can undiluted cream of
  mushroom soup

1 can undiluted cream of
  chicken soup
½ cup heavy cream
⅓ cup dry sherry
Garlic salt
1 teaspoon tarragon

Place chicken breasts in a baking dish. Dot each with 1 tablespoon of the butter. Bake, basting twice, for 40 minutes in a 350° oven. • Sauté the mushrooms in remaining butter and oil. • Whisk together the soups, cream, sherry, garlic salt and tarragon. When blended, stir in the mushrooms. • Pour the sauce over the cooked chicken and return to oven for 5–10 minutes or until thoroughly heated.

Mrs. Charles J. DiBona

CHICKEN AND AVOCADO CASSEROLE   Serves 6–8

6 pound capon
1 quart water
1 onion, quartered
2–3 celery stalks, cut into
  pieces
Salt and pepper
3 tablespoons butter
3 tablespoons flour
1 cup chicken stock
1 cup light cream

½ cup grated sharp cheddar
  cheese
Dash hot pepper sauce
Pinch rosemary and basil
½ pound mushrooms, sliced
2 large ripe avocados, cut into
  large chunks
½ cup slivered toasted
  almonds

Bring 1 quart of water to a boil and add the capon, onion, celery, salt
and pepper. Simmer until tender, about 2–3 hours. Remove meat from
bones and reserve. Return bones to liquid and reduce, strain, cool, and
remove fat. • In a saucepan melt 2 tablespoons of the butter and
whisk in the flour. Whisk in 1 cup of the reduced chicken stock and the
cream. Heat, stirring, until thick. Add the cheese, ½ teaspoon salt,
rosemary, basil and hot pepper sauce. Blend well. • Sauté the
mushrooms in 1 tablespoon butter and place in a casserole with the
chicken meat. Pour sauce over and bake at 350° for 25 minutes. Add
avocado chunks, cover, and bake 10–15 minutes more. Sprinkle with
the slivered almonds.

Frances Humphrey Howard

OVEN CRISP CHICKEN   Serves 4

½ pint sour cream
2 tablespoons lemon juice
2 tablespoons Worcestershire
  sauce
1 teaspoon celery salt
1 teaspoon paprika
½ teaspoon garlic salt

½ teaspoon salt
Dash pepper
1 8-ounce package herb
  seasoned stuffing mix
3 pounds chicken, cut into
  serving pieces
2–3 tablespoons melted butter

Mix together the first 8 ingredients. • Roll stuffing mix into fine
crumbs • Coat the chicken pieces with the seasoned sour cream
mixture. Roll each piece in the stuffing crumbs and arrange on a
shallow, greased baking pan. • Brush with melted butter and cook
at 350° for 1 hour or until tender.

Mrs. A.C. Nielsen

CHICKEN ROSSINI

Serves 4

1 3-pound frying chicken
Salt and pepper
Garlic powder
1 tablespoon butter
3 tablespoons olive or corn oil
1 cup chopped parsley
½ cup chopped onion

3 cloves garlic, minced
2 scallions, chopped
1 teaspoon rosemary
½ teaspoon marjoram
1 cup dry white wine
3 tablespoons tomato sauce

Cut the chicken into pieces and season with salt, pepper and garlic powder. • In a large skillet, melt the butter and oil. Sauté the parsley, onion, garlic, scallions, rosemary and marjoram until golden. Add the chicken and fry on both sides until lightly browned and pour in the wine. When the wine is partly absorbed and the chicken has a deep golden color, add the tomato sauce. Cover and continue to cook over very low heat until the chicken is tender. Serve on a heated platter.

Gill Tatge

CHICKEN DIVAN

Serves 8

8 chicken breasts
1 bay leaf
2 celery stalks
¼ teaspoon thyme
1 tablespoon chopped parsley
2 packages frozen broccoli
2 cans cream of chicken soup

1 cup mayonnaise
1 tablespoon lemon juice
1 teaspoon curry powder
½ pound mushrooms, sautéed
4 ounces grated cheddar
  cheese
Bread crumbs

Boil chicken breasts in enough salted water to cover, with bay leaf, celery stalks, thyme and parsley, until tender—about 45 to 60 minutes. Remove skin and cut meat into bite sized pieces. • Cook broccoli and drain well. Lay it neatly on the bottom of a well buttered, 2½-quart casserole. Layer chicken on top of broccoli. • In bowl, combine soup, mayonnaise, lemon juice, curry powder and sautéed mushrooms. Spread sauce over chicken; sprinkle with cheese and bread crumbs. Bake at 350° for 30 minutes or more, until bubbling hot.

Susan FitzGerald

WATERZOOI DE POULET A LA GANTOISE

Serves 4

"This is chicken stew, Ghent style"

2 stalks celery
2 medium onions
1 carrot
1 leek
3 tablespoons butter
1½ quarts water
2 sprigs parsley

Salt, pepper and nutmeg
1 3-pound chicken cut into
   serving pieces
2 tablespoons flour
2 egg yolks
½ cup light cream
1 teaspoon chopped parsley

Chop celery, onions, carrot and the white portion of the leek. Simmer for 15 minutes in a large covered pot with 1 tablespoon butter. Add the water, bring to a boil and add parsley and seasoning to taste. Add the chicken pieces. Cook over low heat for 1 hour. Strain stock, reserve vegetables and keep chicken warm. • Melt 2 tablespoons butter in a saucepan, add the flour and 2½ cups chicken stock. Stir until thick, but do not boil. • Mix egg yolks into the cream and add carefully to sauce. Correct seasoning. • Bone and skin chicken pieces and add to sauce with reserved vegetables. • Serve in deep plates, sprinkled with chopped parsley and accompany with boiled potatoes.

Mrs. J. Raoul Schoumaker
Wife of the Ambassador of Belgium

President Lincoln's box at Ford's Theatre

CHICKEN WITH CHEESE AND MUSHROOMS   Serves 8

1 pound fresh mushrooms
6 tablespoons butter
Juice of 1 lemon
8 boneless chicken breasts
4 tablespoons finely chopped
   shallots

½ cup dry white wine
1¼ cups heavy cream
Freshly ground black pepper
Swiss cheese, thinly sliced

Chop mushrooms into small pieces. • Melt 2 tablespoons butter over low heat. Cook chopped mushrooms, stirring until they are just wilted, not browned. Add lemon juice. • Cut chicken breasts into medium pieces. Melt 4 tablespoons butter in a skillet and brown chicken pieces on all sides, stirring until cooked to a golden brown, about 12 minutes or less. Remove chicken from pan and set aside. • To the skillet in which chicken was cooked, add chopped shallots, stir for a minute then add white wine and stir to clean pan. Add heavy cream and cook over high heat for about 1 minute. • Arrange chicken pieces in baking dish. Spread mushrooms evenly over the chicken. Season to taste. Cover with very thin slices of Swiss cheese. Pour on cream mixture and bake in a 400° oven for 5 minutes to melt cheese. • Serve with "Rice with raisins and pine nuts."

Lucy Johnson

BAKED CHICKEN IN SOUR CREAM   Serves 2

2 small chicken halves, boned
   or 1 pound boneless
   chicken breasts
Salt and pepper to taste
5–6 sprigs fresh tarragon or
   1 teaspoon dried tarragon

1 pint sour cream
2 tablespoons chopped chives
Butter

Spread boneless chicken, skin side down, on a cutting board and pound lightly. Sprinkle with salt, pepper and tarragon. • Combine sour cream and chives. Spoon ½ the mixture on the chicken and dot with butter. Fold chicken over the filling and secure with toothpicks. Place on a rack in a pan. Sprinkle again with salt and pepper and dot with more butter. Bake 20 minutes at 350°, spread with remaining sour cream and chives and bake 20 minutes more or until juices run clear. (Note: If using chicken breasts, reduce cooking time slightly.)

Robert A. Lamasure

TANDORI CHICKEN
Serves 4

"You might try barbequeing this Indian dish, basting with its marinade instead of oil, for a tasty diet treat."

1 frying chicken, cut up
1 inch piece root ginger
2 cloves garlic
Juice of 1 lime
1 cup plain yogurt
¼ teaspoon red chili powder

1 tablespoon oil
½ teaspoon paprika
Salt to taste
Oil for basting
Scallions and lime
　wedges for garnish

Skin the chicken pieces and cut slits lengthwise in the breast pieces and crosswise in the leg pieces. Tuck tiny slivers of the root ginger and garlic into the slits. Rub salt over all the pieces, sprinkle on lime juice and set aside. • Combine the yogurt and chili powder in a blender and add oil and paprika and mix again. • Spread this marinade over the chicken and refrigerate overnight. • Remove chicken from marinade, baste the pieces with oil, and bake at 375° for 30 minutes. Turn and baste pieces at least once during cooking. • Serve the chicken hot, garnished with chopped scallions and lime wedges. Serve with rice or warm Eastern bread. (Note: The same preparation could be made for boneless fish pieces, one inch thick.)

Mrs. K. R. Narayanan
Wife of the Ambassador of India

HONEY GLAZED CHICKEN
Serves 2–3

1　3-pound chicken, cut into
　serving pieces
2 teaspoons cinnamon
2 tablespoons fresh lime juice
1 small garlic clove, crushed

Salt and freshly ground
　pepper to taste
½ cup honey
½ cup dry sherry

Coat chicken well with cinnamon. • Mix together lime juice, garlic, salt, pepper, honey and sherry. Pour over chicken and turn pieces to coat well. • Refrigerate chicken up to 2 days (at least overnight) in the marinade, turning occasionally. • Bake at 350° for 45 minutes, basting frequently with marinade and pan juices.

Mrs. Warwick M. Carter

ELIZABETH TAYLOR'S ROAST CHICKEN   Serves 4–6

1 6-pound roasting chicken
   with giblets
½ cup chopped celery
1 onion, minced
2 eggs
½ cup milk
1 8-ounce package Pepperidge
   Farm herb seasoned
   stuffing mix

2½ cups water
3–4 tablespoons flour
⅛ teaspoon onion salt
⅛ teaspoon thyme
⅛ teaspoon basil
Salt and pepper
Soy sauce to taste

Combine the celery, onion, eggs, milk and stuffing mix. • Stuff the thoroughly cleaned chicken with this mixture. • Roast the chicken in a 450° oven for 1 hour. Reduce the heat to 300° and roast for 1 hour longer. • While chicken is cooking, simmer giblets in 2½ cups water until tender. Remove giblets and chop fine, reserving liquid. • Thicken giblet cooking liquid with 3–4 tablespoons flour. Beat until smooth. Add seasonings and chopped giblets. Serve with roast chicken.

Elizabeth Taylor

CHICKEN-NOODLE CASSEROLE   Serves 8–10

4 pound frying chicken
¼ pound butter
1 cup chopped green pepper
1 cup chopped celery
1 cup chopped onion
1 cup sliced fresh mushrooms

½ pound Velveeta cheese
1 can cream of mushroom
   soup
1 small jar stuffed green olives
8 ounces noodles
Sliced almonds

Place chicken in a large pot, cover with salted water and simmer until done. Cool, remove meat from the bones, and cut into bite-sized pieces. Reserve cooking liquid. • In a large skillet, melt butter and sauté the green pepper, celery, onion, and mushrooms. Add the cheese, mushroom soup, and sliced olives. Mix in one cup of the reserved stock. • Boil noodles according to package directions using all remaining chicken stock in the cooking liquid. • Combine the noodles, sauce and chicken meat in a casserole dish and top with sliced almonds. • Bake at 350° for 30 minutes.

Mrs. Gary Hart
Wife of the Senator from Colorado

STUFFED TURKEY WITH RICE AND SPICES   Serves 8-10

12–14 pound turkey
Salt and pepper
⅓ cup pine nuts
⅓ cup sliced almonds
¾ cup butter
1½ pounds ground beef

1 teaspoon cinnamon
1 teaspoon allspice
¼ teaspoon ground cloves
2 cups raw rice
3 cups chicken or turkey broth

Wash the turkey, rub it with salt and pepper and set aside. • Sauté the pine nuts and almonds briefly in ½ cup of the butter and set aside. • Brown the ground beef and season it with 1 teaspoon salt and 1 teaspoon pepper, the cinnamon, allspice and cloves. Add the rice and continue cooking for 5 minutes, stirring frequently. Add the chicken or turkey broth, cover and simmer until broth is absorbed. Remove from heat, cool for 15 minutes and mix in the nuts. Stuff the turkey with this mixture and brush it with the remaining butter. Bake the turkey for about 2 hours at 350°. Reduce the oven temperature to 325° and bake 1 hour longer or until turkey is done.

Mrs. Faisal Alhegelen
Wife of the Ambassador of
Saudi Arabia

PARTY TURKEY ROLLS   Serves 8

16 turkey breast cutlets,
   about 2 pounds
2½-ounce jar chipped beef
4 slices of bacon
1 can cream of mushroom
   soup

1 cup sour cream
½ cup dry white wine
   or sherry
Paprika

In the center of each turkey cutlet, place 1 teaspoon of chopped chipped beef. Roll them and place in a well buttered 8 x 12 inch baking dish. Cut each bacon slice in 4 pieces and place 1 piece on top of each turkey roll. • Blend together soup, sour cream and wine. Pour over turkey rolls. Sprinkle lightly with paprika and bake at 275° for 2 hours.

Mrs. Paul F. Petrus

LE PIGEONNEAU EN CHARTREUSE
(Braised boned squab in mold of vegetables)

Serves 4

"Selected for the Presidential Inauguration, January 1981"

10–12 tablespoons clarified
  unsalted butter
4 squab
Salt
Freshly ground pepper
4 slices bacon, diced
1 2-pound cabbage, cored,
  quartered and coarsely
  chopped

2 onions, chopped
2 cups veal stock
1 tablespoon cornstarch
Pinch of sugar
4 large carrots (at least
  1-inch thick), peeled
6 large turnips, peeled
1 small bunch broccoli
Meat glaze (optional)

Heat 6 tablespoons butter in a large, shallow, oven-proof skillet over medium high heat. Season squab with salt and pepper and brown sides and backs in butter (breasts will brown later in oven). Remove squab, discard butter. • Preheat oven to 450°. To the same skillet, add the bacon, then the onion and sauté until onion is translucent. Reduce heat, add the cabbage and cook slowly, uncovered, for 20 minutes, stirring occasionally. • Blend in stock. Set squab, breast side up, on cabbage and bake, uncovered, for 10 minutes. Remove from oven and set squab aside to cool. • Drain liquid from cabbage mixture through a sieve into a large saucepan (cabbage must be very well drained) and set aside for sauce. Season cabbage with sugar, salt and pepper. • Bone the squab as follows: Using a sharp boning knife, cut squab at joints to remove legs and thighs. Cut along sides of breastbone and remove whole breasts, including wings, from each. Separate wings from breasts and remove meat. (Save wing bones for use in making stock.) Chop carcasses and add to saucepan with cabbage liquid. • Generously butter 4 8-ounce soufflé dishes (4-inches in diameter) using at least 1 tablespoon butter in each. • Cook carrots, turnips and broccoli in boiling salted water until just crisp-tender. Drain and cool briefly. Using largest turnips, cut 4 slices ⅛-inch thick and about 3½-inches wide. Cut a 1-inch rosette from the center of each and discard. Set slices in bottom of each mold. Cut carrots into 1½-inch lengths, then cut lengthwise into slices ⅛-inch thick. (You will need about 20 slices.) Slice turnips and cut into 20 pieces the same size as carrots. Alternating carrot and turnip, overlap slices vertically around sides of molds. Set broccoli, floret-side down in center cutout. Cover with layer of drained cabbage, then boned squab, then remaining cabbage. Press with fingers to firm ingredients. (Molds can be made up to 1 day ahead to set.) • When ready to cook, preheat oven to 300°. Cover top of each mold with parchment paper circles. Set in a shallow pan and add hot water to come 1-inch up the sides of molds. Bake

Continued

10–15 minutes, until just heated through. • For sauce: Simmer stock mixture until thickened and reduced. Taste and add meat glaze if needed to highlight flavor and color. Strain through a sieve. • To serve: Turn mold on its side and press with a spoon to remove any excess liquid. Turn each onto a dinner plate and surround with a small amount of sauce.

Chef Jacky Robert
Ernie's Restaurant
San Francisco

RABBIT WITH PINK PEPPERCORN SAUCE   Serves 8–10

2 3-pound rabbits, cut
    into serving pieces
Flour for dredging
2 tablespoons butter
2 tablespoons oil
¼ cup cognac
2½ cups chicken stock
Salt and pepper to taste
2 tablespoons jalapeño
    pepper jelly

2 tablespoons pink
    peppercorns
½ cup crème fraîche
Dash lemon juice
Dash cognac
Dash cayenne
Chopped parsley

Dry rabbit pieces, dredge them lightly with flour and brown on all sides in butter and oil. When all pieces are browned, remove pan from heat and pour off any remaining fat. Add cognac and ignite. Return pan to low heat and burn off all alcohol. Add ½ cup chicken stock and deglaze the pan over high heat. Season with salt and pepper, cover and bake at 350° for 45 minutes or until rabbit is tender; or cook covered, over low heat on top of stove. • Transfer rabbit to a serving dish and keep warm. • Degrease the liquid in the pan if necessary. Add the pepper jelly, pink peppercorns and remaining chicken stock. Reduce by ½ over high heat. Add the crème fraîche and reduce slightly. Correct the seasoning with salt and pepper and enhance the sauce with the lemon juice, cognac and cayenne. Pour a little of the sauce over the rabbit and garnish with chopped parsley. Pass remaining sauce separately. (Note: Chicken pieces or chicken breast may be substituted for the rabbit in this recipe.)

Carol Mason

BAKED RABBIT WITH GARLIC SAUCE

Serves 4–6

3 pound rabbit, cut into
  serving pieces
3–4 cloves garlic, peeled
  and slivered
½ cup olive oil
Salt and pepper
3 ounces tomato paste

¼ cup vinegar
Dash cinnamon
Dash oregano
Dash rosemary
Dash ground allspice
Dash basil
Dash mint

Insert a sliver of garlic in each piece of rabbit. Reserve the rest. Place the rabbit in a shallow casserole, pour on the olive oil and season with salt and pepper. • Purée the remaining ingredients, including the reserved garlic, pour over the rabbit and marinate for 24 hours in the refrigerator. Bake the marinated rabbit at 350° for 1 hour. Serve with garlic sauce.

Garlic sauce and garnish:

4–6 potatoes
Olive oil
Vinegar
10–15 cloves garlic,
  peeled and mashed

Salt and pepper
Chopped walnuts
Chopped parsley

Boil the potatoes until tender, drain and mash them with a little olive oil and vinegar. Add the garlic and season with salt and pepper. Place the rabbit in the center of a ring of the garlic sauce, garnished with chopped walnuts and parsley. Bake the assembled dish at 350° for an additional 10 minutes and serve.

Mrs. Daniel Antonoplos

The plane in which Charles Lindbergh crossed
the Atlantic, now in the Air and Space Museum

RABBIT WITH PERNOD
(Dominique's Restaurant)

Serves 4

*"One of Washington's best known chefs
shares this recipe with us."*

1 rabbit, cleaned and cut
   into 8 serving pieces
⅓ cup Pernod
½ cup pitted green olives
⅓ cup pitted black olives
3 tablespoons olive oil
12 small white onions
1 bouquet garni (4 sprigs
   parsley, 2 bay leaves,
   1 sprig fresh thyme)

1 tablespoon butter
4 cloves garlic, crushed
1 bottle dry white wine
1 cup beef stock, fresh or
   canned
4 large ripe tomatoes, peeled
   and seeded
⅓ cup salt pork, cut into strips
Salt and pepper
Chopped fresh parsley

Rub rabbit pieces with 1 tablespoon of the Pernod. • In a heavy skillet, melt butter over medium heat. Add oil. When butter and oil begin to sizzle, add rabbit pieces and brown evenly. Add onions, bouquet garni and garlic. Reduce heat, cover the pan, and simmer gently for about 45 minutes, stirring contents from time to time. • Add remaining Pernod and ignite. When flame dies down add white wine, beef stock, tomatoes, salt pork, salt and pepper. Remove lid and simmer over medium heat 15 minutes or until tender. • Remove salt pork and bouquet garni. Sprinkle with parsley. Serve immediately with pan juices and mashed potatoes.

Dominique D'Ermo
From his cookbook, **Fish, Game
and Meat Recipes**

CORNISH GAME HEN WITH GRAPES

Serves 4

3 tablespoons butter
4 Cornish game hens
40 white grapes

Juice of 1 lemon
3 tablespoons heavy cream
Salt and pepper

Melt butter in a large pot and brown hens on all sides. Lower the heat, cover and cook gently for 15 minutes. • Plunge the grapes into boiling water for less than a minute. Drain and peel them. • When the hens have cooked for 15 minutes, add the peeled grapes and lemon juice. Cover and cook an additional 5 minutes. • Just prior to serving, stir in the cream to thicken the sauce. Salt and pepper to taste.

Katrina de Carbonnel

MARTHA YOCOM'S DUCK

Serves 8

4 wild ducks
Oil and butter for browning
12 cloves garlic
8 medium onions

4 cups sherry
Worcestershire sauce
4   6-ounce cans sliced
    mushrooms with juice

Soak the ducks in salted water for 24 hours. Drain them and pat them thoroughly dry. Heat oil and butter and brown the ducks, one at a time, on top of the stove. Stuff each duck with 3 cloves peeled garlic and one whole peeled onion and place them in a large roaster. Add the sherry. Chop the remaining onions and add. Sprinkle generously with Worcestershire sauce. Cover the roaster and cook the ducks at 350° for 3 hours. Remove from oven, place ducks on a serving platter, and cool the cooking liquid until fat can be removed. Add the mushrooms to the degreased gravy and reheat. (Note: Tastes even better the second day.)

Mrs. Charles J. DiBona

DUCK WITH HONEY MEAD VINEGAR

Serves 2

1 duck, quartered
   (about 4 pounds)
Salt and pepper
Butter for braising
4 tablespoons honey, or
   to taste

¾ cup honey mead vinegar
¼ cup dry vermouth
¾–1 cup duck stock
1 pear
2 tablespoons sugar

Season quartered duck with salt and pepper. Braise the breast pieces until pink and the leg pieces until well done. • Combine the honey and vinegar. About 5 minutes before duck is done, baste with this mixture to give a caramelized effect to the skin. • To make the sauce, combine the remaining vinegar mixture with the vermouth in a saucepan. Simmer until liquid has reduced by ⅔. Stir in the duck stock and simmer. Correct seasoning. • Lightly poach the pear. Peel, core and slice it lengthwise into 6 pieces. Caramelize the pear pieces using 2 tablespoons sugar and 1 tablespoon water. • To serve: Slice the duck breasts and arrange slices in a fan on 2 plates. Place a duck leg in the center. Garnish with caramelized pears. Spoon a bit of the sauce over all and serve remaining sauce on the side.

Chef William Douglas McNeill
Aux Beaux Champs
Four Seasons Hotel

MEAT

Blair House

Beef

FILET OF BEEF WITH RED WINE SAUCE   Serves 8

8 thick filet steaks   Salt and pepper

Grill or pan fry steaks. Season with salt and pepper and serve on a
heated platter. Spoon some of the sauce over the steaks and serve the
rest on the side.

Sauce:

¼ pound butter   1½ cups red wine
4 large onions, finely chopped   2 tablespoons wine vinegar
½ cup flour   Salt and pepper to taste
2 teaspoons meat extract   ⅓ cup cream

Melt the butter and sauté the onions until golden. Remove from heat
and stir in the flour. Blend the meat extract with ½ cup water and add
to sauce. Stir in the wine, vinegar, salt and pepper. Bring to a boil,
stirring constantly. Blend in the cream just before serving.

Fareeda Kahn

ALICE'S FILET DE BOEUF   Serves 10
WITH BEARNAISE SAUCE

5–6 pounds whole filet   2 teaspoons minced scallions
½ pound butter   1 teaspoon tarragon, crushed
2 tablespoons dry white wine   ½ teaspoon white pepper
1 tablespoon tarragon vinegar   1 cup Hollandaise sauce

Coat the filet with the butter and place on a jelly roll pan or cookie
sheet. Roast in a preheated 400° oven for 50 minutes (35–40 minutes
for rare beef). Remove from oven and allow the meat to rest for 15
minutes before carving. • To prepare the Béarnaise sauce, combine
the wine, vinegar, scallions, tarragon and white pepper in a saucepan.
Cook over high heat until liquid is almost completely absorbed.
• Quickly blend in the Hollandaise sauce and serve over the roasted
filet.

Mrs. John C. Camp

FILET MIRABEAU

Per person

"A different and piquant flavor"

1 medallion of beef tenderloin	Salt and pepper to taste
5 anchovy filets	1 teaspoon lemon juice
4 tablespoons butter,	½ teaspoon tomato purée
softened	Watercress for garnish

Pound 3 anchovy filets to a paste and mix well with the softened butter. Add salt and pepper to taste and the lemon juice and tomato purée. Blend well, spread on both sides of the steak and allow to marinate 1 hour or more. • Broil the steak 3–5 minutes on each side, basting with the juices. Split the remaining 2 anchovy filets in ½ lengthwise, arrange in a lattice on the steak, baste and broil 2 minutes more. Garnish each serving with watercress.

Mrs. Nigel Green

FLANK STEAK ROLL

Serves 6

2 pounds flank steak	1 clove garlic, minced
½ cup red wine vinegar	3 strips bacon, cut into
½ cup oil	small pieces
1 cup beef broth	2 carrots, shredded
2 teaspoons thyme	10-ounce package frozen
2 teaspoons freshly	spinach, thawed and drained
ground pepper	⅓ cup breadcrumbs
1 onion, chopped	2 tablespoons butter

Using a wooden mallet, pound the flank steak until it has flattened out considerably and is well tenderized. In a flat dish or pan, large enough to hold the meat, mix the vinegar, oil, broth, thyme and pepper. Marinate the meat in this mixture for at least two hours, turning it occasionally. • Meanwhile, sauté the onion and garlic with the bacon then mix with the carrots, spinach and bread crumbs. • When ready to assemble, remove meat from marinade. Heat the butter in a large skillet and brown the meat on one side. Remove from heat, lay browned side down and spread the stuffing over it. Roll the steak, tie with string or secure with skewers. Bake at 325° for 1 hour. Place on a heated platter and allow to stand 10 minutes before slicing.

Sandra Foulis

NINITOS ENVUELTOS

Serves 3

6 thinly sliced round steaks,
about 8 x 3 inches
Onion powder
Garlic powder
Salt and pepper
6 slices bacon
2 carrots, cut into thin sticks

1 green pepper, cut into strips
2 hard-boiled eggs
Butter and/or oil
2 cups beef bouillon or
consommé
2 tablespoons flour
Parsley, chopped

Sprinkle each steak with onion and garlic powder, salt and pepper. Lay on each: 1 strip bacon, some carrot sticks, green pepper and sections of hard-boiled egg cut in thirds lengthwise. Roll up and fasten carefully with toothpicks or tie with string. • Sauté the rolls in butter and/or oil until well-browned on all sides. Pour liquid over, cover, and simmer 1 hour. Remove meat and keep warm. Reduce liquid and thicken with flour. Arrange meat on serving platter, pour a little sauce over and garnish with parsley. Pass remaining sauce separately at the table.

Mrs. Stephan M. Minikes

STEAK TARTARE

Serves 1–2

¼ teaspoon freshly ground black
pepper
½ teaspoon salt
1½ teaspoons Dijon mustard
¼ teaspoon wine vinegar
1 egg yolk
1 tablespoon oil
1 teaspoon Worcestershire sauce

1 tablespoon capers
½ pound ground rump or
flank steak
1 tablespoon Cognac
1 heaping tablespoon
minced onion
1 heaping tablespoon
chopped parsley

In a mixing bowl, combine the pepper, salt, mustard and vinegar. Whisk vigorously. Add the egg yolk and oil, continuing to stir. Add the Worcestershire sauce and capers. Crush the capers with a fork and continue to stir until all ingredients are well blended. • Fold in the ground steak, Cognac and onion. When all ingredients are well blended, arrange on a plate, top with the chopped parsley and serve. (Note: If you plan to prepare this recipe in greater quantity, combine all ingredients except the meat, adding it at the last moment.)

Howard de Franceaux

CHINESE PEPPER STEAK

Serves 4

2-pound flank steak
2 tablespoons shortening
3 green peppers, cut into 1½-inch
  pieces
1 package onion soup mix

2 tablespoons soy sauce
½ cup sherry
2 tablespoons cornstarch
½ teaspoon salt
⅛ teaspoon pepper

Cut steak lengthwise into ½-inch strips and then into 1-inch pieces. Melt shortening in a skillet and fry steak in several batches, just long enough for it to change color. Remove meat and sauté the green pepper. • Bring 2 cups water to a boil in a large pot. Add onion soup mix and continue to boil for 10 minutes. Stir in the meat and green pepper and simmer for 30 minutes. Add the soy sauce, sherry, cornstarch (diluted in a little water), salt and pepper. Cook until slightly thickened. For variation, add a can of bean sprouts and a little more cornstarch. Serve over steamed rice.

Mrs. Gerald R. Ford

POT ROAST WITH A DIFFERENCE

Serves 8

½ cup vinegar
1 large onion, chopped
½ cup diced celery
1 teaspoon salt
6 drops Tabasco sauce
2 tablespoons sugar

12 ounces beer or ale
5 pounds boneless rump roast
3 tablespoons oil
6 tablespoons flour
½ cup water

Make a marinade of the first seven ingredients and pour over the meat in a large bowl. Marinate overnight in the refrigerator, turning the meat at least once. • Remove the meat from the marinade and coat with two tablespoons of the flour. • Heat the oil in a heavy kettle and brown meat well on all sides. Add the reserved marinade, cover, and simmer three hours, or until tender. • Remove the meat to a hot platter. • Blend the remaining 4 tablespoons of flour with the water to make a smooth paste and add to the marinade stirring constantly until thickened. • Slice the meat and pour the sauce over it to serve.

Mrs. Paul F. Petrus

MARRON BEEF OLIVES

Serves 4

8 very thin slices beef
 (about 3 x 6 inches)
1 onion, chopped
4 tablespoons butter
3 ounces ground pork
3 ounces chestnut purée

1 stalk celery, chopped
Bouquet garni
Salt and pepper
1 egg yolk
Oil for browning

Sauté the onion in the butter. Add pork, chestnut purée, celery, bouquet garni and salt and pepper to taste. Simmer 10 minutes, remove from heat and add the egg yolk. • Spread each slice of beef with some of this mixture, roll up and tie with thread. • In a large skillet, heat the oil and brown the beef rolls well on all sides. Remove and proceed to braising step using same skillet.

Braising:

2 carrots, chopped
1 turnip, chopped
1 stalk celery, chopped

½ cup red wine
½ cup beef stock
Bouquet garni

Adding more oil if necessary, slowly brown the carrots, turnip, and celery. Place the browned beef rolls on the vegetables, pour in the wine, stock and bouquet garni, cover and braise 1 hour.

Sauce and Finishing:

2 tablespoons oil
2 tablespoons flour
¾ cup stock

½ cup red wine
1 tablespoon tomato purée
Parsley for garnish

While beef is braising, prepare sauce by browning the flour in the oil. Add stock, wine and tomato purée. Simmer 15 minutes. • Remove beef from braising liquid and keep warm. Reduce liquid in pan until syrupy and strain into sauce. Correct seasoning. Arrange beef olives on serving dish, spoon sauce over and garnish with parsley.

Anne Green

Our ball game

TEXAS BARBEQUED BEEF BRISKET
Serves 8–10

4–5 pounds beef brisket
½ cup soy sauce
½ cup lemon juice
16 ounces beer or more
¼ pound butter
1 clove garlic, minced
1 onion, minced
2 jalapeño peppers, seeded
  and diced
1 can tomato sauce
Dash Tabasco sauce

Worcestershire sauce to taste
Coffee, optional
Salt and lemon pepper
Paprika
Cayenne
Garlic powder
Hickory chips, mesquite chips
  or oak bark soaked in water
  for 30 minutes,
plus charcoal

Marinate the beef overnight in the soy sauce, lemon juice and ½ cup of beer. Remove meat and use marinade as a basis for the barbeque sauce. • In a large saucepan, heat the butter and add the garlic, onion, peppers, tomato sauce, Tabasco and Worcestershire to taste. Bring to boil and add the marinade and remaining beer. Simmer slowly at least 2 hours, thinning if necessary with beer or coffee (yes, coffee!). • Prepare a covered grill by making a heavy foil pan to catch the drippings. Place this in the center of the grill and bank the charcoal on the sides. When coals are hot, put brisket on the grill 12–18 inches above the fire and sprinkle with the seasonings and baste with the thin sauce. Sprinkle soaked hickory or other chips over the coals and cover the grill. Smoke the meat, covered, 2½–3 hours, turning the meat every 20 minutes, and basting with the sauce. Sprinkle with additional seasonings twice. Add additional charcoal and soaked hickory chips as necessary. Slice the brisket and pass with any remaining barbeque sauce augmented with pan drippings.

The Honorable Jim Wright
Majority Leader, U.S. House of
Representatives

BENSON'S BARBEQUED BEEF
Serves 4

"A very tasty sauce adds zip to a plain barbeque"

¼ pound plus 3 tablespoons
  butter
4 tablespoons wine vinegar
1 tablespoon soy sauce

1 teaspoon Dijon mustard
2 tablespoons chopped chives
3-pound sirloin steak,
  2 inches thick

Melt butter in a saucepan. Add the wine vinegar, soy sauce, mustard and chives. Mix well and heat. • Barbeque steak to desired doneness. Slice. Pour sauce over the slices, reserving some to pass at the table.

Chris Hunter

MEAT LOAF WITH TOMATO SAUCE

Serves 6–8

2 pounds ground beef
1 pound sausage meat
1 garlic clove, minced
1 medium onion, chopped
1 teaspoon salt
1 teaspoon fresh ground
  pepper
1 teaspoon thyme

1 teaspoon summer savory
1 teaspoon basil
2 tablespoons chopped fresh
  parsley
½ cup dry bread crumbs
2 eggs, beaten
6 strips thick bacon
4 hard-boiled eggs

Thoroughly blend the first 11 ingredients. (The meats should be at room temperature.) Add 2 eggs and mix well. • Cut the bacon strips in half and fry lightly. On the bottom of a baking dish place half the bacon to conform to the size of the meat loaf. • Form half of the meat mixture into a loaf on top of the bacon. Make a well in the middle of the loaf. Place the 4 hard-boiled eggs in a line in the well. Top with the rest of the meat mixture. Place remaining bacon strips on top of the loaf. • Bake for 1¼–1½ hours at 350°, basting 3 or 4 times. Meat thermometer should read 145°. • To serve, slice and top with tomato sauce.

Tomato Sauce:

1   15-ounce can tomato sauce
2 tablespoons tomato paste
1 beef bouillon cube (in ¼ cup
  boiling water)
2 tablespoons chopped fresh
  parsley

1 teaspoon basil
1 teaspoon oregano
1 small garlic clove
½ teaspoon salt
1 teaspoon ground pepper

Place all ingredients in a saucepan and warm for 10 minutes.

Mrs. Joseph W. Henderson, III

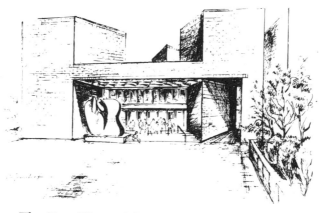

The East Wing of the National Gallery of Art

APPLESAUCE MEAT LOAF

Serves 4

"An interesting and different flavor"

1 pound ground beef	1 teaspoon celery flakes
1 egg, lightly beaten	1 cup applesauce
1 cup bread crumbs	4 teaspoons Dijon mustard
2 tablespoons chopped onion	½ tablespoon vinegar
½ teaspoon salt	1 tablespoon brown sugar
Pepper to taste	

Combine first 7 ingredients, ½ cup applesauce and 1 teaspoon mustard. Blend thoroughly and form into a mound in a loaf pan. • Mix remaining applesauce and mustard with the vinegar and brown sugar. Spread mixture on top of meat loaf and bake at 350° for 1 hour.

Trude Foulis

BOEUF A LA CATALANE

Serves 6

3 pounds lean beef from a rump, round or sirloin tip roast, cut into 2½ x 1-inch squares	Salt to taste
	¼ teaspoon pepper
	2 cloves garlic, crushed
2 tablespoons oil	½ teaspoon thyme
1½ cups sliced onion	Pinch saffron
1 cup white rice	1 bay leaf, crumbled
1 cup dry white wine or vermouth	1 pound tomatoes
2–3 cups beef stock or bouillon	1 cup grated Swiss or Parmesan cheese

Dry the meat on paper towels. Heat the oil until almost smoking in a skillet. Add meat and brown, a few pieces at a time. Place the browned meat in a casserole. • In the same skillet, at moderate heat, lightly brown the onion and add to the casserole. • Still in the same pan, cook the rice, stirring, for 2–3 minutes until it turns a milky color. Scrape into a bowl and set aside. • Add the wine to the skillet, stirring to dissolve the cooking juices. Pour into the casserole. Pour enough beef stock into the casserole to barely cover the meat and stir in seasonings and spices. Bring to a simmer on top of the stove, cover tightly, then bake at 325° for 1 hour on lower oven rack. • Peel, seed and chop the tomatoes. You should have 1½ cups of tomato pulp. Stir it and the rice into the casserole, cover again and return to the oven for 20 minutes, adjusting temperature if necessary, to keep liquid at a full simmer. • Just before serving, fold in the grated cheese.

Mrs. Murray L. Weidenbaum

GERMAN SAUERBRATEN

Serves 6–8

"Guten Appetit!"

3–4 pound beef rump roast

Marinade:

3 cups water
1 cup malt vinegar
3 teaspoons pickling spice

1 small onion, chopped
2 lemon slices
1 carrot, sliced

Marinate meat for 3–7 days. If not covered by the liquid, turn it daily. Before cooking, blot dry with paper towels and remove spices. Reserve marinade.

Butter
1 large onion, chopped
Cooking oil
Flour
Raisins
Sour cream

1 teaspoon sugar, or more
Used marinade
2 tablespoons red wine, or
    more
Salt and pepper

In a dutch oven large enough for the roast, sauté a large chopped onion in a generous amount of butter. Remove onion and set aside. • Add cooking oil to the pot to equal the amount of butter. Brown meat on all sides until very brown, occasionally adding a little water to prevent burning. • When the pot gravy is almost black, add water until meat is half covered. Return sautéed onions to pot, cover and simmer for 1–2 hours until done, turning roast from time to time. • When the meat is fork tender on both sides, remove from pot and place in a warm oven. • Strain the gravy and return to pot. Add flour, dissolved in a little water, stir until smooth and simmer until gravy thickens slightly. • Add to taste: raisins, sour cream, 1 teaspoon sugar, or more. If gravy is not sour enough, add some of the marinade. Add red wine and salt and pepper to taste. • Slice the roast and arrange on a heated serving platter. Pour part of the gravy over the meat and serve the remainder on the side. • Accompany with: dumplings, potato pancakes, spicy red cabbage, cranberry sauce or cooked apples.

Peggy Greer

Balzac by Rodin, at the Hirshhorn Gallery

SAUERBRATEN IN A HURRY

Serves 4–6

"Well named and tasty, too"

1½ pounds round steak,
 ½ inch thick, cut into
 1-inch cubes
1 tablespoon oil
1 envelope brown gravy mix
2 cups water
1 onion, chopped
2 tablespoons vinegar

2 tablespoons brown sugar
½ teaspoon salt
Dash pepper
½ teaspoon ginger
1 teaspoon Worcestershire
 sauce
1 bay leaf
½ cup raisins

Brown the meat quickly in the hot oil. Remove from skillet and set aside. Add the gravy mix and water. Bring to a boil, stirring constantly. Stir in remaining ingredients and return meat to skillet. Cover and simmer 2 hours or until tender, stirring occasionally.

Mrs. Paul F. Petrus

STUFFED CABBAGE

Serves 6

1 large head cabbage
2 tablespoons butter or
  peanut oil
2 onions, sliced
3 cups canned tomatoes
1 beef bone
2 teaspoons salt
½ teaspoon pepper

1 pound ground beef
3 tablespoons raw rice
4 tablespoons grated onion
1 egg
3 tablespoons cold water
3 tablespoons honey
¼ cup lemon juice
½ cup seedless raisins

Immerse the cabbage in boiling water, remove from heat and let stand 15 minutes to loosen the leaves. Carefully remove 12 leaves, 18 if the leaves are small. Set aside. • Heat the butter or oil in a heavy saucepan and brown the onions lightly. Add the tomatoes, beef bone, 1 teaspoon salt and ⅛ teaspoon pepper. Cook slowly for 30 minutes. • Combine the ground beef, rice, grated onion, egg, water and remaining salt and pepper. Place some of this mixture on each cabbage leaf. Tuck in the sides and roll up carefully, securing the roll with toothpicks. Add the cabbage packets to the sauce, cover, and cook 1–1½ hours over low heat. Add the remaining ingredients to the sauce and cook 30 minutes longer.

Patricia Schiller

CAMARGUE STEW

Serves 6

"Robust and delicious"

2 slices bacon, chopped
2 tablespoons olive oil
3 pounds beef chuck, cut
  into 1½–2 inch cubes
2 onions, chopped
2 cloves garlic, minced
¼ pound mushrooms, sliced
2 carrots, chopped
3 cups dry red wine

1 cup small pitted ripe
  olives
Bouquet garni of 3 sprigs
  parsley, ½ teaspoon
  rosemary, ½ teaspoon
  thyme, 1 bay leaf
Salt and pepper
1 tablespoon flour
1 tablespoon soft butter

Sauté the bacon in a skillet with the oil until crisp. Transfer to a Dutch oven or casserole using a slotted spoon. • Brown the meat in the same skillet a few pieces at a time, adding the pieces to the casserole as they are browned. • Again in the same skillet, sauté the onions, garlic, mushrooms and carrots. Add them to the casserole. • Deglaze the skillet with the wine and pour into the casserole. Add the olives, bouquet garni, salt and pepper. Cover and marinate overnight in the refrigerator. • Bring casserole to room temperature and bake, covered at 300° for 3 hours or until beef is tender. Remove from oven. • Knead the flour with the butter and add to the stew. Simmer on top of the stove until thickened. Serve with rice.

Mrs. C.G.A. Ross

POOR MAN'S STROGANOFF

Serves 10–12

1 tablespoon butter
1½ pounds ground beef
½ cup chopped onions
½ pound sliced mushrooms
2 teaspoons salt
1-pound can tomato sauce

1 cup cottage cheese
1 cup sour cream
8 ounces cream cheese
8 ounces Mueller's
   Munchen noodles

Heat the butter in a skillet, add the ground beef, onions, mushrooms and salt and sauté until brown. Add the tomato sauce, cottage cheese, sour cream, and cream cheese. Continue cooking, stirring, until cream cheese melts. • Cook the noodles according to package directions. Drain them and turn them into a 2–2½-quart casserole with the ground beef mixture. Stir to blend well. Bake the casserole at 375° for 30 minutes.

Ruthanna Weber

SHEPHERD'S PIE IN ZUCCHINI BOATS

Serves 4

"A meal in one"

4 zucchini, about 6 inches
   long
1 tablespoon oil
1 onion, chopped
1 carrot, grated
1 pound lean ground beef
1 envelope gravy mix, made
   as directed

1 teaspoon Worcestershire
   sauce
½ teaspoon thyme
½ teaspoon marjoram
Salt and pepper to taste
2–3 cups mashed potatoes

Cut the zucchini in half lengthwise. Scoop out the seeds. Cook in salted water until tender, but still firm. Drain well and place in large greased casserole. • In a large frying pan, heat oil, add onion and carrot. When limp, but not brown, add beef and mix well. Cook until all pink has gone from the beef. Add the prepared gravy, Worcestershire sauce, thyme, marjoram, salt and pepper. Simmer 2–3 minutes. Fill the zucchini boats with the mixture and top with the mashed potatoes, swirling with a fork. Bake in 375° oven 30 minutes or until the tops of the potatoes brown attractively. (Note: If stubborn, pop under the broiler to brown!)

Lu Nielsen

SWEET AND SOUR MEAT BALLS

Serves 8–10

1 package onion soup mix
2 eggs

½ cup water
2 pounds ground beef

Mix the first 3 ingredients. Stir in the meat, blend well and form into balls. In a skillet, brown the meat balls, turning as needed.

Sauce:

16-ounce can sauerkraut
8-ounce can cranberry sauce
¾ cup chili sauce

¾ cup water
⅓ cup brown sugar

Mix all ingredients. Pour ½ the sauce in a large baking dish or casserole. Place the meat balls on top and cover with remaining sauce. Cover and bake at 350° for 20 minutes. Remove cover and bake 20 minutes longer. Serve over hot rice.

Trude Foulis

BOSANSKI LONAC

Serves 8

2 pounds mixed meat, cubed
  (beef, pork and lamb)
½ cup vegetable oil
8 small whole onions
4 carrots, coarsely chopped
3 stalks celery, coarsely
  chopped
3 large tomatoes, coarsely
  chopped
2 tablespoons chopped
  parsley

5 large cloves garlic,
  crushed
1 large potato, peeled and
  diced
2 tablespoons wine vinegar
2 cups white wine
Salt to taste
12 peppercorns
½ cup flour

Brown meat in the oil. Arrange the meat, all the vegetables, garlic and parsley in layers in a heavy lidded casserole. Pour the vinegar and wine over all, adding salt to taste and the peppercorns. • Add just enough water to the flour to make a thick paste. Form into a long strip and attach dough to the rim of the casserole. Seal lid to casserole using dough as the "glue." • Simmer at 300° for 4 hours. (*Note:* This stew is best prepared a day ahead and reheated.)

Mrs. Budimir Loncar
Wife of the Ambassador of Yugoslavia

PASTEL DE CHOCLO

"A delicious Chilean corn pie"

4 tablespoons olive oil
2 pounds diced beef, round
   or sirloin
4 cups coarsely chopped onions
¼ cup raisins
2 teaspoons ground cumin seeds
1 teaspoon paprika
1½ teaspoons salt
¼ teaspoon freshly ground
   black pepper

½ cup pitted black olives
3 hard-boiled eggs, sliced
2½ pounds boned chicken,
   cut into serving pieces
3 cups corn, fresh or frozen
1 tablespoon milk
2 tablespoons butter
3 eggs, separated
1 tablespoon sugar

In a large, heavy skillet, heat 2 tablespoons of oil over high heat. Add diced beef and brown it well, stirring constantly. When meat is brown, reduce the heat to moderate and stir in the onions, raisins, cumin, paprika, salt and pepper. Reduce the heat to low and cook, uncovered, for 15 minutes, stirring occasionally. • Transfer the contents of the skillet to a 4-quart casserole. Spread the olives and hard-boiled eggs on top of the meat mixture. • In the skillet, heat the remaining oil over high heat. Add the chicken and brown the pieces on all sides, regulating the heat so they brown without burning. Reduce heat to low, cover and cook for 25 minutes. Arrange the chicken pieces on top of the meat mixture. • In an electric mixer or food processor, combine the corn (thoroughly thawed if frozen) and milk. Blend at medium speed for about 30 seconds. Cook the corn mixture over moderate heat for 10 minutes, stirring constantly so it does not burn. Add the butter, mix well and remove from heat. Beat the egg yolks slightly and beat the whites until stiff. Fold separately into the corn mixture and pour it over the chicken and meat. Spread the corn mixture evenly and sprinkle with sugar. • Bake at 350° for 30 minutes or until the top is golden brown. Serve hot.

Embassy of Chile
For cooking classes to benefit
The Washington Opera

JAIL HOUSE CHILI

Serves 10–12

2 pounds pinto beans
2 tablespoons bacon fat
3 pounds ground beef
1 pound Italian garlic
   sausage or chorizo
5 large onions, chopped
4 garlic cloves, minced
3 28-ounce cans tomatoes
2 6-ounce cans tomato paste
3 4-ounce cans green chilies
   chopped

1 tablespoon oregano
1 tablespoon cumin
1 teaspoon paprika
5 teaspoons salt
4 tablespoons chili powder
¼ teaspoon black pepper
¼ teaspoon cayenne
¼ teaspoon dried red chilies
4 tablespoons masa flour,
   softened in water

Soak the pinto beans in cold water overnight. • In a skillet, melt the bacon fat and brown the ground beef and chopped sausage. Remove the meat to a Dutch oven or other covered casserole. • Add the onions and garlic to the skillet, sauté until limp and add to the meat in the Dutch oven. • Drain the beans, reserving the water in which they soaked. Add the beans to the meat and onion mixture along with the tomatoes, paste, chilies and remaining seasonings. Pour in enough of the bean water to barely cover. • Mix the masa flour with a little water to soften. Stir into the meat mixture. Stir well and simmer, covered, over low heat until the beans are tender, about 2 hours.

Jean Page

TALLARINI

Serves 6

1 large green pepper,
   chopped
1 large onion, chopped
1 clove garlic, minced
½ pound sausage meat
1 pound ground beef
6-ounce can tomato paste
8-ounce can tomato sauce
¼ cup ketchup or chili sauce
28-ounce can tomatoes

¼ pound cheddar cheese,
   cubed
1 can ripe unpitted olives
½ pound mushrooms,
   sliced
8 ounces seashell
   marcaroni, cooked and
   drained
Parmesan cheese
Fresh parsley

Sauté the green pepper, onion, garlic, sausage and ground beef together in a large skillet. Turn into a crock pot or other large pot, add all remaining ingredients and simmer together 1–2 hours. Serve with Parmesan cheese and fresh parsley.

Maxine Polsky

Veal

Scene from "L'Enfant et les Sortilèges"

VEAL SHOULDER ROAST

Serves 4–6

Veal roast, about 3 pounds,
  boned, rolled and tied
Lemon-soy butter
  (recipe below)

8 large carrots, peeled
10 small new potatoes,
  peeled
2 tablespoons sugar

Place veal roast, fat side up on a rack in a roasting pan. Roast in a 325° oven for about 2½ hours, basting frequently with lemon-soy butter. • Cut carrots diagonally in 2–2½ inch pieces. Boil carrots and potatoes until barely tender. Drain. About 30 minutes before meat is done, arrange the carrots and potatoes around the roast in pan, removing rack if necessary. • Into remaining lemon-soy butter, stir 2 tablespoons sugar and generously baste vegetables and meat. Continue cooking until meat thermometer registers 155°–160° inserted in center of veal. • Arrange meat and vegetables on a heated serving platter and pour pan juices over them.

Lemon-soy butter:

⅓ cup butter
2 cloves garlic, crushed
2 tablespoons soy sauce

1 tablespoon lemon juice
1½ teaspoons thyme
½ teaspoon grated lemon peel

Melt butter in a small saucepan and stir in other ingredients.

Mrs. James R. Patton, Jr.

EDITH'S POLISH VEAL ROAST

Serves 6–8

4 pounds leg or rump veal
   roast
Salt
6 slices bacon
4 carrots, chopped
3 stalks celery, chopped
2 large onions, sliced
3 ounces red wine

¾ cup chicken broth
1 teaspoon peppercorns
1 bay leaf, crumbled
1 tablespoon soft butter
   blended with 1 tablespoon
   flour
Juice of 1 lemon
3 ounces caviar

Sear the roast in a heavy pan and then salt it. • Line a casserole with the bacon slices, cover them with the carrots, celery and onion and place the meat on top. • Drain any fat from the searing pan and deglaze it with the wine and chicken broth. Add to the casserole. Add the peppercorns and crumbled bay leaf. Cover the casserole and cook in a 325° oven for 1½ hours. • When the meat is tender, remove it from the casserole and keep warm. Sieve the vegetables and cooking liquid or purée in a food processor. Return to the casserole. Bring to a boil on top of the stove, and add the butter and flour paste to thicken the sauce. Stir in the lemon juice. Just before serving, gently stir in the caviar. Place the roast on a platter and spoon the sauce over it.

Mrs. John E. Chapoton

VEAL BIRDS

Serves 4–6

1½ pounds veal steak, cut into
  6 ⅛-inch thick slices,
  measuring about 4 x 6 inches
5 tablespoons oil or butter
1 tablespoon minced onion
1 tablespoon minced celery
1 cup diced peeled apples
3 tablespoons raisins

2 tablespoons fine, dry
  bread crumbs
½ teaspoon salt
¼ teaspoon pepper
¼ pound sliced mushrooms
¾ cup white wine
2 tablespoons flour
½ cup cream

Lightly pound the veal slices to flatten them. • Heat 2 tablespoons butter or oil in a skillet, add the onion and celery and sauté 5 minutes. Add the apples, raisins, bread crumbs, salt and pepper, blend well, and remove from heat. Place equal amounts of this stuffing mixture on each veal slice, roll up and tie or secure with toothpicks. • Heat 2 tablespoons oil or butter in a large saucepan or Dutch oven and brown the veal birds evenly on all sides. • Sauté the mushrooms in 1 tablespoon oil or butter and add to the meat with the white wine. Cover and cook 45 minutes. Remove the veal to a serving dish and keep warm. Blend the flour and cream together and add to the pan juices. Heat, stirring constantly, until the sauce is thick and pour over the veal.

Paula Jeffries

MEDAGLIONI DI VITELLO ALLA BOLOGNESE CON TARTUFI

Serves 6

6 oval ½-inch slices of
  veal, cut from the upper leg
Juice of 2 lemons
2 teaspoons salt
½ teaspoon freshly
  ground pepper
2 eggs, beaten

1 cup fresh bread crumbs
½ cup grated Parmesan cheese
6–8 tablespoons butter
6 slices prosciutto
6 slices Fontina cheese
6 slices white truffle

Combine the lemon juice, salt and pepper and stir until salt has dissolved. Brush the veal slices with the mixture and let them stand in a bowl for 2 hours, turning them occasionally. Dry the veal slices on paper towels, dip them in the beaten egg, then coat them thoroughly with the bread crumbs mixed with the Parmesan cheese. • Heat the butter in a skillet large enough to hold the veal without crowding, or use 2 skillets and the larger amount of butter. Brown the veal quickly, about 3 minutes on each side. Top each slice with a slice of prosciutto, a slice of cheese and a slice of truffle. Cover the pan, reduce the heat slightly, and cook about 4 minutes longer or until the cheese melts. Transfer the veal to a serving platter and spoon a little of the pan juices over each slice.

Chef Armando
Restaurant Tartufo

VEAL SAUTE

Serves 8–10

*"Serve over green noodles for a most
attractive buffet supper dish."*

3 pounds veal, cubed
3 tablespoons olive oil
2 medium onions, chopped
1 large clove garlic, crushed
¼ cup dry Madeira
35-ounce can Italian tomatoes
Salt and pepper

½ teaspoon thyme
1 teaspoon basil
½ pound mushrooms
1 tablespoon butter
½ cup sour cream
¼ cup chopped fresh parsley
  and basil

Brown the veal quickly over high heat in a skillet with 3 tablespoons olive oil. Remove to a casserole. Add onions to the same pan, cover, and cook slowly over low heat for 10 minutes. Add garlic. Add to the casserole. Deglaze the pan with the Madeira and pour over all. Add the tomatoes, seasonings and herbs. Bring casserole to a boil, reduce heat and cook slowly, covered, for 1¼ hours. (Recipe may be prepared ahead to this point.) • Before serving, gently reheat. Add mushrooms which have been sautéed in the butter. Stir in the sour cream and correct seasoning. Garnish with parsley and basil.

Sally Boasberg

VEAL MOZZARELLA

Serves 4

2 medium eggs
Salt and pepper
Oregano
¼ cup flour
¼ cup Italian seasoned bread
  crumbs
¼ cup Parmesan cheese
1 large white sweet onion
½ cup clarified butter
Basil

Dash of sugar
1 pound veal, sliced
  ¼-inch thick
2 medium tomatoes, sliced
8 ounces mozzarella, sliced
  ⅛-inch thick
White wine
Olives (green or black)
  or anchovies

Beat the eggs with a little salt, pepper and oregano. • Combine flour, seasoned bread crumbs and Parmesan cheese. • Thinly slice the onion and sauté in 2 tablespoons clarified butter until golden and season with basil, sugar, more oregano, salt and pepper. • Dip each slice of veal into beaten egg mixture, then into flour mixture. Sauté very quickly in remaining butter until golden brown on both sides. Arrange the veal in a single layer in a shallow casserole. Cover each piece with some of the sautéed onions, then a slice or 2 of tomato. Sprinkle with more herbs and top with mozzarella slices. If using anchovies, place filets on cheese, one to each veal slice. Pour in eough white wine to just cover casserole bottom and bake at 350° for about 15 minutes to heat through and melt the cheese. If not using anchovies, sprinkle with parsley and olives to garnish. (Note: A suggested accompaniment is Italian rice cooked in chicken broth with fresh mushrooms.)

Ann Brasfield

PICCATA DI VITELLO

Serves 4

1 pound veal medallions,
  pounded as thin as possible
  and cut into 3 x 4 inch pieces
¼ cup flour
Salt and pepper to taste
4 tablespoons butter

2 tablespoons olive oil
2 tablespoons lemon juice
2 tablespoons chopped parsley
10 rolled anchovy filets
  stuffed with capers
10 slices lemon

Lightly dredge the veal pieces in the flour and season with salt and pepper. • Heat 2 tablespoons of butter and the oil in a large skillet until bubbling. Add the veal, a few pieces at a time and brown for 1–2 minutes on each side. Remove to a warm serving platter. Discard any remaining fat in the pan, then add the remaining butter with the lemon juice and parsley. Return the veal to the pan and heat, spooning the lemon sauce over the slices. Arrange on the serving platter and garnish with the anchovies and lemon slices.

Mrs. Sander Vanocur

The Air and Space Museum

BLANQUETTE DE VEAU

Serves 6

4 tablespoons butter
2 large onions, finely chopped
2 pounds veal, cut into
   small cubes
2 pounds veal bones
1 teaspoon salt
¼ teaspoon pepper

¼ teaspoon thyme
1 bay leaf
1 tablespoon flour
2 carrots, diced
5 tablespoons sour cream
2 egg yolks
Juice of 1 lemon

Melt butter in a large skillet and sauté onions until golden. Add the cubed veal and sauté until meat is lightly browned. Stir in the bones, salt, pepper, thyme, bay leaf, and sprinkle with the flour. Mix well and cook for 2–3 minutes. ● Cover with water (2–3 cups) and simmer over low heat for about 1½ hours. ● Carefully remove all the bones and stir in the carrots. Simmer ½ hour longer. ● In a small mixing bowl, combine the sour cream, egg yolks and lemon juice. When ready to serve, stir this mixture into the meat. Reheat but do not boil. Serve with rice. (Note: If desired, diced mushrooms may also be added along with the carrots.)

Gertrude deP. d'Amecourt

VEAL WITH CASHEW NUT SAUCE

Serves 8–10

2 teaspoons salt
1 teaspoon black pepper
2 cloves garlic, minced
3 pounds veal, cut into
   1-inch cubes
4 tablespoons butter

3 tablespoons tomato sauce
2 onions, chopped
1 teaspoon flour
1 teaspoon Worcestershire
   sauce
2 cups cashew nuts

Mix the salt, pepper and garlic to a smooth paste. Combine with veal and stir well until pieces are coated. • Melt the butter in a casserole or Dutch oven and brown the veal. Add tomato sauce, 1½ cups water and chopped onions. Cover and cook over low heat for 1 hour. • Mix the flour and Worcestershire sauce and add to the gravy, stirring constantly. Add the cashew nuts and cook, uncovered, for 30 minutes, until veal is very tender. Correct seasoning and serve with boiled rice.

George T. Wittie

VEAL IN CREAM SAUCE

Serves 6–8

2 tablespoons unsalted butter
3 pounds veal, cubed
2 teaspoons finely chopped
   onion
½ teaspoon thyme
½ teaspoon salt
½ teaspoon freshly
   ground pepper
½ teaspoon paprika
2 bay leaves
½ teaspoon garlic powder

1 teaspoon Maggi seasoning
1 tablespoon freshly chopped
   parsley
1 teaspoon lemon juice
2 tablespoons sherry
2 tablespoons butter
1 teaspoon Worcestershire
   sauce
1 pound mushrooms, sliced
½ cup sour cream

Melt the unsalted butter in a skillet and brown the veal and onions. • Stir in all seasonings, parsley, lemon juice and sherry. Cook over low heat until tender, about 45 minutes. • In a separate pan, melt the butter, add the Worcestershire sauce and cook the mushrooms until tender. • Add the mushrooms and the sour cream to the veal and stir until thoroughly blended. Thicken the sauce with cornstarch if necessary. Serve with wild rice.

Mrs. J. Donald Annett

VEAL AND HAM SAUCE

Serves 3–4

1 pound veal or chicken
  scallops
Flour for dredging
3 tablespoons olive oil
5 tablespoons unsalted butter
¾ cup minced onion
½ cup plus 3 tablespoons
  Madeira or red wine
2½ teaspoons sage
1 bay leaf

2 cups beef broth
1 tablespoon arrowroot
  or flour
1 pound mushrooms, sliced
6 ounces baked ham, diced
½ cup red peppers,
  cut into strips
Salt and pepper to taste
Chopped parsley for garnish

Cut the meat into 1 x 4 inch strips and dredge with flour. Heat the olive oil and 2 tablespoons butter in a skillet, add the meat, brown 3–5 minutes, remove it and keep warm. Add the onions to the skillet and cook 3 minutes until soft. Stir in ½ cup wine, sage and bay leaf and reduce by ½. Add the beef broth, mix well, purée in a blender or food processor and strain, if desired. Return to pan and add the arrowroot or flour blended with 3 tablespoons wine. Simmer, stirring, until thickened. Add the meat. Heat 2 tablespoons butter in another skillet, sauté the mushrooms for 3 minutes and add them to the meat and sauce. Add the ham. • Sauté the red peppers in 1 tablespoon butter for 3 minutes. Add to the mixture. Season with salt and pepper. Sprinkle with parsley and serve.

Mary A. McGrade

VEAL KIDNEY STEW

Serves 4

"Make it ahead. . . . the flavor will only improve"

2 veal kidneys
2 tablespoons butter
2 medium onions, thinly sliced
20 large mushrooms, quartered
1½ cups chicken broth

2 tablespoons tawny port
1 teaspoon thyme
1 bay leaf
Salt and pepper

Cut kidneys into bite-sized pieces, including center fat. • Sauté onions in the butter in a large skillet. Add the mushrooms and sauté briefly. Add the kidneys and cook, stirring, over medium high heat until they lose their pink color. Turn into an ovenproof casserole and set aside. • Pour chicken broth into skillet, bring to a boil, and add port and seasonings. Add to casserole. • Bake in a preheated 400° oven for 45 minutes. Serve over rice.

Diane Rehm

VEAL AND WATER CHESTNUT CASSEROLE   Serves 12

"A truly outstanding party dish"

1 cup butter
4 pounds cubed veal
2 onions, sliced
2 cloves garlic, minced
2 teaspoons salt
½ teaspoon pepper
3 dashes cayenne pepper
2 pounds mushrooms, quartered

2 cups beef bouillon
¼ teaspoon nutmeg
1 bay leaf
4   5-ounce cans sliced
   water chestnuts
2 cups heavy cream
½ cup Cognac
¼ cup chopped parsley

Melt ½ the butter in a large skillet. Brown the veal, a few pieces at a time. Add the onions and garlic to the skillet, brown them and season with salt, pepper and cayenne. Turn the veal and onion mixture into a casserole. • Sauté the mushrooms in the remaining butter. Add to the casserole. • Deglaze the pan with the bouillon and add to the casserole. Add the spices and water chestnuts. Cover and bake at 375° for 1–1½ hours or until meat is tender. Remove from oven, add the cream and Cognac and return to the oven for 10 minutes to blend the flavors and thicken the sauce. Sprinkle with parsley and serve on green noodles.

Mrs. C. Michael Price

MARINATED VEAL WITH SCALLIONS   Serves 2

1 teaspoon dill
1 teaspoon rosemary
Juice of 1 lemon
1 cup plus 2 tablespoons
   olive oil
2 veal loin chops, ½ inch
   thick or more

2 tablespoons butter
6–8 scallions, sliced, using
   both green and white parts
½ cup dry vermouth

Combine the dill, rosemary, lemon juice and 1 cup of olive oil in a shallow dish. Marinate the chops in this mixture for at least ½ hour, turning occasionally and piercing the chops with a fork. Remove chops from marinade, and blot with paper towels to absorb excess oil. Heat the remaining oil and butter in a heavy frying pan and sauté the chops uncovered for 25 minutes until cooked and evenly browned. Remove chops from pan and keep warm. Add the scallions and brown lightly, stirring with a wooden spoon. Add the vermouth and simmer 3–4 minutes more. • Arrange chops on a serving dish and pour warm vermouth and scallions over them. (Note: Chops are good served on a bed of wild rice or a long grain and wild rice mixture.)

Sally Davidson

Lamb

The C and O Canal, Georgetown

MARINATED LEG OF LAMB

Serves 10

6-pound leg of lamb, boned
   and butterflied
8-ounce jar Dijon mustard
1 cup soy sauce
1 cup peanut oil

1 small onion
1 clove garlic, chopped
Cherry tomatoes
Tiny cooked buttered carrots
Chopped parsley for garnish

Combine the mustard, soy sauce, peanut oil, onion and garlic in a blender or food processor and blend well. Pour over the boned, butterflied lamb and marinate at least 4–6 hours or overnight.
• Broil the lamb for 10 minutes on each side, reduce oven heat to 325° and bake 30–40 minutes longer, using the shorter cooking time for rarer lamb. Place the lamb on a serving platter and surround it with cherry tomatoes and tiny buttered carrots. Sprinkle on chopped parsley and serve.

Mrs. Mark Hatfield
Wife of the Senator from Oregon

MARINATED BUTTERFLIED LEG OF LAMB Serves 8

"A superb barbeque"

1 6–7 pound leg of lamb,
   boned and butterflied
1¼ cups olive oil
¾ cup soy sauce
¼ cup Worcestershire sauce
2 tablespoons Dijon mustard
¼ teaspoon salt

1 tablespoon pepper
¼ cup red wine or
   wine vinegar
1½ teaspoons rosemary
⅓ cup fresh lemon juice
2 cloves garlic, crushed

Remove excess fat from boned and butterflied lamb. • Combine all remaining ingredients in a large bowl and marinate the lamb overnight in the refrigerator. Remove meat from marinade and pat dry. • Mound coals in center of grill and sear meat, then bank coals on either side and continue cooking, covered, over indirect heat for about 40 minutes. Lamb should be rosy pink inside. (Note: Lamb can also be baked in a 375° oven for 40–50 minutes.)

Nancy Holway

The Botanical Gardens

ARNI PSITO   Serves 6

1 leg of lamb
¼ cup lemon juice
½ cup corn oil
Salt and pepper to taste

1 large tomato, sliced
½ cup water
3 large potatoes, peeled
   and quartered

Trim excess fat from lamb, place it in a roasting pan and pour the lemon juice and corn oil over it. Sprinkle with salt and pepper and lay tomato slices on top. Add ½ cup water to the pan and place it in a preheated 450° oven. Reduce heat to 325° and bake the lamb for 2 hours, adding the potatoes after 1 hour. Turn the potatoes at least once during the cooking time.

Mrs. Andrew Jacovides
Wife of the Ambassador of Cyprus

LAMB STUFFED ACORN SQUASH   Serves 6

3 medium acorn squash
1 pound ground lamb
2 garlic cloves, minced
½ cup chopped onion
2–3 tablespoons butter
1½ cups cooked brown rice

4 cups water or broth
1 teaspoon salt
1 teaspoon cumin
¾ cup raisins
¾ cup raw cashew pieces

Cut squash in half, scoop out membrane and seeds and parboil for 15 minutes. Drain, cut a slice off the bottom of each so they will stay upright and set them aside. • Combine lamb, garlic and onion and sauté in butter until meat is just browned. Drain off excess liquid. Stir in the rice and sauté a few minutes longer. Add remaining ingredients and bring to a boil. Reduce the heat, cover and simmer gently until liquid is absorbed. • Fill each squash half with the lamb mixture, piling it to form a mound. Set stuffed squash in a shallow baking pan. Pour in enough water to cover the bottom of the pan. Cover with foil and bake at 350° until squash is soft, 30–45 minutes.

Sandra Foulis

LAMB WITH YOGURT   Serves 4

3 tablespoons butter
1 onion, chopped
1 pound lean lamb, cut into
   1-inch cubes
2 tablespoons flour

16 ounces plain yogurt
1 clove garlic, crushed
1 tablespoon dried mint
Salt to taste

Melt ½ the butter in a saucepan and brown the onion. Remove onion pieces from pan, add remaining butter and brown the lamb chunks. Lower the heat, cover and cook ½ hour. Add a little water, if needed, to prevent burning. • In a separate saucepan, combine the flour and yogurt. Mix well. Cook slowly, stirring, until thickened. Add to lamb along with the onions, garlic, mint and salt. Serve with rice.

Anne Shultz

ARCADIAN LAMB   Serves 6–10

5–6 pound leg of lamb
1½ cloves garlic
½ cup plus 1 tablespoon butter
Salt and pepper to taste
1 teaspoon beef extract

3 bay leaves
3 sprigs parsley
2 cups jumbo pimento-
   stuffed green olives

Remove all excess fat from the leg of lamb. With a sharp knife make an incision at the small end of the leg and insert ½ clove garlic. • Melt ½ cup butter in a roasting pan and brown the lamb quickly on top of the stove. Rub the browned meat with a cut clove of garlic and sprinkle with salt and pepper. • Dissolve the beef extract in 1 cup boiling water and add to the roasting pan along with the bay leaves and parsley. Bring the liquid to a boil and remove from heat. Cover the roasting pan and place in a 300° oven for 1 hour. • Remove the meat to a serving platter and keep it warm. Skim the fat from pan juices. Pour the liquid into a small saucepan and reduce over high heat to the consistency of a glaze. • Scald the pimento-stuffed olives in boiling water. Drain and cut in half lengthwise. Heat the olives in the roasting pan with 1 tablespoon butter, turning them to coat with the melted butter. Arrange the olives around the lamb and pour the glaze over all. Garnish with parsley and serve with rice pilaf.

Deena Speliakos Clark

LORD WHAT FOOLES
THESE MORTALS BE!

Statue of Puck at the Folger Library

DOLMAS   Serves 6–8

"Stuffed grape leaves are a Greek favorite"

2 tablespoons butter
2 tablespoons olive oil
½ pound ground beef
½ pound ground pork
½ pound ground lamb
2 tablespoons chopped onion
1 teaspoon salt
⅛ teaspoon pepper
2 cups cooked rice

2 tablespoons chopped mint
1 clove garlic, minced
1   16-ounce jar vine leaves
Juice of 1 lemon
1 cup tomato juice
2 cubes beef bouillon
    dissolved in 2 cups hot water
Cornstarch for thickening

Melt the butter and oil in a skillet and brown the meat and onion. Add the salt and pepper. Stir in the rice, mint and garlic. Mix well. • Unroll the leaves, shiny side down. Place a rounded teaspoon of the meat mixture on each leaf and carefully roll it up. • Arrange the rolls, seams down, on a rack in a large pot. • Make a sauce of the lemon juice, tomato juice and bouillon. Pour over the stuffed grape leaves and bring to a boil. Simmer for 30 minutes. • Remove from heat. Gently remove rolls from pot and arrange on a platter. Thicken the sauce with cornstarch and pour over the rolls. (Note: If using fresh grape leaves, wash thoroughly, cover with cold water and 1 tablespoon baking soda. Bring to a boil, simmer for 5 minutes and drain. Place shiny side down and carefully cut off the stem and tough part of lower leaf around it. Stuff and roll.)

Trude Foulis

CURRIED LAMB WITH GRAPES

Serves 6

2 pounds boneless shoulder
  or leg, of lamb
¾ cup finely chopped onion
1 tablespoon curry powder
½ cup salad oil or shortening
1 cup hot water or beef or
  lamb stock
1 bay leaf

¼ teaspoon ground cardamon
¼ teaspoon ground ginger
¼ teaspoon powdered
  mustard
2 teaspoons salt, or to taste
¼ cup evaporated milk
1½ cups green, seedless grapes

Trim and discard excess fat from lamb. Cut meat into 1 inch pieces. Set aside. • Sauté onions and curry powder in oil or shortening until onions are golden, stirring frequently. Add lamb and cook until browned on all sides, about 10 minutes. Add the next 6 ingredients. Cover and cook 50 minutes, or until lamb is tender. Stir in milk and grapes. Heat thoroughly, but DO NOT BOIL. Serve hot with rice.

George T. Wittie

SOUTH AFRICAN MEAT STEW

Serves 8

1½ cups dried white beans
1 tablespoon olive oil
1 tablespoon butter
3 onions, chopped
4 pounds lamb, cut from
  leg in 2-inch cubes
2 pounds canned tomatoes
2 teaspoons salt

¼ teaspoon chili powder
2 tablespoons curry
1 teaspoon sugar
¼ cup water
2 tablespoons vinegar
1 cup chopped green (sour)
  apples
½ cup raisins

Cover beans with water, soak them overnight and drain. Place them in a heavy saucepan, cover with water and boil them until tender. Drain. • Heat the oil and butter in a large pot and sauté the onions until limp, not brown. Remove to a side dish and brown the meat in the same oil. Add the onions, tomatoes, salt and chili powder, cover, and cook over very low heat for 30 minutes. • Blend the curry powder with the sugar, water and vinegar until smooth. Add to the meat with the apples, raisins and cooked, drained beans. Bake the stew in a 325° oven for 2½–3 hours until meat is very tender.

Dorothy B. Wexler

JELLIED LAMB
Serves 8–12

"Something different for a cold buffet, or serve as a first course"

1½–2 pounds lamb shoulder
1½–2 pounds fresh pig's feet
1 large unpeeled onion
1 large carrot, peeled
2 cloves garlic, halved

8 cups water
4 bay leaves
8 whole black peppercorns
1 tablespoon salt

Combine the first 6 ingredients in a large saucepan and bring to boil. Skim off the foam and add the seasonings. Reduce the heat and simmer, partially covered, for 3¼ hours. Remove the meat and let it cool. • Strain the stock through a fine sieve, cook and skim off surface fat. Bring the stock to a boil again and reduce it to 4 cups. • Trim fat from the cooled meat and discard the bones. Cut the meat into ¼-inch shreds and stir into the cooled stock. Correct the seasoning. Pour meat and stock into a 2-quart mold and refrigerate until firm, about 4 hours.

Mrs. G. William Miller

DO PIYAZA
Serves 6

"A spicy lamb dish from Pakistan."

3 pounds leg of lamb
  meat, cubed
4 tablespoons corn
  or vegetable oil
3 pounds onions

12–14 cloves garlic, chopped
2 teaspoons salt
6 whole dried red
  peppers, crushed
1 cup plain yogurt

In a large skillet, brown the lamb in the corn oil. • Cut the onions into fine rings. Add to browned meat, along with the garlic, salt and crushed pepper. Add ½ cup water and cook over medium heat until tender. • Add yogurt and simmer gently over low heat for 10 minutes. Remove from heat and serve hot.

Mrs. Shahida Azim
Wife of the Ambassador of Pakistan

Pork

Decatur House

JAMBON BOURBON

Serves 5

1   1½-pound canned ham
2 cups Kentucky bourbon
1 tablespoon cinnamon
1 teaspoon nutmeg
4 tablespoons maple syrup

4 tablespoons butter
2 tablespoons Dijon mustard
½ cup Cognac
½ cup water

Marinate the ham overnight in the bourbon, cinnamon and nutmeg.
•   Place ham and marinade in a covered pot and simmer 1 hour. Add
maple syrup and butter and cook 10 minutes more.   •   Remove ham,
cool and slice.   •   Add the mustard and Cognac and ½ cup water to
the marinade mixture. Boil, uncovered, until reduced. Pour over ham
slices and serve.

Justine Hughes

CROWN ROAST OF PORK WITH CORN STUFFING

Serves about 8

1 crown roast of pork,
  2 ribs per person

Cover ends of bones with foil. Salt and pepper the meat. Place in a preheated 450° oven, reduce heat to 350° and roast 35–40 minutes a pound.

Stuffing:

3 onions, diced
¼ cup chopped parsley
1 cup chopped celery
½ cup butter
12 slices day old bread,
  cubed

1 beaten egg
8¾-ounce can whole kernel
  corn, drained
8½-ounce can creamed corn
Salt and pepper

Sauté onions, parsley and celery in the butter for 8 minutes and place in a mixing bowl. Add cubed bread, beaten egg, corn, salt and pepper. Toss together and mound in the center of the crown roast for the last 1½-hours of its cooking time, covering loosely with foil until the last 30 minutes. • To serve, add frills to the pork bone ends. Make pan gravy if desired.

Mrs. Milton Traer

STUFFED ROAST PORK

Serves 6–8

1 cup brandy
12 pitted prunes
6 dried apples, cut in half
2 tablespoons raisins
3½–3¾ pound pork loin,
  boned

½ teaspoon cinnamon
¼ teaspoon allspice
¼ teaspoon mace
⅛ teaspoon ground cloves
2 ounces currant jelly
1 cup bread crumbs

The night before, combine brandy and fruits. Let stand overnight. • Cut a pocket into the boned pork loin large enough for the fruit. Stuff the fruit into the pocket. Roll the roast and tie it closed with string. • Combine the spices and rub them over entire roast. • Bake uncovered for 1½ hours at 350°. • Remove from oven, coat with currant jelly and roll in the bread crumbs. Return to oven and continue baking another 1½ hours.

JoAnne Nicholson

HOT PORK ROLL WITH MUSTARD SAUCE   Serves 6

"Hot or cold this is deliciously different"

2 pounds boneless pork, loin
  or shoulder
¼ pound boiled ham
1 medium onion, chopped
2 cloves garlic, minced
2 slices white bread with
  crusts, ground into crumbs
½ teaspoon thyme
¼ teaspoon nutmeg
½ teaspoon ground allspice

¼ teaspoon sage
1 teaspoon oregano
2 teaspoons salt
1 teaspoon pepper
4 tablespoons butter,
  softened
½ cup heavy cream
2 eggs
2 quarts chicken or
  veal stock

Grind the pork and ham in a meat grinder or food processor and turn
into a large mixing bowl. Add the onion, garlic, bread crumbs, all herbs
and seasonings, and softened butter. Mix thoroughly with your hands.
• Beat cream and eggs together, add to the meat mixture and mix
again. Fry a teaspoon of the meat at this point, taste and correct
seasoning. Chill meat mixture. • Spread a strong dish towel or 2
layers of cheesecloth on a counter and pat chilled meat into a 12 x 4
inch roll on top near one of the long edges. Roll cloth tightly around
the meat and tie the ends with string. • Pour stock into a heavy pot
and heat. Gently immerse meat roll in the stock adding enough hot
water to cover. Return to simmer, cover the pot and gently poach the
roll for 45–60 minutes. • Lift cooked roll from stock and allow to
drip 5 minutes. Carefully remove cloth wrapping, slice meat, and
arrange on warm serving platter. Spoon some mustard sauce (see
below) over the top and pass the rest of the sauce separately.

Mustard Sauce:

1 teaspoon salt
2 tablespoons sugar
¼ teaspoon pepper
2 teaspoons dry mustard

1 teaspoon cornstarch
1 egg, lightly beaten
½ cup water
¼ cup vinegar

Combine dry ingredients in a saucepan. Stir in the egg, water and
vinegar. Cook, stirring, over medium heat until sauce thickens, about 3
minutes.

Carol Cutler

SPARERIBS WITH FRUIT

Serves 6

"A tangy and different flavor"

6 pounds meaty spareribs
¾ cup soy sauce
1 cup marmalade
½ teaspoon ground ginger
½ teaspoon rosemary
½ teaspoon thyme
½ cup brown sugar

1½–2 cups orange or
    pineapple juice
Juice of 1 lemon
Salt and pepper
12–18 pitted prunes
12–18 dried apricots

Combine soy sauce, marmalade, ginger, rosemary, thyme, brown sugar and fruit juices for marinade. Pour over ribs and marinate for at least 2 hours. Best if allowed to marinate 6–8 hours in the refrigerator ● Salt and pepper the ribs generously and place under broiler for a few minutes, just until brown. Do not overcook. Remove and reduce oven temperature to 300°. ● Place ribs and marinade in a roasting pan and cover tightly. Baste the ribs every 20–30 minutes. ● After ribs have cooked for 1 hour add softened pitted prunes and apricots (or just one). Cook for 1 hour more, continuing to baste, for a total cooking time of 2 hours. ● Cut ribs into pieces of 2 ribs each and arrange on a heated platter.

Karen Fawcett

SMOTHERED PORK

Serves 8–10

4–5 pound loin of pork
2 cups red wine
2 cloves garlic, sliced
Assorted herbs, dried or
    fresh: basil, thyme,
    marjoram, oregano, bay leaf
8 small potatoes
8 carrots

4 peppers, green or red
8 stalks celery
2 turnips
4–8 onions or leeks, sliced
Additional vegetables: broccoli
    cauliflower, brussel sprouts,
    etc. to taste (use leftovers)

Marinate pork loin for 8 hours in red wine, garlic and herbs. ● Place pork in a Dutch oven or large covered roasting pan. Cut vegetables into bite-sized pieces or slices and add to roast in pan. Pour in marinade, cover and bake at 350° for 1½ hours. Remove cover and bake ½ hour longer so meat will brown.

Dorothy B. Wexler

PORK TENDERLOIN IN TOMATO SAUCE   Serves 2

½ pound pork tenderloin
1 cucumber
2 tablespoons sugar
1 teaspoon sherry
1 tablespoon vinegar
Salt to taste

Pinch cornstarch
3 tablespoons water
3 tablespoons tomato paste
1 cup flour
2 egg whites, lightly beaten
7 tablespoons oil

Slice the pork and the cucumber. • Combine sugar, sherry, vinegar, salt, cornstarch and water with tomato paste. • Coat the meat slices with flour and dip in the egg whites. Heat 5 tablespoons of oil in a skillet and add meat. Brown on both sides, about 3 minutes. • In a clean skillet, heat 2 tablespoons oil and stir-fry cucumber slices quickly. Add tomato mixture and bring to a boil. Add cooked meat slices, mix well and serve.

Mrs. Zemin Chai
Wife of the Ambassador of
the Peoples' Republic of China

Sculling on the Potomac

CHICK PEA AND SAUSAGE CASSEROLE   Serves 6–8

"Nourishing cold weather supper"

1 pound hot sausage meat
2 tablespoons butter
3 slices bacon, chopped
4 scallions, chopped
1 large green pepper, chopped
2 cloves garlic, chopped
1   8-ounce can tomato sauce

1½ teaspoons chili powder
¼ teaspoon cumin
Salt and pepper to taste
2   1-pound cans chick peas,
   drained
½ cup sliced black olives
3 tablespoons chopped parsley

Sauté sausage meat and set aside.   •   In 2 tablespoons butter, sauté the bacon, scallions, green pepper and garlic. Cook for 5 minutes. • Mix in the rest of the ingredients and simmer for 5 minutes. • Add the sausage meat and put mixture in a casserole. Bake for 30 minutes at 350°.

Joy J. Hamm

CHICONS AU JAMBON GRATINES

Serves 4

"Belgian endives with ham combine
beautifully for this light supper or luncheon dish."

8 stalks Belgian endives
1 tablespoon lemon juice
½ cup water

½ teaspoon salt
8 slices cooked ham

Place endives in a saucepan with the water, lemon juice and salt. Weight with an overturned saucer, cover and simmer gently for about 40 minutes. Strain well, reserving cooking liquid. • Roll each stalk of endive in a ham slice. Set aside.

Sauce Mornay:

2 tablespoons butter
2 tablespoons flour
1½ cups liquid (cooking liquid
 from endives plus milk)
Nutmeg, salt and pepper
 to taste

4–5 tablespoons grated Swiss
 cheese
1 egg yolk (optional)
Bread crumbs

Melt butter and when very hot, but not brown, add flour all at once. Cook together over medium heat 1 minute. Off heat, add *cold* liquid all at once, mixing with a wire whisk. Return to heat and bring to a boil, stirring constantly. Off heat again, add cheese and egg yolk, if desired. • Cover the bottom of a baking dish with a small quantity of sauce and arrange endives and ham rolls on top. Cover with remaining sauce, sprinkle with bread crumbs, dot with butter and brown under the broiler.

Mrs. J. Raoul Schoumaker
Wife of the Ambassador of Belgium

SUGAR BACON

"What could be simpler or more delicious?"

Bacon
Dark brown sugar

Allow 3 strips of bacon for each serving and place the strips on a baking sheet. • Put dark brown sugar in a strainer and sprinkle enough over the bacon to cover it well. • Bake the sugared bacon strips in a 300° oven for about 30 minutes, checking often to see that it does not burn and that both sides are cooked. • When done, remove from oven, cool, cut into small pieces and serve.

Mrs. David K. E. Bruce

EGGS AND CHEESE

The Washington Cathedral

GRIPSHOLM EGG

Serves 10

10 large hard-boiled eggs
8 ounces bacon
6 tablespoons butter
6 tablespoons flour
4 cups milk

Salt and pepper to taste
1 cup freshly grated Parmesan
cheese
Chopped parsley

Press 4 of the egg yolks through a fine sieve and set aside. Chop the remaining 6 eggs plus 4 whites. • Cook the bacon until crisp, cool, and chop it finely. • Melt the butter in a saucepan, whisk in the flour and add the milk slowly, stirring constantly with the whisk until the sauce has thickened. Season with salt and pepper. Stir in the Parmesan cheese. When ready to serve, fold the chopped eggs into the hot sauce, cook ½ minute and turn into a serving dish. Garnish with rows of sieved egg yolks, chopped bacon and chopped parsley.

Embassy of Sweden
For cooking classes to benefit
The Washington Opera

SCOTCH EGGS

Any quantity

"Great picnic fare"

Hard-boiled eggs, peeled
Beaten eggs, one for every
four hard-boiled eggs
Italian seasoned bread crumbs

¼ pound hot, spicy sausage
meat, uncooked, for each
egg
Oil

Take one peeled egg, dip in beaten egg, roll in bread crumbs and place in center of the sausage meat which has been flattened into a patty. Fold sausage around egg, sealing and pressing meat as though making a snowball. Dip sausage-covered egg into beaten egg again and coat meat. Roll in bread crumbs and dip back into the beaten egg. Roll again in bread crumbs. Let eggs stand 5 minutes, then fry in hot oil in a skillet, wok or deep fryer until dark brown. Drain, cool and refrigerate. Serve hot or at room temperature.

William J. Kerns, Jr.

WINE AND CHEESE OMELET   Serves 12–15

1 large loaf French bread, cut
  in small cubes
6 tablespoons butter
¾ pound Swiss cheese,
  shredded
½ pound Monterey Jack
  cheese, shredded
9 slices Genoa salami,
  shredded

16 eggs
3¼ cups milk
½ cup white wine
4 scallions, chopped
1 tablespoon Dijon mustard
¼ teaspoon cayenne
1½ cups sour cream
⅔ cup Parmesan cheese

Butter 2 (9 x 13 inch) baking dishes. Spread bread in bottom and
drizzle with melted butter. Sprinkle with Swiss and Monterey Jack
cheeses and salami. • Beat the eggs, milk and wine. Add the scallions, mustard and cayenne and stir until completely blended. Pour
over cheese and salami. Cover with foil and refrigerate overnight.
• Bake covered at 350° for 1 hour and 15 minutes. Remove foil,
spread with sour cream and Parmesan. Bake 15 minutes longer.

Susan Koehler

MEXICAN CANAPE   Serves 2

2   8-inch flour tortillas
Peanut oil for frying
Salt
½ cup shredded Monterey
  Jack cheese

⅓ cup shredded cheddar
  cheese
¼ cup chopped hot green
  chilies
⅓ cup chopped onion

Fry the tortillas quickly in hot oil. Prick them with a fork so they will
remain flat. When golden on both sides, drain and sprinkle with salt.
• Place 1 fried tortilla on a cookie sheet. Sprinkle the cheese to cover
the entire tortilla, then the chilies and then the onion. Place the other
tortilla on top and press lightly. • Bake at 375° for 10 minutes, or
until cheese begins to run. • Cut in pie-shaped pieces and serve on
a warm platter while crispy and hot. Have plenty of napkins on hand.
People go crazy over these!

Ann Brasfield

PACK-A-PICNIC PIE   Serves 6

"Don't wait for a picnic!"

Pastry for a two-crust pie
  (9½ inch)
3 medium onions, chopped
2 tablespoons olive oil
1 tablespoon butter
1 frozen spinach soufflé,
  defrosted
12 ounces diced cooked ham
1½ cups grated Parmesan
  cheese

1 cup ricotta cheese
4 eggs, beaten with
  ¼ teaspoon pepper
Pinch nutmeg
8 ounces mozzarella cheese,
  shredded
1 egg beaten with a pinch
  of salt

Sauté onions in butter and oil. Remove from heat and add spinach soufflé, broken into small pieces. Add ham, Parmesan, ricotta, the 4 eggs beaten with ¼ teaspoon pepper and nutmeg. • Roll out one half of the pastry and line a 9½ inch pie dish. Pour in ham and cheese mixture. Top with mozzarella. • Roll out remaining pastry, fitting on top and turning the edges from the bottom up over the top crust. Flute edges and brush top with beaten egg. Cut a vent in the top of the pie. • Bake on center oven rack for 25 minutes at 425°. (Cover crust with foil half way through baking if it is browning too quickly). • Let pie rest 20 minutes before serving—warm or cold.

Pat Young

EGG AND MUSHROOM CASSEROLE   Serves 4

"A tasty addition to your brunch or luncheon repertoire."

4 eggs, hard boiled
8 ounces mushrooms,sliced
3 ounces butter

2 cups light cream
2 ounces bread crumbs
4 ounces grated cheddar cheese

Shell and slice the eggs. • Sauté the mushrooms in 2 ounces of the butter for 5 minutes. • Grease a medium-sized casserole and pour in 1 cup cream. Cover with half the bread crumbs, a layer of sliced egg, the remaining cream and the mushrooms. Sprinkle with grated cheese, top with the remaining bread crumbs and dot with remaining butter. • Bake at 350° for 30 minutes.

Lili-Charlotte Sarnoff

SEAFOOD CREPES

Makes 8–10 crêpes

"Delicious with tossed salad as a light lunch or supper"

8–10 crêpes
2 tablespoons butter
½ cup sliced scallions
¾ cup sliced celery

6 ounces crab meat
½ cup mayonnaise
2 tablespoons diced pimento
1 teaspoon lemon juice

Melt the butter in a small skillet and sauté the scallions and celery. Combine remaining ingredients in a bowl. Add sautéed scallions and celery. Mix well and correct seasoning. Place 2 heaping tablespoons across the center of each crêpe, brown side out, and role. • Place filled crêpes in a buttered baking dish and cover with foil. Bake 15–20 minutes at 350°. Serve with hot sauce.

Sauce:

1 can cream of mushroom
  soup

1 teaspoon lemon juice
½ cup sherry

Combine all ingredients in a saucepan. Stir over low heat until thoroughly blended and hot. Serve immediately.

Christa Annett

Information booth and dinosaur on the Mall

SPINACH AND SAUSAGE CREPES

Serves 6

Crêpes:

1½ cups milk
⅔ cup flour
3 eggs

½ teaspoon salt
Butter

Use a food processor or blender to make a batter of the milk, flour, eggs and salt. • Melt 1 teaspoon butter in a 9-inch skillet and pour in just enough batter to thinly cover the pan. Cook the crêpe 2 minutes, turn it and cook 1 minute more. Repeat until all batter is used, stacking the finished crêpes on a plate. You should have 12 crêpes.

Spinach and Sausage Fillings:

12 breakfast sausage links, cooked
2 packages Stouffer's frozen spinach soufflé, cooked
2 cups grated cheddar cheese

On each of 6 of the crêpes place 2 sausage links, sprinkle with 1 cup of the cheese, roll up and place in a large buttered baking dish. • On each of the 6 remaining crêpes, place about 2 tablespoons of the cooked spinach soufflé, sprinkle with the remaining cup of cheese, roll up and add to the baking dish.

Sauce:

2 tablespoons butter
2 tablespoons flour

1 cup milk
1 cup grated cheddar cheese

In a saucepan, melt the butter and stir in the flour using a whisk. Continue stirring while adding the milk. Heat almost to boiling, add the cheese and stir until melted. Pour the sauce over the crêpes. • To serve, heat the crêpes in a 350° oven. This will take beween 5 and 30 minutes depending on whether the dish has been assembled ahead and refrigerated.

Leslie Anne Gottfred

BACON, CORN AND ONION QUICHE

Serves 6–8

1 partially baked pie shell
1½ cups sour cream
3 eggs
1 cup grated Gruyère cheese
½ cup grated Swiss cheese
Salt and pepper to taste
1 pound bacon

1½ tablespoons butter
1 onion, sliced
1½ cups corn kernels, about
  3 ears
¼ teaspoon nutmeg
2 tablespoons cream

Beat the sour cream with the eggs. Add the cheeses, salt and pepper. Chill 15 minutes. • Cook the bacon, reserving 1 tablespoon of the grease. Crumble the bacon into the sour cream mixture. • Heat the bacon grease with the butter, add the onion and sauté 5 minutes. Add the corn and cook 5 minutes. Remove from heat and stir in the nutmeg and cream. Combine this with the sour cream mixture and pour into the pie shell. Bake at 375° for 45 minutes.

Susan Koehler

ZUCCHINI AND HAM QUICHE

Serves 6–8

2 tablespoons butter
¼ cup finely chopped onion
1 small clove garlic, minced
Salt and pepper
1¼ pound zucchini, sliced
¼ pound boiled ham,
  finely diced

4 large eggs
¾ cup milk
½ cup heavy cream
¼ cup Parmesan and cheddar
  cheese, mixed

Preheat oven to 350°. • Heat butter in skillet and add onion and garlic. Cook, stirring, until softened. Add salt and pepper to taste. Add zucchini and cook for 5 minutes, stirring gently and shaking pan. Add chopped ham and remove from heat. • Break eggs into a mixing bowl. Beat well and add milk, cream, salt and pepper to taste. Mix with zucchini and pour into Pyrex dish. Sprinkle with cheese. • Increase oven temperature to 375°. • Place Pyrex dish on a baking sheet and bake for 30 minutes. • Reduce oven temperature to 350° and bake 15 minutes longer. It is a good idea to have a bit of water in a pan on the rack under the baking sheet. (Note: This is best with no crust, however if you prefer a crust, use pastry to line a 10-inch quiche pan.)

Mrs. Malcolm Price

COUNTRY QUICHE   Serves 6

5 2–3 ounce cans whole green   5 eggs
   chilies   13 ounces evaporated milk
2 pounds Monterey Jack   1–2 tablespoons flour
   cheese, grated   Salt and pepper to taste

Split the chili peppers lengthwise and remove seeds. • Make a layer
of ½ the peppers in the bottom of a 9 x 13-inch pan. Add a layer of ½
the cheese, follow with the remaining peppers and end with a layer of
the remaining cheese. • Blend the eggs, milk, flour and salt and
pepper together. Pour over the layered green chilies and cheese. Bake
at 350° for 35–45 minutes. Let set 5–10 minutes before cutting to
serve.

Mrs. James A. Baker, III

SOUFFLE AUX EPINARDS   Serves 6

"A classic spinach soufflé plus cheese"

¾–1 cup grated cheese   4½ tablespoons butter
1½ cups chopped spinach,   4½ tablespoons flour
   cooked and drained   1½ cups milk
Pinch nutmeg   6 egg yolks
Salt and pepper to taste   8 egg whites, room
2 tablespoons minced shallots   temperature

Generously butter an 8-cup soufflé dish and sprinkle with 1–2 tablespoons grated cheese to coat the sides and bottom. • Season the
cooked, drained spinach with nutmeg, salt and pepper. Sauté the
shallots in 1 tablespoon butter for 2–3 minutes, stir in the spinach and
set aside. • Heat 3½ tablespoons of butter in a saucepan, add the
flour and stir with a whisk. Add the milk and heat, stirring with the
whisk, until smooth. Beat in the egg yolks, one at a time, with the
whisk. Remove from heat. • Beat the egg whites until stiff. • Stir
the spinach into the egg yolk mixture, then fold all but 2 tablespoons of
the cheese into the egg whites. Stir a little of the egg white mixture
into the yolk mixture and fold in the rest. Turn into the prepared
soufflé dish and sprinkle 2 tablespoons of cheese over the top. Place
the soufflé on the middle rack of a preheated 400° oven, reduce the
temperature to 375° and bake for 30 minutes or until puffed and
brown. Bake 5 minutes more to firm it and serve immediately.

Lili-Charlotte Sarnoff

CRAB QUICHE

Serves 8

"Very light and good"

1   10-inch unbaked pie shell
4 eggs
2 cups light cream
⅓ cup minced onion
1 teaspoon salt

⅛ teaspoon cayenne pepper
8 ounces crab meat
1 cup shredded mozzarella
   or Swiss cheese
Snipped parsley

Beat eggs until fluffy. Stir in cream, onion, salt and cayenne. Pat crab meat dry with paper towels if frozen or canned. Sprinkle crab and cheese evenly in pie shell. Pour in the egg mixture and sprinkle with parsley.   •   Bake 15 minutes at 400°. Reduce heat to 300° and bake 30 minutes more or until knife comes out clean. Let stand 10 minutes before cutting.

Pam Burge

MUSHROOM SOUFFLE

Serves 6

½ pound firm white
   mushrooms
1 medium onion, minced
5 tablespoons butter
2 cups milk
4 tablespoons Cream of Wheat

½ teaspoon marjoram
Dash freshly ground black
   pepper
½ teaspoon salt
3 eggs, separated

Wash the mushrooms, chop them finely and sauté them with the minced onions in the butter.   •   Scald the milk, sprinkle in the Cream of Wheat, stir until thick and add to the mushrooms. Add the seasonings and the beaten egg yolks and blend well   •   Beat the egg whites until stiff but not dry. Fold them into the mushroom mixture. Pour into a well greased 1½-quart baking dish. Bake at 300° for about 1 hour.

Paula Jeffries

The Lee Mansion and the John F. Kennedy grave

CRAB AND SPINACH SOUFFLE   Serves 6 as a first course

**1 package fresh spinach, do
    not use frozen spinach
Salt and pepper
4 egg whites**

**1 cup homemade mayonnaise
1 pound backfin crab meat
½ cup buttered bread crumbs**

Clean the spinach, removing the stems and steam or blanch until
wilted. Drain well, sprinkle lightly with salt and pepper and set aside.
• In a large bowl, whip egg whites until stiff but not dry. Fold in
mayonnaise. Carefully pick over the crab meat, removing any bits of
shell. Fold into mayonnaise mixture. • Spread the spinach in a
buttered 11 x 8 inch baking dish. Lightly pile crab and mayonnaise
mixture over spinach. Sprinkle bread crumbs over the top. Bake at
350° for 20 minutes or until lightly browned.

Robin Jacobsen

FRITADA DE BERENJENA (EGGPLANT SOUFFLE)

Serves 8

"In the tradition of Sephardic Jews"

2 large eggplants
1 cup grated Romano or
  Parmesan cheese
½ cup cracker or bread
  crumbs

4 eggs
Salt and pepper to taste
1 tablespoon oil

Place whole eggplants on foil in 350° oven. Bake until soft. • Remove skin and seeds and chop eggplant very fine. Stir in cheese (reserving some for topping), crumbs, eggs, salt and pepper. Place in shallow, greased baking dish and top with remaining cheese and a little oil. • Bake, uncovered, in 350°–400° oven until browned and inserted knife comes out clean.

Mrs. K. Norman Diamond

CHEESE SOUFFLE

Serves 4–6

"Unflappable and always successful!"

6 slices bread, spread with
  garlic butter
6 eggs
½ pound Swiss cheese, grated
½ cup light cream or milk

1 cup dry white wine
1 cup chicken broth
½ teaspoon dry mustard
½ teaspoon paprika

Line a casserole dish with alternate layers of bread and cheese, beginning with bread, buttered side down. • Beat eggs well and combine with cream (or milk), wine, chicken broth and seasonings. Mix well. Pour over layers of bread and cheese. • Bake at 350° for 25 minutes or until browned on the top.

Pauline Innis

PEPPER SOUFFLE

Serves 4

2 4-ounce cans Ortega green
chili peppers, drained
and diced
1 pound cheddar cheese, grated

3 eggs
3 cups milk
1 cup Bisquick

Put peppers in the bottom of a greased Pyrex baking dish and top with the grated cheese. • Beat the eggs and add the milk and Bisquick. Blend well, and pour over the pepper and cheese mixture. • Bake at 350° for one hour.

Randa Mendenhall

SALMON SOUFFLE

Serves 4

4 tablespoons butter
4 tablespoons finely
chopped onion
4 tablespoons flour
1 cup milk
5 eggs, separated
1 tablespoon ketchup

15-ounce can salmon, drained
well
1½ teaspoon dill seed, crushed
1 teaspoon salt
1 tablespoon lemon juice
Dash cayenne pepper

Preheat oven to 400°. Using 1 tablespoon butter, grease the bottom and sides of a 2 quart soufflé dish. • Melt remaining butter in a medium sacuepan. Add chopped onion and sauté for 3 minutes. Remove from heat. Add flour all at once, and stir to make a smooth paste. Add milk all at once, and beat with a whisk. Cook over medium heat, stirring constantly, until thick and smooth. Remove from heat. Beat in egg yolks one at a time. Stir in remaining ingredients except egg whites and set aside. • Beat egg whites until stiff. Stir a heaping tablespoon of whites into salmon mixture. *Gently* fold in the rest of the egg whites until no white streaks remain. • Pour into soufflé dish and place in preheated oven. Reduce oven temperature to 375° and bake, without disturbing, for 35–40 minutes. Serve immediately.

JoAnne Nicholson

PASTA AND RICE

Watergate, overlooking the Kennedy Center

CANNELLONI

Serves 8

Fresh pasta, cut into 16
  3 x 4-inch rectangles or
  16 pieces cannelloni
1 package frozen chopped
  spinach, thawed
2 tablespoons butter
3 tablespoons minced onion
1 egg yolk

1 cooked chicken breast,
  chopped
1 teaspoon salt
Pepper to taste
1 cup ricotta cheese
½ cup freshly grated
  Parmesan cheese
¼ teaspoon nutmeg

Cook the pasta according to directions, drain and dry on paper towels. • Cook the spinach in a large pot of boiling water 5 minutes and drain, pressing out the moisture. • Melt the butter in a large skillet, add the onion and sauté 5 minutes. Add the spinach and sauté 2–3 minutes more. Cool slightly and purée in a blender or food processor. Turn the purée into a bowl, add the remaining ingredients and mix well. • Spread 1–2 tablespoons of the spinach mixture on each pasta rectangle. Roll the pasta up lengthwise and place in a buttered baking dish seam side down. Dot with butter and cover with foil.

Béchamel Sauce:

6 tablespoons butter
5 tablespoons flour

2½–3 cups light cream

Melt the butter in a saucepan. Stir in the flour and cook 2 minutes without browning the flour. Remove from heat and slowly add the cream. Return to heat and cook, stirring, until the sauce has the consistency of thick cream.

Tomato Sauce and Assembly:

2 1-pound cans tomato sauce
3 tablespoons tomato paste
½ cup chopped onions
Salt and pepper to taste

1 teaspoon dried basil or 1
  tablespoon fresh
1 teaspoon sugar

Combine all ingredients in a saucepan and simmer, partially covered, for 40 minutes, stirring occasionally. Sieve the sauce and correct the seasoning. • Bake the filled cannelloni at 350° for 15 minutes, remove from oven and let stand 10 minutes. To serve, place 2 on each plate, spoon the béchamel sauce over them, covering well, and spoon 2 tablespoons of the tomato sauce over the béchamel.

Chris Hunter

CRAB CANNELLONI

Serves 8–12

14–18 manicotti noodles
½ pound butter
8 tablespoons flour
5 cups milk
1 teaspoon nutmeg
1½ pounds crab meat
2 egg yolks

1 pound mozzarella cheese
1 cup freshly grated
  Parmesan cheese
3 tablespoons tomato paste
½–1 pound mushrooms, sliced
5–8 tablespoons fresh sage,
  crushed

Cook manicotti noodles according to package instructions. Drain very carefully. • Melt 6 ounces of the butter in a saucepan. Add flour, stirring constantly, to make a smooth paste. Gradually add the milk, 1 cup at a time, stirring until sauce thickens. Add nutmeg. Remove ½ the sauce and set aside. • Clean the crab meat and mix with 2 egg yolks. Cut the mozzarella cheese into squares and combine with crab meat. • Boil the sauce remaining in the pan until very thick (consistency of oatmeal). Add 4 tablespoons grated Parmesan cheese. Blend this mixture into crab meat and season to taste. • With a teaspoon, carefully stuff each noodle with the crab mixture. Place in a single layer, sides touching, in a shallow buttered baking dish. • To remaining portion of white sauce add tomato paste and ½ cup Parmesan cheese. Spoon over noodles. • In 2 tablespoons butter, sauté mushrooms and sage. Place on top of sauce. Top with remaining Parmesan cheese, dot with butter and bake at 400° for 20–25 minutes. Do not brown. Let sit 10 minutes before serving.

Mrs. Andrew E. Manatos

NOODLE PUDDING

Serves 10–12

1   12-ounce box broad egg
  noodles
½ cup sugar
½ cup butter
1 cup sour cream
1 cup cottage cheese

4 eggs, beaten
1 teaspoon vanilla
2 teaspoons cinnamon
1   6-ounce can frozen
  orange juice concentrate
1 large cooking apple

Prepare noodles according to package directions. Do not overcook. Drain the noodles and toss with ½ cup sugar. In a large mixing bowl, combine the butter, sour cream, cottage cheese, eggs, vanilla, cinnamon and orange juice concentrate. • Peel, core and chop the apple. Add apple and noodles to the moist ingredients and blend thoroughly. Place in a 9 x 13 inch baking dish. Sprinkle with additional sugar and cinnamon if desired. Bake at 350° for 50 minutes.

Jill Alexander

GREEN NOODLE BOLOGNAISE

Serves 6

3 cloves garlic
¼ cup oil
1 pound lean ground beef
1   8-ounce can tomato sauce
1   6-ounce can tomato paste
¾ cup dry red wine
½ cup water
½ teaspoon oregano
¼ teaspoon basil
½ teaspoon salt

Freshly ground pepper
1   12-ounce package spinach
    noodles
1 cup milk
3 tablespoons butter
3 tablespoons flour
6 tablespoons light cream
1 cup grated Parmesan cheese
1 cup grated Gruyère cheese

Mince the garlic and place in a heavy saucepan with the oil. Cook over low heat until lightly browned. Add ground beef and stir with a wooden spoon to prevent burning. Add the tomato sauce and paste, wine, water, oregano, basil, ¼ teaspoon salt and pepper. Cover and simmer over low heat for 25 minutes. The sauce is done when oil rises to the surface. • Prepare the noodles according to package directions. • Prepare the béchamel sauce as follows: Scald the milk. Melt the butter in a skillet and stir in the flour. Slowly add the hot milk, stirring constantly over low heat for 3–5 minutes or until thickened. Remove from heat and stir in cream, ¼ teaspoon salt and pepper. • Drain the noodles and arrange in a well buttered casserole or ovenproof serving dish. Sprinkle with ¾ cup Parmesan and ¾ cup Gruyère. Pour the béchamel sauce over the noodles and sprinkle with remaining cheese. Heat in a 350° oven for 15–20 minutes. • Serve very hot with meat sauce.

Mrs. John N. Parker

MULYATYZ

Serves 10

*"It's an Italian noodle pie! Serve with meat at dinner
or as a main luncheon dish (serves 5)."*

6 eggs
¾ cup sugar
15 ounces ricotta cheese
½ pound fine noodles, cooked
1 tablespoon butter

¼ cup Cream of Wheat
3 cups milk
½ cup raisins
¼ cup pine nuts

In a large bowl combine eggs, sugar and ricotta cheese and beat well. • Cook the noodles according to package directions, drain well and toss with butter. Add to egg mixture. • Cook ¼ cup Cream of Wheat in 3 cups of milk and add to eggs and noodles. Add raisins and pine nuts and stir well with a wooden spoon. • Pour the mixture into a greased 13 x 9 inch baking pan and bake at 350° for 30–40 minutes. Knife inserted in center should come out clean.

Johanna S. Kramer

GNOCCHI ALLA CIPRIANI

Serves 6

1 quart milk
1 cup semolina or Cream of
    Wheat
2 egg yolks
½ teaspoon salt

Pepper
1 cup grated Swiss cheese
½ cup grated Parmesan cheese
¼ pound chopped prosciutto
2 tablespoons butter

Bring milk to a boil in a heavy saucepan, preferably non-stick. Slowly stir in semolina. Bring to a boil, lower heat and cook for 15 minutes, stirring often. Mixture will be very thick. • Remove from heat. Add some of the mixture to 2 beaten egg yolks. Then add the rest of the semolina mixture, salt, pepper, cheeses and prosciutto. • Spread out ½-inch thick to cool on buttered cookie sheet. When cold, cut into 1½-inch squares. Arrange overlapping in buttered baking dish, dot with butter and sprinkle with a little more Parmesan cheese. • Heat at 350° for 15–20 minutes until cheese begins to brown and butter bubbles.

Sally Boasberg

PESTO WITH CHICKEN AND ALMONDS

Serves 10

*"A wonderfully adaptable and expandable
dish to serve hot or cold"*

1 boneless chicken breast
8 ounces slivered almonds
1 pound vermicelli
½ cup plus 1 tablespoon
    vegetable oil
2 cups fresh basil leaves
1 clove garlic, minced

1 teaspoon salt
¼ cup olive oil
1–1½ cups grated Parmesan
    cheese
Bay leaves, extra almonds
    and extra cheese for
    garnish

Cover chicken with water and gently poach until done. Shred or cut the chicken into bite-sized pieces and place in a mixing bowl. Add the almonds. • Boil the vermicelli in salted water until "al dente." Drain, rinse in cold water, drain again and toss with 1 tablespoon vegetable oil. Add to the chicken and almonds and mix well. In a blender or food processor, combine ½ cup vegetable oil, basil leaves, garlic, salt, olive oil and 1 cup of the cheese. Blend for 15–20 seconds. Add more cheese to the pesto sauce to taste. Combine the pesto sauce with the vermicelli mixture, transfer to a serving dish, garnish and serve. If serving hot, transfer to a casserole or baking dish and heat in a 350°–375° oven.

Mrs. Nicholas Benton

VEGETARIAN LASAGNA

Serves 6–8

1 pound lasagna noodles
1 medium onion, chopped
1 clove garlic, minced
1 tablespoon butter
3–4 cups grated zucchini
16 ounces Italian style
tomato sauce

1 egg
12 ounces cottage cheese
12–16 ounces mozzarella
cheese, shredded
¾ cup grated Parmesan cheese

Cook lasagna noodles according to package directions. Drain and separate. • Sauté onion and garlic in the butter. Add the zucchini and tomato sauce and simmer 10 minutes. •˙ Beat the egg and mix well into the cottage cheese. • Grease a baking dish about 2 inches deep. Layer the lasagna, zucchini mixture, cottage cheese and mozzarella in the dish, ending with a layer of zucchini. Sprinkle with Parmesan cheese. • Cover and bake at 325° for 30 minutes. Uncover and bake 15 minutes longer to brown the top.

Mrs. Thomas F. Lenihan

STRAW AND HAY PASTA

Serves 10

1½ pounds fresh mushrooms
10 tablespoons butter
2 cloves garlic, minced
1 pound prosciutto ham,
minced
2 cups heavy cream

1 pound fresh egg pasta
1 pound fresh spinach pasta
1 cup freshly grated
Parmesan cheese
Salt
Freshly ground pepper

Clean and slice mushrooms. Melt 5 tablespoons of butter in a large skillet. Sauté the garlic and mushrooms for 10 minutes, until browned. • In a separate pan, melt remaining butter and fry the prosciutto until browned. • In a double boiler, heat the cream. Keep all ingredients hot. • Boil the noodles in separate pans for 1 minute. When they are tender but still firm (al dente), drain and toss them together in a heated serving dish. Over the top, add the mushrooms, prosciutto, cream and grated cheese. Season with salt and pepper. Serve immediately.

Mrs. Richard Landfield

SPAGHETTI IN CLAM-SCALLOP SAUCE

Serves 4

"A quick light meal"

1 pound extra-thin spaghetti
2 tablespoons butter
½ pound shucked clams
  with juice
½ pound scallops

1 bunch parsley, stemmed
  and chopped
2 tablespoons arrowroot
½ cup white wine
Freshly grated Parmesan cheese

Cook spaghetti according to package directions. • While spaghetti is boiling, melt the butter over high heat in a large skillet, add the clams and their juice and sauté quickly. Add the scallops and parsley and cook a few seconds to heat scallops through. • Blend the arrowroot with the wine and stir into the clam mixture. Cook about 45 seconds more to lightly thicken the sauce. Do not overcook. Serve over drained, cooked spaghetti and top with the grated Parmesan cheese.

Mr. and Mrs. Bruce D. Smith

FETTUCINE AL BURRO

Serves 4

¼ pound butter, softened
¼ cup heavy cream
1 cup freshly grated imported
  Parmesan cheese
1 pound fettucine

Salt and pepper
1 canned white truffle, sliced
  very thin or chopped
  (optional)

Cream the softened butter by beating it vigorously against the sides of a heavy bowl with a wooden spoon until it is light and fluffy. Gradually, beat in the cream and then, a few tablespoons at a time, beat in ½ cup of the Parmesan cheese. Cover and set aside. • Bring water to boil in a large pot, add 1 tablespoon salt and fettucine, a few strands at a time, stirring gently to prevent sticking. Boil 5–8 minutes or until pasta is tender. Drain well and transfer to a hot serving bowl. Add the creamed butter mixture and toss to coat the pasta well. Season generously with salt and pepper and stir in the truffle if desired. Serve immediately, passing remaining Parmesan cheese in a separate bowl.

Frances Humphrey Howard

RICE AND MUSHROOMS

Serves 4–6

" Great with dolmas"

¼ pound butter
¾ cup sliced fresh mushrooms
½ cup chopped celery,
  include leaves

¼ cup chopped scallions
1 teaspoon salt
2½ cups beef bouillon
1½ cups uncooked rice

In a saucepan, melt the butter and sauté the mushrooms, celery and scallions. Stir in the salt and bouillon. Combine with the uncooked rice in a 2-quart, tightly covered casserole and bake at 350° for 30–40 minutes.

Mrs. Charles W. Barker

GREEN RICE

Serves 6–8

3 tablespoons finely
  chopped onion
½ teaspoon minced garlic
3 tablespoons butter
2 cups cooked rice

¾–1 cup finely chopped
  parsley
1¼ cups milk
2 eggs, slightly beaten
1–2 cups grated cheddar cheese

Sauté onion and garlic in butter. Add rice, parsley and milk. Blend in beaten eggs and ½ the grated cheese. Pour in a buttered casserole and sprinkle the rest of the cheese on top. Set the casserole in a pan of hot water and bake at 350° for about 40 minutes or until firm.

Mrs. James R. Patton, Jr.

RICE WITH RAISINS AND PINE NUTS

Serves 8

4 tablespoons butter
6 tablespoons finely chopped onion
1 teaspoon minced garlic
2 cups rice

½ cup raisins
3 cups chicken broth
½ cup pine nuts

Melt 2 tablespoons butter in a saucepan. Add the onions and garlic, stirring until softened. Add rice and stir. Add raisins. Pour in chicken broth and bring to boil. Cover and simmer for exactly 17 minutes. Add pine nuts and remaining 2 tablespoons butter. Stir to fluff the rice while blending in the nuts. (Note: Serve with "Chicken with Cheese and Mushrooms".)

Lucy Johnson

WILD RICE AND MUSHROOM CASSEROLE   Serves 4–5

*"Plan ahead for this delicious casserole
for the rice must soak overnight"*

⅔ cup uncooked wild rice
¼ cup onion, chopped
1 cup sliced mushrooms
2 tablespoons butter
1 tablespoon flour

1 cup beef bouillon
½ teaspoon salt
⅛ teaspoon pepper
2 tablespoons blanched,
    slivered almonds

Prepare the wild rice as follows: Wash ⅔ cup uncooked wild rice and soak overnight in cold water. Wash rice again in several changes of water and stir into 3 cups boiling water. Cover, boil 5 minutes, drain and wash again. Add rice and ½ teaspoon salt to 3 cups boiling water, cover and cook 15–20 minutes until tender. Yield 2½ cups. • Sauté onions and mushrooms in butter until the onion is transparent, about 5 minutes. Blend in the flour, gradually add the bouillon, and cook, stirring, until smooth and thickened. Season the mixture with salt and pepper and combine with the cooked wild rice. • Turn into a buttered casserole, sprinkle with almonds and bake 30 minutes at 350°.

*Mrs. Peter Towe
Wife of the Ambassador of Canada*

BROWN RICE PILAF   Serves 6–8

3 cups chicken broth
1½ cups raw brown rice
1 teaspoon turmeric
¼ cup currants
¼ cup Madeira wine

½ cup minced scallions
⅓ cup pine nuts
1 tablespoon minced
    preserved ginger

In a large saucepan combine chicken broth, rice and turmeric. Cover and bring to a boil. Stir it once and reduce the heat. Over very low heat, cook the rice, covered, for 45 minutes. Remove from heat and allow rice to stand, covered, for 10 minutes. • Soak the currants in Madeira for 30 minutes. Drain and combine them with the scallions, pine nuts and ginger. Stir the mixture into the rice and serve.

*Embassy of the Federal Republic of Germany
For cooking classes to benefit The
Washington Opera*

TABOULEE

Serves 12–16

"This is an Algerian recipe"

1 cup couscous (bulgar wheat)
2 cups chicken broth
1 cup olive oil plus
  2 tablespoons
3 large bunches parsley, finely
  chopped

Salt and pepper
4 cups finely diced and
  drained tomatoes
3 cups chopped scallions
1½ cups freshly squeezed
  lemon juice

Slowly pour the couscous into the boiling chicken broth. Add 2 table-spoons olive oil and ½ teaspoon salt. Continue to boil until liquid is absorbed, 2–5 minutes, stirring constantly. Remove from heat. Let stand 10–15 minutes. Fluff with a fork. Cool. • Mix together parsley, tomatoes, scallions, lemon juice and 1 cup olive oil. Stir in couscous. Season with salt and pepper to taste and chill before serving. (Note: This is a wonderful accompaniment for lamb.)

Monir MacNeally

NEW ORLEANS RED BEANS AND RICE

Serves 8

1 pound dried red kidney
  beans
1 onion, coarsely chopped
3 cloves garlic, minced
½ green pepper, chopped
1 tablespoon oil
¼ pound salt pork, cut into
  strips
½ teaspoon red pepper

¼ teaspoon thyme
1 bay leaf, crumbled
1 teaspoon sugar
1 tablespoon red wine vinegar
4 cups cooked rice
2 pounds smoked sausage,
  cooked
Tabasco sauce

Pick over the beans and wash them. Cover them with water in a bowl and set aside to soak. • In a Dutch oven, or 6-quart pot, sauté the onion, garlic and green pepper in the oil until soft. Add the beans with the water, the salt pork, red pepper, thyme, bay leaf, sugar and vinegar. Stir and bring to a boil. Cover and simmer slowly for 2–3 hours until beans are tender and mixture is thick and creamy. Add water as needed to keep mixture covered. Taste for salt. • Serve beans over the cooked rice with the cooked sausage on the side. Pass the Tabasco.

Mrs. David C. Stephenson

VEGETABLES

St. John's Church, Lafayette Square

HOT ASPARAGUS VINAIGRETTE

Serves 8

Fresh asparagus, allow 4–5
  stalks per person
1 teaspoon salt
¼ teaspoon paprika
1 tablespoon tarragon vinegar
2 tablespoons cider vinegar

6 tablespoons olive oil
1 tablespoon chopped pickles
1 tablespoon chopped green
  pepper
1 teaspoon chopped parsley
1 teaspoon chopped chives

Place asparagus on board and cut into uniform lengths. Lightly pare
the tough end of the stalks with a vegetable peeler. Tie the asparagus
in bundles and stand them upright in boiling water. Cover and simmer
for 15 minutes, or until the lower stem is tender. • Combine the
remaining ingredients to make the vinaigrette sauce. Whisk it well and
serve on the side with the hot asparagus. (Note: May also be served
cold.)

Mrs. Albert E. Ernst

BROCCOLI WITH SOUR CREAM SAUCE

Serves 8–10

3 bunches (about 3 pounds)
  broccoli
2 tablespoons butter
2 tablespoons chopped onion
1½ cups sour cream

2 teaspoons sugar
1 teaspoon white vinegar
1 teaspoon salt
Dash pepper
¼ cup chopped nuts (optional)

Wash, trim and cook broccoli until tender. Transfer to serving dish.
• In a saucepan melt butter, add chopped onion and cook until soft.
Add sour cream, sugar, vinegar, salt and pepper. Cook over low heat
until heated through. • Pour sauce over broccoli, sprinkle with
chopped nuts and serve.

Chris Hunter

BROCCOLI EXTRAVAGANZA

Serves 6–8

2 10-ounce packages frozen
  broccoli or 1½ pounds fresh
2 eggs, lightly beaten
1 pound can stewed tomatoes

1 can cheddar cheese soup
Grated Parmesan cheese
Oregano

Cook the broccoli until just tender in boiling salted water and drain
well. Place in a buttered casserole and top with beaten eggs. Add the
stewed tomatoes and cover all with the undiluted cheese soup. Sprinkle with grated Parmesan cheese and oregano. Bake the broccoli
uncovered at 350° for 30 minutes.

Mary Doremus

Japanese Bonzai at the National Arboretum

STUFFED ARTICHOKES

Serves 6

"Terrific for a brunch"

6 medium sized artichokes
Boiling salted water
2 tablespoons lemon juice
3 tablespoons olive oil
¼ cup chopped onion
1 clove garlic, mashed
1-pound can tomatoes
½ cup halved, pitted,
  ripe olives

½ teaspoon salt
½ teaspoon thyme
½ teaspoon oregano
Dash pepper
Parsley Scrambled Eggs
  (recipe below)
Grated Parmesan cheese

Slice off the top fourth of each artichoke. Cut thorns from tips of lower leaves. Peel stem and remove leaves from around base. Scoop out chokes and a few center leaves with a spoon to make a cup. Place artichokes in boiling salted water to cover. Add lemon juice and 1 tablespoon of the oil. Cover and cook until stems are tender (about 30 minutes). Drain. Cut off stems so that the artichokes will stand flat; chop and reserve stems for sauce. Stand artichokes in a baking dish.
• Sauté onion and garlic in the remaining oil until soft; stir in tomatoes, chopped artichoke stems, olives and seasonings. Bring to a boil then simmer, uncovered, for about 20 minutes. Spoon sauce around artichokes in baking dish. Cover and bake in a 350° oven for 10 minutes, or until artichokes are heated. Fill artichokes with Parsley Scrambled Eggs. Serve with cheese.

Parsley Scrambled Eggs:

6 eggs, beaten
3 tablespoons cream
½ teaspoon salt

Dash of pepper
3 tablespoons chopped parsley
2 tablespoons butter

Beat eggs with cream, salt, pepper and parsley. Scramble in frying pan with 2 tablespoons of melted buter.

Mrs. George F. Will

CABBAGE AU GRATIN AMANDINE

Serves 8

3½–4 pounds cabbage
1 cup blanched toasted almonds, chopped
1 can Campbell's cheddar-cheese soup, undiluted

4 ounces sharp cheddar cheese
¾ cup buttered bread crumbs

Wash, clean, and quarter the cabbage. Steam or cook it in boiling salted water for 15 minutes. Cabbage should be just tender. Drain and chop the cabbage, turn it into a casserole dish and mix in the almonds.
• Heat the soup and sharp cheddar cheese, stirring until the cheese has melted. Pour the sauce over the cabbage and sprinkle the bread crumbs on top. Bake at 400° until the crumbs have browned.

Mrs. A. C. Liggett

CARROTS WITH FENNEL

Serves 4

1 fresh fennel bulb
4 tablespoons chopped onion
2 tablespoons butter
1 tablespoon oil

1 pound carrots
⅓–½ cup heavy cream
Salt and pepper
Parsley for garnish

Chop 4 tablespoons fennel close to the heart of the bulb. If you have some leaves on your fennel, chop and reserve 1–2 teaspoons for garnish. • Sauté the chopped onion slowly in butter and oil for about 5 minutes. Add chopped fennel and continue to sauté until onion has softened, another 5 minutes. • Scrape carrots and divide in half crosswise. If carrots are large, divide in half again lengthwise. Blanch the carrots in a large quantity of salted water for 10–15 minutes or until a knife will easily pierce the ends. Drain and refresh with cold water. Cut into smaller pieces and purée in a food processor with the cream. Start with ⅓ cup cream and add more to attain desired consistency. Continuing to purée, add the fennel, onion and butter mixture a spoonful at a time. • To serve, reheat in a double boiler or in the oven with additional butter, if desired. Garnish with the chopped fennel leaves or parsley.

Allen L. Thomas

SWEET AND SOUR CABBAGE

Serves 6–8

"Simple and good"

1 head red cabbage, about
  2½ pounds
2 tablespoons butter or
  margarine
2 medium tart apples,
  cored, peeled and chopped

1 cup water
3 tablespoons cider vinegar
3 tablespoons sugar
Salt and pepper to taste

Clean and shred cabbage—cutting out and discarding core. Melt butter in large saucepan. Add cabbage and remaining ingredients. Mix well and cook slowly, covered, about 50 minutes, or until cabbage is tender. Check for seasoning and add a little more vinegar, if desired.

Renee Zlotnick Kraft

HUNT BREAKFAST CARROTS

Serves 3–4

2 dozen raw Belgian carrots or
  2 packages frozen Belgian
  carrots
1 bottle Good Seasons
  Italian dressing

1 cup sour cream
1–2 tablespoons mayonnaise
Parsley for garnish
Crisp lettuce leaves

Peel, split and parboil the raw carrots. If using frozen carrots, prepare according to package directions. • Submerge coooked carrots in the Italian dressing and refrigerate overnight. • The next day, drain carrots and combine with sour cream and mayonnaise. Sprinkle with parsley and serve on crisp lettuce leaves.

Justine Hughes

WHISKEY CARROTS

Serves 4

6 carrots
1 tablespoon honey
1 tablespoon minced parsley

2 tablespoons butter
2 tablespoons whiskey
Salt and pepper

Scrape carrots and sliver them lengthwise. • Cook the slivered carrots in boiling water for 5 minutes. Drain thoroughly. • Return carrots to pan with remaining ingredients and cook for 5 additional minutes.

Mrs. David J. Tinkham

CARROT STUFFED PEPPERS

Serves 12

"Cool and colorful summer side dish"

5 tablespoons salad oil
1 large onion, coarsely
    chopped
28-ounce can stewed tomatoes,
    discard seeds
2 tablespoons ketchup

Salt and pepper
1 tablespoon sugar
12 Cubannello peppers (small,
    light green ones)
8 large carrots, coarsely grated

Heat 3 tablespoons of the oil in a large skillet and sauté the onion. Add the tomatoes, ketchup, salt, pepper and sugar and simmer 20 minutes. Set aside. • Slice the tops off the peppers and remove the seeds and membrane. Place the peppers in a large saucepan of boiling salted water for 2 minutes. Drain them and set aside. • Heat 2 tablespoons of oil in a large skillet, add the grated carrots and sauté them 3-4 minutes. • To assemble, stuff the peppers with the carrots and arrange them in a 2-quart casserole. Sprinkle any remaining carrots over the top and cover all with the tomato sauce. Bake, covered, at 350° for 45 minutes. Chill in the refrigerator and serve cold.

Mrs. G. William Miller

CELERY VICTOR

Serves 8

1 bunch celery
1 cup light chicken stock
6 tablespoons olive oil
2 tablespoons lemon juice
Salt and pepper to taste
Yolk of 1 hard-boiled egg,
    sieved
½ teaspoon minced parsley

½ teaspoon minced chives
1 teaspoon capers
1 tin flat anchovy filets
8 lettuce leaves
16 strips pimento
16 Mediterranean olives
4 eggs, hard-boiled and
    quartered

Trim the celery and cut each stalk into 3–4 inch pieces. • Poach the celery, covered, in the stock about 20 minutes or until tender. Remove it to a glass dish. • Combine the olive oil, lemon juice, salt and pepper, sieved egg yolk, parsley, chives, capers and 1 teaspoon oil from the anchovy tin. Pour this dressing over the celery, cover and refrigerate several hours. • To serve, place a lettuce leaf on each of 8 individual plates. Top with some of the celery and garnish with 2 anchovy filets and 2 strips pimento in a crisscross design. Arrange olives and hard-boiled egg quarters on the side.

Mrs. Tom Page

CARROT AND SPINACH TIMBALES WITH NUTMEG SAUCE

Serves 12

½ pound butter
½ cup flour
3 cups milk
2 packages frozen chopped spinach, cooked and drained

3 cups cooked, grated carrots
3 eggs, beaten
¾ teaspoon minced onion
Salt to taste

Melt the butter, stir in the flour and cook until golden brown. Remove from heat and stir in the milk. Return to stove and cook until thickened. Add the cooked carrots and spinach. Gradually add this hot mixture to the beaten eggs. Add the onion and salt to taste. Pour into greased timbale cups. Set the cups in 1 inch hot water in a large pan and bake at 350° for 40 minutes or until set. Serve with nutmeg sauce.

Nutmeg Sauce:

4 tablespoons butter
¼ cup flour
3 cups milk

3 egg yolks, beaten
Nutmeg
Salt and pepper to taste

Melt the butter, stir in the flour and cook until golden brown. Remove from heat and stir in the milk and egg yolks. Continue cooking over low heat until thickened. Season with nutmeg, salt and pepper (light on the nutmeg).

Chef Forest Bell
Congressional Country Club

Skating on the Reflecting Pool near the
Lincoln Memorial

CORN PUDDING

Serves 6

3 tablespoons butter
3 tablespoons flour
1½ teaspoons salt
2 tablespoons sugar
⅛ teaspoon pepper
Dash nutmeg
1½ cups light cream

2¼ cups cooked corn, cut from
the cob (8–9 medium ears) or
frozen white shoepeg corn, thawed
3 beaten eggs
¾ cup buttered soft bread crumbs
Paprika

Heat the butter in a saucepan, add the flour and blend with a wire whisk. Season with salt, sugar, pepper and nutmeg. • Bring cream to a boil and add all at once to flour mixture, stirring vigorously with the whisk until the sauce is thickened and smooth. Remove from heat and add the corn. Slowly add the beaten eggs, stirring constantly. Pour the mixture into a greased 1½ quart casserole and top with the crumbs. Sprinkle with paprika. Place casserole in a shallow pan of hot water and bake at 350° for 45–50 minutes.

Karin G. Weber

LEEKS IN RED WINE

Serves 6–8

"May be served hot or cold"

6–8 fresh leeks
3 tablespoons butter
1 cup dry red wine

½ cup beef or chicken broth
Salt and pepper
Parsley for garnish

Cut leeks into evenly sized pieces, the narrow ones about 2 inches in length, the larger ones about 1 inch in length. Melt the butter in a skillet large enough to hold the leeks in one layer. Brown the leeks evenly, shaking the pan and turning them as needed. Add wine, broth and salt and pepper to taste. Cover and simmer 5–10 minutes or until leeks are just tender. Remove leeks from the pan. Continue to simmer the liquid until it is reduced to about 1 cup. Pour over the leeks and serve hot, garnished with chopped parsley. (Note: May also be served chilled. Prepare as above, adding reduced liquid to leeks and chill. Just before serving, add 2 tablespoons capers and mix gently. Garnish with parsley and serve as a salad or summer vegetable.)

Mrs. Stuart C. Davidson

QUICK CORN PUDDING

Serves 4

2 eggs
1 cup milk
1 tablespoon Bisquick

4 teaspoons sugar
17-ounce can cream-style corn

Beat the eggs and add the milk, Bisquick and sugar, blending well. Stir in the corn, mixing thoroughly. Pour the corn pudding into a well buttered 1-quart casserole and bake at 350° for 1 hour.

Mrs. Peter M. Nelson

TILA'S CREAMED ONIONS

Serves 8

6–7 large onions
8 tablespoons butter
4 tablespoons flour
2 cups hot milk (of which
⅔ may be half and half)

Salt and pepper to taste
Garlic powder
Parmesan cheese

Slice the onions very thin. Heat 4 tablespoons of the butter and cook the onions slowly uncovered for 30 minutes. Do not brown them. • While onions are cooking, melt the remaining butter and stir in the flour. Add hot milk and cook, stirring, until the white sauce is smooth and thickened. • To assemble: Place a layer of ½ the onions in the bottom of the casserole. Pour in ½ the sauce and sprinkle with garlic powder and Parmesan cheese. Repeat. Bake at 350° for 45 minutes.

Dorothy B. Wexler

DAUPHINOIS POTATOES

Serves 4–6

4 large potatoes
1 clove garlic, minced
Salt and pepper to taste
1 cup heavy cream

1 tablespoon grated Gruyère cheese
1 tablespoon grated Parmesan cheese

Peel and slice the potatoes very thin. Place in an ovenproof dish and sprinkle with minced garlic, salt and pepper. Pour the cream over the potatoes and mix well. • Sprinkle the 2 cheeses over the top and bake at 350° for 45 minutes or until potatoes are done.

Embassy of Belgium
For cooking classes to benefit
The Washington Opera

PAM'S POTATOES

Serves 12–16

"Terrific ahead-of-time dish for company"

5 pounds new potatoes
Salt and pepper
5 tablespoons butter

1 pint cream
1 pint half and half
Paprika

Boil potatoes for 40 minutes. Cool and peel them. • Grease a three-quart baking dish. • Grate the potatoes into the baking dish in layers, adding salt, pepper and one tablespoon of butter to each layer. Pour cream and half and half over potatoes. Shake a very generous amount of paprika on top, cover and bake at 450° for 30 minutes. Remove cover and bake 15 minutes more. Should be crisp on top. (Note: If preparing ahead, refrigerate. Do not add cream, half and half or paprika until ready to bake.)

Mrs. Raymond Howar

HUNGARIAN POTATOES AU GRATIN

Serves 6–8

6 eggs, hard-boiled
6 pounds potatoes
1 pound onions
½ pound bacon

1 pound Hungarian, Italian
  or Polish sausage
Butter
¾–1 cup sour cream
Paprika

Slice hard-boiled eggs evenly. • Boil potatoes and onions in just enough salted water to barely cover. Do not overcook. Reserving cooking liquid, drain. Cool, peel and slice both vegetables as thinly as possible. • Cook the bacon just until fat is released and chop. • Use bacon fat to grease a gratin dish and layer ingredients as follows: sliced potatoes, onions, eggs, potatoes, bacon, potatoes, sliced uncooked sausage. Repeat the layers as far as possible, ending with a layer of potatoes. Dot some of the layers with butter and/or sour cream if desired. Pour some of the reserved cooking liquid over the layers, but keep below top layer. Spread thinly with sour cream, dot with butter and sprinkle with paprika. • Bake 30 minutes at 300°. Brown under the broiler during last few minutes.

Nicolas M. Salgo

National Archives

SOUR CREAM POTATOES SUPREME   Serves 6

"Make it ahead for maximum flavor"

6 medium potatoes, boiled   1 bunch scallions
  with skins on   Salt and pepper
1 pint sour cream   Paprika
1½ cups grated sharp cheddar cheese

Skin and chill the boiled potatoes. When cold, grate the potatoes with a medium cheese grater. • Mince the scallions and combine with potatoes and 1 cup of grated cheese. Sprinkle with salt, pepper and paprika. Turn into a buttered casserole, top with remaining ½ cup cheese. Chill for several hours. • Bake at 350° for 30 minutes or until brown and bubbly.

Frances Humphrey Howard

IRISH POTATO CAKES

Serves 4–5

2 tablespoons butter or
   bacon grease
1½ cups self-rising flour
Pinch of salt

1½ cups freshly boiled and
   mashed potatoes
¼ cup milk

In a mixing bowl, rub the butter or bacon grease into the flour with your fingertips. Add a large pinch of salt. Mix in the mashed potatoes, add the milk and blend well. Roll out the potato mixture on a floured board, cut into squares or circles. Transfer cakes to cookie sheet and bake in 400° oven for 30–40 minutes or until golden brown.

Mrs. Sean Donlon
Wife of the Ambassador of Ireland

MOYIN MOYIN

Serves 10–15

2 cups black-eyed peas
1½ teaspoons salt
½ teaspoon cayenne
1 large tomato, chopped

1 large onion, chopped
1 cup cooking oil
3 hard-boiled eggs
½ pound sliced corned beef

Soak the black-eyed peas in lukewarm water for about 2 hours. This helps remove the skin. Wash thoroughly to make sure all skin is peeled off. Drain. Grind in a blender or food processor with a little water. When smooth, pour into a bowl. Add the salt, cayenne, chopped tomato and onion and cooking oil and stir well. Pour ½ the batter into a greased 8 x 11 inch baking pan. • Cut each hard boiled egg into 4 slices. Arrange the 12 egg slices and the corned beef in a layer on the batter. Pour remaining batter evenly over the top. Cover with foil and bake at 350° for 1 hour, or until an inserted toothpick comes out clean. Cool and serve.

Mrs. Abudu Y. Eke
Wife of the Ambassador of Nigeria

SCALLOPED MUSHROOMS   Serves 8

1½ pounds mushrooms
3 cups French bread crumbs
¾ cup butter, melted

Salt and pepper to taste
½ cup dry white wine

Wash, drain, and slice the mushrooms. • Whirl French bread in a blender or food processor to make 3 cups crumbs. • In a buttered 2 quart baking dish place ⅓ of the mushrooms, cover with ⅓ of the crumbs and drizzle ⅓ of the melted butter over the crumbs. Sprinkle with salt and pepper. Repeat these layers. • Spread remaining mushrooms over the top, sprinkle with salt and pepper, and pour the wine over all. • Cover and bake in a 325° oven for 35 minutes. • Combine remaining butter and crumbs, spoon over the mushrooms and bake, uncovered, 10 minutes more.

Pat Boeke

HOT SPINACH   Serves 6

"Spicy, hot and unusual"

2 packages frozen chopped
  spinach
4 tablespoons butter
2 tablespoons flour
½ cup evaporated milk
½ teaspoon black pepper
¾ teaspoon celery salt
¾ teaspoon garlic powder

1 teaspoon Worcestershire
  sauce
Dash red pepper
6-ounce roll jalapeño cheese
1 cup bite-sized bread crumbs
  sautéed in 2 tablespoons
  butter

Cook the spinach in unsalted water and drain well, reserving ½ cup of the liquid. • Melt the butter, add the flour and whisk in the milk and reserved spinach liquid. Cook, stirring, until thickened and add the seasonings. • Cut up the cheese and add to the sauce to melt. Add the spinach. Turn the mixture into a casserole dish and top with the buttered crumbs. Bake at 350° until bubbly, about 30 minutes.

Mrs. Charles S. Robb
Wife of the Governor of Virginia

GREEK SPANAKOPITA (SPINACH PIE)　　　　Serves 16

*"A versatile recipe that may be used as
an appetizer, side dish or main course"*

3 pounds fresh spinach	Generous dash oregano
1 pound butter	Salt and pepper
1 large onion, minced	6 eggs, separated
1 clove garlic, minced	1 pound feta cheese
1 tablespoon dill	1 pound phyllo dough
½ cup chopped parsley	

Wash, stem and dry spinach. Chop into small pieces and set aside.
• Melt ¼ pound of the butter in a large skillet, add onion and garlic
and cook slowly until soft. Add spinach, herbs and seasoning. Cover
and cook for 1 minute. Remove from heat. • Beat egg yolks until
foamy; blend in crumbled feta cheese, add spinach mixture and stir
well. • Beat egg whites until stiff and fold into spinach mixture. Set
aside. • Melt remaining ¾ pound of butter. • To assemble, use a
pastry brush to coat a 9 x 13 inch baking dish with some of the melted
butter. Lay a sheet of phyllo dough in the pan and brush with more
butter. Continue to layer and butter phyllo sheets until ½ pound has
been used. If sheets tear, patch, butter and go on. Spread on spinach
filling and continue layering and buttering remaining phyllo sheets.
• With a sharp knife, cut through top half of the phyllo dividing the
pie into serving squares. Bake at 350° for 45–60 minutes. Cool slightly
and cut through the filling and bottom layer of phyllo. (Note: If used as
an appetizer, use a larger dish such as a 22 x 16 inch pan.)

Peggy Greer

SPINACH SURPRISE　　　　Serves 8

2 10-ounce packages frozen chopped spinach	Salt to taste
	Nutmeg
¼ pound butter	2 6-ounce cans tomato paste
½ pound fresh mushrooms or ¾ cup canned	1 cup sour cream
	Paprika
2 tablespoons grated onion	

Prepare spinach according to package directions. Set aside to drain.
• Melt the butter and sauté the mushrooms and onions. Season the
spinach with salt and nutmeg. In a casserole dish, mix the spinach with
the mushrooms and onions. Spread the tomato paste on top and cover
with sour cream. Sprinkle with paprika. Bake, uncovered, at 350°
about 20 minutes or until heated thoroughly.

Mrs. Norbert L. Anschuetz

SPINACH DELIGHT   Serves 6–8

2   10½-ounce packages frozen
    chopped spinach
15 tomato slices, ¾" thick
15 zucchini slices, ½" thick
1 tablespoon minced onion
¼ cup melted butter
2 eggs, beaten

¼ teaspoon garlic powder
¼ teaspoon salt
Pepper to taste
½ teaspoon thyme
¼ cup breadcrumbs
⅓ cup Parmesan cheese

Cook spinach slightly to thaw. Drain well. • Line a shallow, greased baking dish with the tomato slices. Cover with zucchini slices. • Combine spinach, minced onion, melted butter, beaten eggs and seasoning. Spread evenly over tomatoes and zucchini. • Toss breadcrumbs with Parmesan cheese and sprinkle over the top of the spinach mixture. • Bake for 30 minutes at 350°.

Bettejane Middleton

SPINACH–MUSHROOM–TOMATO–CHEESE   Serves 6
CASSEROLE

2 tablespoons butter
2 medium-large onions,
    chopped
28 ounces canned Italian
    tomatoes cut into pieces
12 ounces canned mushrooms,
    drained or 1 pound sliced
    fresh mushrooms
12 ounces shredded
    mozzarella cheese
2   10-ounce packages frozen
    spinach, steamed
    and drained

¾ teaspoon salt
½ teaspoon nutmeg
¼ teaspoon pepper
3 large eggs
1 cup evaporated skim milk,
    evaporated milk or
    heavy cream
⅓–½ cup grated Parmesan
    cheese

Sauté the onions in the butter in a large covered pan. Add the tomatoes and mushrooms and cook 4–5 minutes longer. Drain thoroughly. • Mix the mozzarella, drained spinach and seasonings in a large greased casserole. Add the drained tomato mixture and stir to blend. Cover and set aside. • In a separate bowl, beat the eggs with the milk or cream. • Remove any excess liquid from the cheese-vegetable mixture and add the eggs and milk, stirring with a fork. Sprinkle on the Parmesan cheese and use the fork to push the cheese just under the top of the mixture. Bake the casserole, uncovered, at 350° for 1 hour.

Mrs. Alan Fisher

SUPER SQUASH

Serves 4–6

1 large onion
1 green pepper
2 zucchini
2 yellow squash
2 small ripe tomatoes
2–3 tablespoons peanut oil
1–2 cloves garlic, minced
2 tablespoons tomato paste
2 tablespoons ketchup

Oregano
Basil
Thyme
Sugar
Salt and pepper
½ cup grated cheddar cheese
½ cup grated mozzarella
½ cup grated Parmesan cheese

Cut the onions vertically. Cut other vegetables into 1½-inch pieces. Heat the oil in a large skillet and add the garlic, onion and green pepper. Sauté until golden. Add the squash and cook 2–3 minutes. Add the tomatoes, tomato paste, ketchup and seasoning to taste. Stir in about ¾ of each of the cheeses and turn the mixture into a casserole, sprinkling remaining cheese over the top. Bake at 400° for 10 minutes or until bubbly hot and cheeses are melted.

Mrs. George F. Brasfield, Jr.

Space capsule at the Air and Space Museum

SQUASH CASSEROLE

Serves 6

"Can be easily doubled, even tripled, for a party"

2 pounds summer squash or
  zucchini
8-ounce package herb stuffing mix
1 can cream of chicken soup
1 cup sour cream

8-ounce can water
  chestnuts, drained
1 medium onion, diced
1 cup butter

Steam squash only until just tender and cut into ½ inch slices.
• Lightly grease a casserole dish and spread ½ the stuffing mix on the
bottom. Layer ½ the squash over this. • Combine the soup, sour
cream, water chestnuts and diced onion. Pour ½ this mixture over the
layer of squash and top with remaining squash. Cover with remaining
soup mixture and sprinkle the rest of the stuffing mix over all. Dot
with the butter and bake the casserole at 350° for 30 minutes.

Ann Lewis

BERNICE'S SUMMER SQUASH

Serves 6

6 medium yellow squash,
  cubed
4 tablespoons butter
1 egg beaten
1 tablespoon chopped onion
4 Saltine crackers, crumbled

½ cup grated sharp cheddar
  cheese
Salt to taste
Pepper to taste
⅛ teaspoon paprika
Bread crumbs

Steam or cook squash in a small amount of salted water until tender.
Drain well and mash. • Add the butter, the beaten egg, onion,
crackers, cheese, salt, pepper and paprika and blend well. • Turn
the squash mixture into a casserole dish, sprinkle with bread crumbs,
and bake at 350° for about 20 minutes or until firm and golden in
color.

Mrs. John C. Camp

TOMATO PUDDING

Serves 4

10-ounce can tomato purée
¼ cup hot water
1 cup brown sugar
¼ teaspoon salt

1 cup fresh white bread,
cut in 1-inch squares
½ cup melted butter

Pour tomato purée into a saucepan. Add ¼ cup hot water to can, shaking to dislodge any remaining purée. Add to saucepan with sugar and salt. Boil 5 minutes. • Place bread squares in a casserole and pour the melted butter over them. Add the hot tomato mixture. Bake at 350° for 30 minutes. Serve with meats. (Note: Recipe may be prepared ahead and frozen.)

Mrs. John T. Gibson

RATATOUILLE

Serves 10–12

½ cup olive or peanut oil
2 large onions
2 medium or 1 large eggplant
4–5 medium-sized zucchini
2–4 green peppers
4–6 ripe tomatoes
1 pound fresh mushrooms

½–¾ cup chopped fresh
parsley
1 teaspoon oregano
1½ teaspoon basil
2 teaspoons salt
¼ teaspoon garlic powder

In a large covered pot, place ¼ cup oil and the onions, cut into medium-sized chunks. Cook over medium heat while preparing the rest of the vegetables. • Wash and cut up the eggplant, zucchini and green peppers. Wash the mushrooms and halve or quarter the larger ones. Add these vegetables to the pot along with enough of the remaining oil to keep them from sticking. Stir in the seasonings and simmer over low heat for 25–30 minutes. • Cut tomatoes into bite-sized pieces and add to the pot. Stir and simmer an additional 15 minutes. Cool and refrigerate for up to a week. To serve, reheat desired amount and serve with the juice.

Dr. Alan A. Fisher

TOMATO PIE   Serves 8

1 unbaked pie shell
8–10 tomatoes, peeled and seeded
Salt and pepper to taste
2 tablespoons sweet basil

3 tablespoons chives
1½ cups mayonnaise
1½ cups grated sharp
  cheddar cheese

Partially bake pie shell at 400° for 8–10 minutes to avoid sogginess.
• Cut the tomatoes into thick slices and arrange them in the pie
crust. Sprinkle with salt, pepper, basil and chives. • Combine the
mayonnaise and grated cheese and spread the mixture over the tomatoes. Bake at 400° for 35 minutes or until browned.

Mrs. Peter McCoy

VEGETABLE MOUSSE   Serves 10–12

"This is almost too pretty to eat."

1 pound carrots, cut into
  chunks
1 package frozen artichoke
  hearts
2 tablespoons butter
1 package frozen chopped
  spinach, thawed
  and squeezed dry
1 medium onion, minced

3 tablespoons fresh or
  1½ tablespoons dried dill
5 large eggs
1 cup heavy cream
½ cup Parmesan cheese
½ cup milk
Salt and pepper
Nutmeg

Grease an 8½ x 4½ inch loaf pan, line it with wax paper, grease again
and set aside. • Cook or steam carrots in a small amount of water.
• Cook artichoke hearts. • Melt the butter in a saucepan and add
the spinach, onion and dill. Cook over medium heat until onion is
tender and spinach is dry. • Combine eggs, cream, milk, salt, pepper and nutmeg and blend until smooth. • In a blender or food
processor combine ⅓ of the egg mixture with each of the vegetables.
Arrange in even layers in the loaf pan with artichokes on the bottom,
then carrots, then spinach on top. Place in a pan of simmering water
that reaches half-way up the loaf pan and bake 1¼ hours at 375°. Let
stand 10 minutes. Invert onto a serving dish to unmold and remove
wax paper. Let stand 20 minutes before serving or refrigerate and
serve very cold.

Howard de Franceaux

TOMATOES CREOLE   Serves 8

"A fine addition to a meat platter"

4 medium tomatoes
1 onion, finely chopped
1 green pepper, finely chopped
Brown sugar

Butter
Salt and pepper
Thinley sliced white bread,
   toasted

Cut tomatoes in half. Cover with chopped onion, green pepper, salt, pepper and a little brown sugar. Top with a generous lump of butter. Bake at 350° for about 20 minutes. • Prepare 8 rounds of buttered toast. Place tomato half on each round.

Mrs. Albert E. Ernst

ZUCCHINI SILVER DOLLARS   Serves 6

3 small zucchini, peeled
   and grated
2 eggs
2 scallions with tops,
   chopped, or 1 large onion,
   minced
½ cup fresh mint leaves,
   chopped

½ cup fresh chopped parsley
½ cup grated Gruyère cheese
½ cup flour
Salt and pepper
Dash cayenne
Salad oil

Combine the grated zucchini, eggs, scallions, mint, parsley and cheese in a mixing bowl. Gradually add the flour, then the seasonings. • Heat the oil in a heavy saucepan for deep fat frying and drop the zucchini mixture into the oil by teaspoons if serving as an appetizer, or by tablespoons if serving as a vegetable side dish. Fry until golden brown and drain on paper towels.

Mrs. Alpheus W. Jessup

SALADS AND
SALAD DRESSINGS

Fountain by Bartholdi

BEET SALAD WITH CUCUMBER SAUCE   Serves 6

3 envelopes unflavored
  gelatine
2 16-ounce jars pickled beets
1 16-ounce jar plain beets

½ cup sour cream
½ cup mayonnaise
Salt and pepper to taste

In a medium saucepan, sprinkle gelatine over ¾ cup cold water. Stir over low heat until it is disssolved. • Purée the beets, one jar at a time. With the second batch of beets, slowly add the gelatine. • Combine all ingredients and mix thoroughly. Pour into an oiled 6 cup ring mold and refrigerate. • When set, serve with cucumber sauce.

Cucumber sauce:

3 cucumbers
1 teaspoon minced onion
2 tablespoons lemon juice

½ teaspoon salt
1 teaspoon sugar
2 tablespoons sour cream

Peel, halve and remove seeds of cucumbers. Grate on large side of grater. Add onion, lemon juice, salt and sugar. Refrigerate. • Just before serving, stir in the sour cream.

Mrs. G. William Miller

ENDIVE-AVOCADO SALAD   Serves 4–6

8 stalks Belgian endive
1 large avocado
Juice of ½ lemon
4 scallions, chopped
Salt
Freshly ground pepper

¼ cup olive oil
1 tablespoon white wine
  vinegar
¼ teaspoon dry mustard
2 tablespoons chopped parsley

Wash and chill endive to crisp. When dry, remove a few outer leaves (8–10) and set aside. Cut endive stalks into large crosswise slices, ½–¾ inches. Thinly slice the avocado and sprinkle with lemon juice. • In a salad bowl, combine endive slices, avocado and scallions. Season to taste with salt and freshly ground pepper. Combine olive oil, vinegar and dry mustard. Whisk until thoroughly blended and pour over salad. Toss lightly until vegetables are coated. Garnish with chopped parsley and arrange reserved leaves around the edge of the bowl.

Mrs. Stuart C. Davidson

AUTUMN SALAD — Serves 6

"Dense and delicious"

4 tart apples, peeled, cored
   and diced
1 cup chopped walnuts
1 cup diced avocado
1 cup diced cheddar cheese
1 endive, coarsely chopped
3 tablespoons olive oil

2 teaspoons lemon juice
1 teaspoon chopped dill
Salt and freshly ground black
   pepper
½ cup chopped celery and
   mushrooms, (optional)
Lettuce

Combine all ingredients except lettuce and toss well. Make a bed of lettuce in the bottom of the serving bowl and arrange autumn salad on it.

Mrs. Richard Beeston

GRAPE AND ALMOND RICE SALAD — Serves 4–5

8 ounces Patna or long grained
   rice
1 tablespoon oil
2 tablespoons vinegar
Salt and pepper

2 ounces blanched almonds
2 ounces black grapes
3 ounces green grapes
1 bunch watercress

Boil the rice, covered, in 2½ cups water for 20–30 minutes. Drain and run cold water through it. • When cold, stir in oil, vinegar, salt and pepper. Toast almonds and stir into rice. • Halve and pit grapes and toss with the rice. • Garnish with watercress. (Note: Serve with "Cold Chicken with Curry Cream Dressing".)

Lady Parkinson
Wife of the Ambassador of Australia

CURRIED SALAD — Serves 4–6

Your favorite greens
Slices of pickled beets
Mandarin oranges
Thin slices of sweet onions

½ cup homemade mayonnaise
½ teaspoon curry powder
1 tablespoon chutney

Arrange first 4 ingredients on a plate. Mix dressing ingredients and spoon over salad. Serve immediately.

Jean Arnold

CURRIED PEA SALAD

Serves 4

1   1-pound can early peas
2 tablespoons chopped
   scallions
2 tablespoons chopped and
   seeded cucumber
2 tablespoons yogurt or sour
   cream

2 tablespoons mayonnaise
1–2 teaspoons curry powder
Freshly ground black pepper
1 avocado, sliced

Drain the peas and mix with chopped scallions and cucumbers.
• Make a dressing of yogurt or sour cream, mayonnaise and curry
powder. Season with freshly ground pepper. • Chill at least 2 hours,
overnight if possible, and serve on a bed of lettuce with sliced avocado.

Mrs. Warwick M. Carter

CRISPY SALAD

Serves 4

1 bunch watercress,
   stems removed
1 bunch scallions, chopped
½-head red cabbage, chopped
2 stalks celery, cut in
   ¼-inch slices

Oil to taste
Vinegar to taste
1 tart apple, chopped
½ cup Stilton cheese,
   crumbled

Combine the first 4 ingredients in a salad bowl. Lightly dress them
with oil and vinegar. Add the chopped apple and cheese and toss 5
times.

Mrs. Frank N. Ikard

SAUERKRAUT SALAD

Serves 8

"Sit back and enjoy the raves"

2 cups sauerkraut, drained
1 cup chopped celery
16 ounces garbanzo beans
1 green pepper, chopped
3 scallions, chopped

3 tablespoons chopped
   pimentos
½ cup oil
¼ vinegar
½ cup sugar (optional)

Combine all the ingredients in a salad bowl. Refrigerate for 12 hours
before serving.

Betty Hosn

SPINACH AND MUSHROOM CAESAR SALAD   Serves 6

"Two classics meet"

½ cup salad oil
2 tablespoons lemon juice
1 teaspoon Worcestershire
  sauce
2 cloves garlic, minced
½ teaspoon salt
⅛ teaspoon ground pepper

¼ cup chopped onions
1 egg
½ pound fresh mushrooms,
  sliced
½ pound fresh spinach
1 cup croutons
¼ cup grated Parmesan cheese

Combine first 8 ingredients in a jar, cover, and shake until blended.
• Clean spinach and tear into bite-sized pieces. • Place spinach
and mushrooms in a salad bowl, pour dressing over them and toss. Add
croutons and cheese and toss again.

Mrs. Marvin L. Stone

SALADE DE MAISON   Serves 8–10

Juice of 1 lemon
3 cloves garlic, crushed
1 teaspoon salt
½ teaspoon pepper
¾ cup vegetable oil
¼ pound bacon, diced
2 heads romaine lettuce or
  equal amount of spinach
2 cups cherry tomatoes, halved

1 cup coarsely grated
  Swiss cheese
⅔ cup slivered almonds,
  toasted
⅓ cup freshly grated
  Parmesan cheese
Salt and pepper to taste
1 cup croutons

Make dressing by combining lemon juice, garlic, salt and pepper.
Beating continuously with a fork, slowly add vegetable oil. Let dressing stand for 3 hours. • Sauté bacon until crisp. Drain. • Tear the
romaine or spinach into small pieces and combine in a salad bowl with
the tomatoes, Swiss cheese, almonds, and bacon. • Toss with the
dressing and add Parmesan cheese, salt and pepper. Garnish with
croutons.

Mrs. Andrew E. Manatos

MIXED VEGETABLE SALAD

Serves 8

¾ cup olive oil
¼ cup wine vinegar
Salt and pepper
1 teaspoon Dijon mustard
3 cloves garlic, crushed
1 pound zucchini
1 pound yellow squash

4 scallions with tops
8 radishes
¾ pound green beans
½ pound snow peas
2 stalks broccoli
¾ pound cherry tomatoes
Lettuce

Combine the first 5 ingredients to make a vinaigrette. Let stand 1 hour to allow garlic to permeate the dressing. Remove garlic before tossing salad. • Thinly slice cleaned and trimmed zucchini, yellow squash, scallions and radishes. • Clean and cut green beans into 1-inch lengths. Blanch in boiling water for 4 minutes, drain, and refresh with cold water. • Blanch the snow peas in boiling water for 1 minute. • Cut the broccoli into flowerets and blanch them in boiling water for 1 minute. • Marinate the green beans and tomatoes for 1 hour in the vinaigrette dressing. Then toss them and the other vegetables with the dressing. Line a salad bowl with lettuce and mound the vegetable salad on it.

Mrs. John E. Chapoton

CRANBERRY CREAM AMERICANA

Serves 8–12

"Either a molded salad or dessert"

1 cup fresh or frozen
   cranberries, chopped fine
⅓ cup sugar
⅓ cup orange juice
8 ounces cream cheese,
   softened
1 teaspoon vanilla

1 orange, chopped
1 apple, chopped
½ cup chopped dates
1 cup whipping cream
A few whole berries or
   grapes for garnish

Combine cranberries and sugar and let stand for 10 minutes or more to blend. • Beat together orange juice, cream cheese and vanilla until fluffy. Stir in chopped orange, cranberries, apple and dates. • Whip the cream to soft peaks and fold into the cheese mixture. Put into a 5 cup mold and cover with plastic wrap. Seal and freeze for at least 4 hours, or as long as 4 weeks. • To serve, let stand at room temperature 15 minutes to soften slightly. Unmold onto a lettuce lined plate and add garnish. (Do not allow to thaw completely as it becomes mushy.)

Dennis Cory

SWEET SPINACH SALAD
Serves 4–6

"Summery and refreshing"

1 pound spinach, washed and
stemmed
11-ounce can mandarin
oranges
1 cup coarsely chopped
walnuts

½ cup plain yogurt
Honey to taste
Raisins, optional
Coconut, optional

Toss spinach, oranges and walnuts together in a salad bowl. • Combine the yogurt with honey to taste. Stir in raisins and or coconut if desired. Toss the salad with the dressing and serve.

Tara Lechia Hardiman

SRI LANKA GREEN SALAD
Serves 3

1 bunch parsley, watercress
or spinach
½ cup freshly grated coconut
or packaged coconut and
½ cup milk

1 small onion, minced
Salt to taste
Lime juice to taste

Wash, dry and chop the greens finely. If using packaged coconut, soak it, covered, in the milk for 10 minutes, rinse in cold water, then squeeze out extra moisture. Toss the greens with the coconut and onions. Season with salt and lime juice to taste.

Mrs. Ernest Corea
Wife of the Ambassador of Sri Lanka

ZUCCHINI VINAIGRETTE
Serves 8–10

8 medium zucchini, trimmed
and scrubbed
½ cup olive oil
½ cup lemon juice
2 teaspoons salt
½ teaspoon pepper

½ teaspoon thyme
2 teaspoons coriander
2 bay leaves
2 cloves garlic, crushed
4 tablespoons chopped parsley

Slice the zucchini ¼-inch thick. • Combine the remaining ingredients in a large saucepan, add the zucchini and bring to a boil. Reduce the heat and simmer about 8–10 minutes until zucchini is tender. Chill the zucchini in the liquid. When ready to serve, drain and place zucchini in a serving bowl.

Mrs. Robert C. Eisele

WHOLE AVOCADO STUFFED WITH CRAB MEAT

Serves 6–8

"The ideal summer luncheon"

2 pounds fresh lump crab
  meat
8–9 medium tomatoes
2 tablespoons chopped chives
1 teaspoon chopped parsley
1½ cups mayonnaise
4 tablespoons chili sauce

2 teaspoons Worcestershire
  sauce
Juice of ½ lemon
2 teaspoons tarragon vinegar
6–8 whole ripe avocados
1 head romaine lettuce

Clean crab meat of shells, being careful to keep as many large lumps as possible. • Peel, seed, chop and drain 5 of the tomatoes. Combine them with the chives, parsley, mayonnaise, chili sauce, Worcestershire sauce, lemon juice and vinegar. Gently fold this mixture into the crab meat, again being careful not to break up the lumps. • For each serving, halve an avocado and remove the pit. Cut bottom of ½ avocado so that it will lie flat and place it in the center of a large leaf of romaine. Stuff it with 5–6 ounces of the crab meat salad. • Peel and slice the remaining ½ avocado. Slice ½ a tomato. Arrange avocado and tomato slices alternately around the stuffed avocado. Repeat for each serving.

Le Jardin Restaurant

GRAPEFRUIT-AVOCADO SALAD WITH ROQUEFORT DRESSING

Serves 8

2 grapefruit
2 avocados
1 head crisp, leafy lettuce
  (Boston or bibb)
¼ pound Roquefort or bleu
  cheese
Juice of ½ lemon

2 tablespoons vinegar
9 tablespoons oil
¼ teaspoon dry mustard
Salt to taste
Sugar to taste
Paprika to taste

Peel and separate sections of grapefruit. Peel and slice avocados into long thin slices. Arrange alternately on a bed of crisp lettuce leaves either on a platter or individual salad plates. • Make the dressing as follows: Mash the Roquefort or bleu cheese to very fine pieces. Add remaining ingredients and whisk to blend well. Chill and serve over grapefruit and avocado slices.

Mrs. Albert E. Ernst

JUDY BELTON'S SALAD

"Nice accompaniment for fish or ham dishes"

New potatoes
Fresh green beans

Dressing:

Oil
Tarragon vinegar
Salt
Freshly ground pepper
Sugar

½ teaspoon capers
1 hard-boiled egg, finely
   chopped
4–5 sweet gherkins, finely
   sliced

Boil the potatoes and drain. • Steam green beans and cut into 2-inch lengths. • When potatoes have cooled to room temperature, slice and combine with green beans. • Add dressing. Garnish with sliced gherkins.

Mrs. Parker T. Hart

MEGABEAN SALAD   Serves 15

"Low-cal, low-fat, high-protein and divine"

Beans of all sorts: pinto,
   kidney, all cuts of green and
   yellow, large and small
   limas, garbanzo, etc.,
   enough to equal 3 quarts.
   Beans may be fresh, frozen,
   canned or a combination.

1 large can pitted black olives
14-ounce can artichoke
   hearts
Pimentos or roasted red
   peppers

Begin with all ingredients at room temperature. If you have cooked any fresh beans, cool them. Drain all ingredients, place in a large bowl and toss with vinaigrette (recipe below). Mix well and let stand a few hours before serving.

Dressing:

½ cup good olive oil
¼ cup tarragon vinegar
2 cloves garlic, crushed
1 lemon slice, peeled
1 tablespoon dried chervil

1 tablespoon dried tarragon
1 tablespoon dried parsley
Dashes of salt, pepper and
   cayenne

Whisk together all ingredients or mix in a blender.

Beverly Jackson

Chinese New Year

CHICKEN SALAD   Serves 4

"A great summertime lunch from the Hong Kong Peninsula Hotel."

2 large cantaloupes
3 cups cooked chicken, in
  chunks
4 medium tomatoes, peeled
  and chopped
2 medium green peppers,
  chopped

¼ cup ketchup
¾ cup mayonnaise
2–3 cans mandarin oranges
40 cashew nuts
Parsley to garnish

Slice the cantaloupes crosswise. Remove the meat, cut into balls, leaving a rim of about ½ inch inside the cantaloupe halves. • In a large bowl, mix the chicken chunks, chopped tomatoes, green peppers and the cantaloupe balls. • In a small bowl, mix the ketchup and mayonnaise and combine with the chicken salad. Toss to blend thoroughly. • Pile the salad to the rim. Place Mandarin orange slices, close together, around the cantaloupe rim. • Place 10 cashew nuts on each salad and parsley at the very top. To serve, place cantaloupe halves in a bowl surrounded by crushed ice.

Mrs. John H. Groth

SUMMER SALAD   Serves 4–6

½ head iceberg lettuce
½ head romaine
1 bunch watercress
6 tablespoons salad oil
6 tablespoons lemon juice
Salt
Freshly ground black pepper
3 whole chicken breasts,
  cooked

4–6 hard-boiled eggs, finely
  chopped
4 tablespoons Roquefort
  cheese, crumbled
3 medium tomatoes
½ pound bacon, cooked
1 bunch scallions, sliced
¼ bunch parsley, chopped

Wash and chop salad greens and mound in a salad bowl. • Make a dressing of the lemon juice, salad oil, salt and pepper and sprinkle over greens. • Dice cooked chicken. • Combine chopped egg with Roquefort cheese and sprinkle with lemon juice and salt. • Chop tomatoes. • Arrange decorative bands of chicken, eggs and tomatoes over the salad greens. Sprinkle crumbled bacon, scallions and parsley over all. Drizzle on remaining salad dressing.

Mabelle Brower

ORIENTAL SALAD   Serves 4

6 cucumbers
Dash salt
Dash sugar
1 teaspoon curry powder
1 tablespoon honey
1 teaspoon fresh orange juice
1 teaspoon grated orange peel
½ cup vinegar
½ cup sesame seed oil

1 teaspoon tartar sauce
2 cups cooked, shredded
  chicken or crab meat,
  shrimp or lobster
1–2 eggs, hard-boiled and
  sieved
½ cup raisins
1 orange, peeled and sliced
Pineapple slices

Peel cucumbers, trim ends and remove seeds. Rub them with salt and sugar and cut them in quarters lengthwise. Lightly crush the cucumbers with the back of a heavy spoon. • Combine the curry powder, honey, orange juice, grated peel, vinegar and sesame oil and marinate the cucumber in the mixture for 2 hours. Add the tarter sauce. • Mound chicken or shellfish on a serving dish and surround with the marinated cucumbers. Arrange orange and pineapple slices decoratively on top and sprinkle the sieved eggs and raisins over all.

Anna Chennault

SANDE-KO-CHARA   Serves 6

"A low calorie luncheon chicken salad"

½ teaspoon cumin seeds
½ teaspoon minced fresh
  ginger
4 cloves
3 cardamon
3 bay leaves
2 cloves garlic, crushed
6–8 black peppercorns
5 cups water
2 chicken bouillon cubes

4 whole chicken breasts,
  about 2½ pounds
½ teaspoon garlic powder
½ teaspoon ginger powder
1–1½ teaspoons salt
½ teaspoon red chili powder
2 tablespoons oil
½ teaspoon fenugreek
½ teaspoon turmeric

Combine the cumin, ginger, cloves, cardamon, bay leaves, garlic, peppercorns, water and bouillon cubes in a large saucepan and bring to a boil. Add the chicken, reduce heat and cook slowly, covered, until done, about 20 minutes. Remove and sliver the chicken meat. • Combine the chicken meat with the garlic powder, ginger powder, salt and chili powder. Set aside. • In a small skillet, heat the oil, add the fenugreek and sauté until dark. Remove from heat and add the turmeric. Add this while hot to the chicken mixture, blending well. Serve at room temperature.

Mrs. Bhekh B. Thapa
Wife of the Ambassador of Nepal

CURRIED CHICKEN SALAD   Serves 4

4 whole chicken breasts
1 teaspoon curry powder
½ teaspoon salt
Pepper
1 tablespoon lemon juice
1 cup diced cantaloupe
1 cup seedless grapes

½ cup walnuts
2 tablespoons slivered candied
  ginger *or* grated fresh ginger
  to taste
¼ cup sour cream or plain
  yogurt
½ cup mayonnaise

Steam the chicken breasts for 15 minutes until just cooked through. When cool, bone and skin the chicken, cut into 1-inch cubes, and toss with curry powder, salt, pepper and lemon juice. Refrigerate until cold. • Combine the cold chicken with the remaining ingredients and refrigerate until ready to serve.

Phyllis Richman

CORN AND AVOCADO SALAD   Serves 6

2 10-ounce packages frozen
   whole kernel corn, cooked
⅔ cup chopped green pepper
2 tablespoons finely chopped
   onion
½ cup mayonnaise

1 teaspoon chili powder
1 teaspoon chopped pimento
⅛ teaspoon seasoned salt
⅛ teaspoon pepper
3 avocados, seeded and
   halved.

Combine all ingredients, except avocados, and chill. When ready to
serve, fill avocado halves and serve with chili mayonnaise.

Chili Mayonnaise:
1 cup mayonnaise
1 teaspoon chili powder
½ teaspoon seasoned salt

Dash pepper
1 teaspoon lemon juice

Blend all ingredients and chill before serving.

Mrs. Ferd Nauheim

TOFU POTATO SALAD   Serves 1

*"A lovely luncheon salad from a popular
Washington restaurant."*

½ cup diced boiled potatoes
½ cup tofu, boiled once to
   firm, diced
¼ cup chopped green pepper
¼ cup chopped bread-and-butter
   pickles
½ cup chicken or shrimp

2 tablespoons chopped
   parsley
Salt and pepper
¼ cup chopped hard-boiled
   egg
½ cup mayonnaise
2 tablespoons French dressing

Combine first 9 ingredients. • Thin mayonnaise with French dressing and combine well with salad mixture.

Trader Vic's Restaurant

RUTHIE'S FRUIT SALAD

Serves 6

Dressing (about 1 cup):

Rind of 1 lemon
Rind of 1 lime
Rind of 1 orange
3–4 slices crystalized ginger

1½ cups sugar
¾ cup cold water
¼ teaspoon cream of tartar

Slice rinds of lemon, lime and orange very thin, like threads. Combine with the ginger in a saucepan, cover with cold water and bring to a boil. Simmer 5–7 minutes until limp. Strain and rinse under cold water. • Combine sugar, ¾ cup cold water and cream of tartar in a saucepan, bring to a boil and stir until sugar is dissolved. Add sliced rinds and boil 5 minutes. Cool and refrigerate until ready to use. (Note: Dressing may be stored in the refrigrator indefinately.)

Fruit (about 4 cups):

Blueberries
Watermelon balls
Canteloupe balls

Honeydew melon balls
Mandarin oranges
Mint leaves, for garnish

The above are only suggestions. Use these or fruits of your own choice, keeping the proportions of 4 cups of fruit to 1 cup of dressing. Pour dressing over the fruit and garnish with mint leaves.

Dorothy B. Wexler

RICE SALAD

Serves 8

¼ cup French dressing
¾ cup mayonnaise
1 tablespoon lemon juice
1 tablespoon minced onion
1 cup chopped celery
¾ teaspoon curry powder

½ teaspoon dry mustard
½ teaspoon salt
Pepper to taste
1½ cups cooked rice
1   16-ounce can mixed
   vegetables

Combine first 9 ingredients to make dressing. Mix well. • Warm the rice and stir into dressing. • When the rice and dressing have cooled, add the mixed vegetables. Refrigerate several hours before serving.

Mrs. Ferd Nauheim

CONRAD'S SCALLOP SALAD   Serves 6

"Elegant picnic fare"

1 pound scallops	½ cup mayonnaise
1 cup dry white wine	¼ cup lemon juice
1 scallion, chopped	Capers to taste
½ teaspoon thyme	Garlic salt to taste
¼ cup chopped parsley	Several drops Tabasco sauce

Rinse the scallops and poach them for 2 minutes in the white wine mixed with ½ the chopped scallion and the thyme. • Combine all remaining ingredients, stir in the scallops and chill until ready to serve.

David P. Fogle

PASTA SALAD   Serves 12

"Great for a summer party"

1 pound tortellini	1 pint cherry tomatoes
2–2½ pounds broccoli	½ pound red onions
½ pound green beans	1 green bell pepper
1 pound mushroom caps	1 red bell pepper
2 14-ounce cans artichoke hearts	

Prepare the tortellini according to package instructions. Set aside. • Prepare the vegetables as follows: Cut the broccoli into bite-sized pieces and blanch for 2 minutes. Trim the ends of the green beans, cut the larger ones in half and blanch for 2 minutes. Cut the mushroom caps into quarters. Cut the artichoke hearts in half. Slice the red onions very thin. Julienne the green and red peppers. • Combine the tortellini, the vegetables and dressing (recipe below). Toss well and chill for several hours. Toss every hour until served.

Dressing:

1½ cups olive oil	½ teaspoon crushed bay leaves
6 ounces red wine vinegar	½ teaspoon rosemary
1 tablespoon minced garlic	½ teaspoon thyme
1 teaspoon basil	Salt and pepper
1 teaspoon oregano	

Whisk together all ingredients until well blended. Correct seasoning.

Clyde's of Georgetown

PASTA SEAFOOD SALAD   Serves 8

1 pound backfin crab meat
¾ pound bay scallops
1 pound thin spaghetti
1 package frozen artichoke
  hearts
6 carrots
3 small yellow squash

18 spears asparagus
½ cup chopped scallions
½ cup chopped parsley
½ cup chopped fresh dill
Cherry tomatoes
Watercress
Lemon slices

Prepare ingredients separately as follows and set aside. Carefully pick over crab meat to remove bits of shell. Briefly parboil the scallops. Cook spaghetti, rinse with cold water and drain. Cook, drain and chill the artichoke hearts. Cut the carrots in 1½ inch matchsticks, parboil briefly and chill. Scoop seedy center out of squash, cut into 1½ inch matchsticks, parboil briefly and chill. Parboil the asparagus, cut into 1½ inch pieces and chill. • Combine drained spaghetti with lemon-mustard dressing (recipe below). Add crab meat, scallops, chilled vegetables, scallions and all but 2 tablespoons of parsley and dill. Let chill for several hours or overnight to blend flavors. • To serve, sprinkle with remaining parsley and dill. Garnish around edge of platter with cherry tomatoes, watercress and lemon slices.

Lemon-mustard dressing:

1 egg yolk
2 tablespoons lemon juice
1 small clove garlic, crushed
1 teaspoon salt

Pepper
2 teaspoons Dijon mustard
¾ cup olive oil
1 tablespoon heavy cream

Beat yolk with lemon juice, garlic, salt, pepper and mustard. Whisk in olive oil gradually until thick. Beat in cream. Correct seasonings.

Mrs. Kenneth Bacon

ACCOMPANIMENTS

The entrance to Union Station

GLAZED CHESTNUTS   Serves 6

"A wonderful accompaniment for turkey or other fowl"

1 pound chestnuts
Milk
4 tablespoons butter
5 tablespoons sugar

2 teaspoons cornstarch or
  arrowroot
3 tablespoons beef stock

Cut across the flat side of each chestnut with a sharp knife. Place the chestnuts in a saucepan, cover with water and boil them for 10 minutes. Drain and peel the chestnuts immediately. • Place the peeled chestnuts in a clean saucepan with enough milk to cover them. Add 1 tablespoon butter and 1 tablespoon sugar and simmer the mixture at least 15 minutes. Drain the chestnuts, discarding the milk. • In a skillet, brown 3 tablespoons butter with 4 tablespoons sugar. Combine the cornstarch or arrowroot with the beef stock and add to the butter-sugar mixture. Cook 1–2 minutes, add the chestnuts, and cook over low heat, shaking the pan, until the chestnuts are glossy and well coated with the glaze.

Mrs. Alpheus W. Jessup

ZUCCHINI RELISH   Makes 8 pints

10 cups ground firm,
  unpeeled, zucchini
4 cups ground onions
4 red or green peppers,
  ground
5 tablespoons salt
5 cups sugar

2½ cups white vinegar
1 tablespoon cornstarch
1 tablespoon turmeric
1 tablespoon dry mustard
2 tablespoons celery seed
1 teaspoon black pepper

The vegetables are to be ground together in a meat grinder. Do not use a food processor as relish will be too mushy. Sprinkle the ground vegetables with the salt and let stand at least 12 hours. Rinse them in a colander, then squeeze out liquid with your hands. Mixture should still be very moist. • Place the vegetables in a large saucepan with the remaining ingredients, bring to a boil, reduce heat and simmer slowly for 30 minutes. Pour into hot sterile jars and seal tightly. (Note: Any screw lid jar will do if relish is not to be stored too long.)

Mrs. Peter Ellenshaw

SUPER STUFFING   Serves 12–16

"Excellent as a stuffing or served as a side dish"

16-ounce package herb
  stuffing mix (Pepperidge
  Farm)
2 cups chicken broth
1 pound hot sausage meat,
  cooked and drained
2 celery stalks, chopped

1 green pepper, chopped
1 medium onion, chopped
16-ounce can white
  corn, drained
3 eggs
2-3 cloves garlic, chopped
Salt and pepper to taste

Prepare stuffing mix according to package directions, substituting chicken broth for water. • Add all other ingredients and blend thoroughly. Put in a well buttered casserole and bake at 350° for 30 minutes. (Note: This dish freezes well.)

Shirley Neal

FAVORITE BARBEQUE SAUCE   2¾ Cups

"Especially good on chicken or fish"

Rind of 1 lemon, grated
Rind of 1 orange, grated
1 cup orange juice
½ cup lemon juice
½ cup onion, minced

¼ cup oil
¼ cup honey
¼ cup vinegar
¼ cup ketchup
1 tablespoon molasses

Combine all ingredients in saucepan and heat for several minutes to blend the flavors. Refrigerate or freeze until ready to use.

Jenne W. Jones

MINT SAUCE   Serves 12

"Easy and refreshing dressing for fresh fruit"

2 large handfuls fresh
  mint leaves
2–4 teaspoons sugar
1 cup fresh cream

2 cups sour cream
Juice of 3–4 limes

In a food processor or blender chop the mint, add the sugar and half the cream. Slowly add remaining cream, then sour cream and lime juice. • Refrigerate until ready to serve over fresh fruit such as blueberries, peaches, strawberries, kiwis, etc.

Mrs. Newton I. Steers, Jr.

CECIL'S CHOCOLATE SAUCE   Makes 2¼ cups

"Fabulous for parfaits or sundaes"

3 ounces unsweetened
   chocolate
1¾ cups light cream
1 cup sugar
¼ cup flour

¼ teaspoon salt
1 tablespoon butter
1 teaspoon vanilla
½ cup toasted almonds,
   optional

Melt the chocolate in the cream over hot water in the top of a double boiler. Cook until smooth, stirring occasionally. • Combine sugar, flour and salt. Add just enough of the chocolate mixture to make a smooth paste. Add to the remaining chocolate mixture and continue cooking until smooth and slightly thickened, about 10 minutes. Remove from heat and stir in remaining ingredients. Serve hot or cold.

Mrs. Alpheus W. Jessup

LEMON CURD   Makes 1 pound

"Delicious as a pie or, in the old English way, spread on bread"

3 lemons
1¼ cups sugar

¼ pound butter
3 eggs, beaten

Pare the rind from the lemons in strips. Set aside. • Squeeze and strain the lemon juice. • In a double boiler, melt the butter. Stir in the sugar, lemon juice and rind. Continue stirring over boiling water until sugar is dissolved. Add the eggs and stir gently as mixture thickens. Continue cooking until it reaches a consistency to coat the spoon. Remove from heat. Let stand a few minutes to thicken a bit more then strain through a course sieve.

Anne Green

STRAWBERRY-RHUBARB CONSERVE   6–8 half-pint jars

1½ pounds raw rhubarb
1 quart ripe strawberries
5 cups sugar

1 cup golden raisins
2 oranges or 1 orange
   and 1 lemon, ground

Wash the rhubarb and cut it into 1-inch pieces. • Wash and hull the strawberries. • Combine all ingredients in a large pot, mix them together well, cover the pot and allow to stand 30 minutes to 1 hour. • Bring to a boil and then simmer, stirring frequently, 45 minutes to 1 hour until thick. Pour into hot sterilized jars and seal.

Paula Jeffries

BREADS

Pierce Mill in Rock Creek Park

CRANBERRY COFFEE CAKE

Serves 8–10

"University Administrator's favorite"

¼ pound butter
1 cup sugar
2 eggs
2 cups flour
1 teaspoon baking powder
1 teaspoon baking soda

½ teaspoon salt
½ pint sour cream
1 teaspoon almond extract
1   7–8-ounce can whole
   cranberry sauce
½ cup chopped walnuts

Cream butter and add sugar gradually. Add eggs, one at a time. Sift dry ingredients together; add alternately with sour cream, ending with dry ingredients. Add almond extract.   •   Grease and flour a tube pan. Put half of the batter in the botton of the pan, add half the cranberry sauce and spread evenly. Add remaining batter and top with the rest of the cranberries. Sprinkle with walnuts.   •   Bake in 350° oven for 55 minutes. Cool for 5 minutes and remove from pan.

Topping:

¾ cup powdered sugar
2 tablespoons warm water

½ teaspoon almond extract

Mix ingredients well. Spread over top of coffee cake after it has been removed from the pan. Let topping run over sides of the cake.

Meredith A. Gonyea

SOUR CREAM COFFEE CAKE

Serves 8–10

1 cup sour cream
1 teaspoon baking soda
½ pound butter
1 cup sugar
2 eggs
2 cups sifted flour
1 teaspoon baking powder

¼ teaspoon salt
1 teaspoon vanilla
Streusel topping of ⅓ cup
   chopped nuts, 5 tablespoons
   sugar and ½ teaspoon
   cinnamon

Mix the sour cream with the baking soda and set aside.   •   Cream the butter and sugar together with an electric mixer. Add the eggs, beat them in and add the flour, baking powder and salt. Mix well. Add the vanilla and sour cream mixture. Spoon ½ the batter into a greased tube pan and sprinkle on ½ of the streusel mixture. Add the remaining batter and top with the rest of the streusel mixture. Bake the coffee cake at 350° for 45 minutes.

Joanne Mason

APPLE OR PEACH COFFEE CAKE

2 cakes, each
serving 8–10

"Excellent for a special weekend"

½ pound butter
½ cup milk
2½ cups flour
½ teaspoon salt
1¼ cups sugar
2 packages yeast
¼ cup warm water

3 eggs, separated
1 cup chopped nuts
1 cup chocolate chips
1 cup raisins
Cinnamon and sugar mixed
Apples or peaches (drained well
   if using canned)

Heat butter and milk over low heat. • In a mixing bowl combine flour, salt, and 2 tablespoons sugar. • Dissolve the yeast in warm water. Beat the egg yolks and combine with the yeast mixture. Pour this and the warm butter and milk into the flour mixture and blend very well. Cover and refrigerate overnight. • Next day beat the egg whites, gradually adding 1 cup of sugar. Continue beating until syrupy—about 15 minutes. • Take dough from refrigerator and divide in half. Roll out dough and using a pastry brush, generously coat with egg white mixture. Combine the nuts, chocolate chips, raisins and drained fruit and spread half the mixture on each cake. Roll, brush with egg white, and place in a greased baking pan. • Bake at 350° for 30–45 minutes until browned. • If desired, make a paste of orange juice and sugar, or milk and sugar, to put on top after the cake has cooled. Sprinkle with cinnamon and sugar mixture. (Note: the cake freezes very successfully.)

Renee Zlotnick Kraft

ZUCCHINI BREAD

Makes 2 loaves

3 eggs
2 cups sugar
1 cup vegetable oil
2 cups grated, unpeeled
   zucchini
1 tablespoon vanilla

3 cups flour
1 teaspoon salt
1 teaspoon baking soda
¼ teaspoon baking powder
1 tablespoon cinnamon
1 cup chopped walnuts

Beat eggs until foamy. Add sugar, oil, zucchini and vanilla, mixing lightly but well. • Combine flour, salt, baking soda, baking powder and cinnamon and add to zucchini mixture. Blend well and stir in the nuts. • Pour into 2 greased bread pans and bake at 350° for 1 hour. • Cool 20 minutes in the pans before removing to serve or freeze.

Chris Hunter

AUNT OLGA'S BASIC SWEET ROLL   Serves 6–8

½ cup scalded milk
¼ cup sugar
¼ teaspoon salt
1 rounded tablespoon
  shortening

1 package dry yeast or 1 cake
  compressed yeast
1 egg
2½ cups flour

Heat milk in a saucepan to just below boiling. Pour into a mixing bowl containing sugar, salt and shortening. Stir until dissolved and set aside to cool. • Dissolve yeast in ¼ cup water. Set aside. • When milk mixture is cool, add 1 cup flour and stir to make a smooth batter. Add yeast, being sure to scrape it all from cup, and stir well. Add the egg and beat until thoroughly blended. Stir in 1½ cups flour. If dough looks shiny, add a little more flour (no more than ¼ cup). • Flour a bread board or pastry cloth and knead dough for about 5 minutes, using quick movements. When dough is smooth and does not stick to fingers, form it into a ball. • Put ball into a greased bowl large enough to allow the dough to double in size. Cover with a cloth and set in a warm place to rise until it has doubled. This will take an hour or more. Punch it down and allow to rise again. When it has doubled once again, form into rolls and place on baking sheet or in tins and allow to rise a third time for about an hour. • Bake at 275° for 20 minutes or until nicely browned. (Note: This basic recipe may be used for crescents, clover leaf rolls, buns or cinnamon rolls. For variation, use nuts, fruit and cheese.)

Frances Humphrey Howard

PUMPKIN BREAD   Makes 3 loaves

"Save your empty coffee cans for this bread."

2 cups canned pumpkin
2½ cups sugar
1 cup vegetable oil
⅓ cup water
4 eggs
3½ cups flour

1 teaspoon cinnamon
1 teaspoon nutmeg
1½ teaspoons salt
2 teaspoons baking soda
1 cup chopped nuts

Combine all the ingredients in a large mixing bowl and blend well.
• Divide dough into 3 well-greased and floured 1-pound coffee cans.
• Bake for 1 hour at 350°. Cool 10 minutes and remove from cans.

Mrs. David J. Tinkham

CAPE COD CRANBERRY BREAD   Makes 1 loaf

"Tangy and delicious"

1 cup whole raw cranberries
1 cup chopped walnuts
2 cups sifted flour
1 cup sugar
½ teaspoon salt
1½ teaspoons baking powder
½ teaspoon baking soda

2 eggs, lightly beaten
2 tablespoons melted
   shortening
Juice and grated rind
   of 1 orange
Boiling water

Mix the cranberries and nuts in a bowl with 1 tablespoon of the flour. • Combine all dry ingredients. • In a measuring cup, combine the eggs, shortening, orange juice and grated rind, adding enough boiling water to make 1 cup liquid. Stir this mixture into the dry ingredients, blending well. Fold in the cranberries and nuts. Turn into a greased loaf pan and bake at 350° for 1 hour. Remove from pan, cool on a rack and wrap in foil to store or freeze. (Note: This recipe can be doubled or tripled.)

Mrs. Elliot L. Richardson

Mule drawn barge on the Canal

TASA JARA LEMON BREAD   Serves 8–10

1 cup sugar	½ teaspoon salt
½ cup oil	½ cup milk
2 eggs, lightly beaten	½ cup chopped nuts
1 ¼ cups flour	Juice of 1 lemon
1 teaspoon baking powder	Grated peel of 4 lemons

Cream the sugar and oil. Blend in the eggs. • Sift together the flour, baking powder and salt. Alternately add sifted ingredients and milk to creamed mixture, stirring constantly. • Mix in nuts, lemon juice and peel. • Pour in a greased and floured 5 x 9 inch loaf pan. Bake at 350° for 1 hour.

Topping:

¼ cup sugar	Juice of 1 lemon
Grated peel of 1 lemon	

Combine all ingredients and pour over the top of the hot loaf when it comes from the oven.

Mrs. Ernest G. Rafey

MAKE-AHEAD CHEESE PAN BREAD   Makes 6–8 wedges

"Serve warm with your favorite soup."

½ cup chopped onion	2 eggs
1 tablespoon butter	1 cup Bisquick
1½ cups shredded sharp	⅓ cup milk
cheddar cheese	1 tablespoon poppy seeds

Sauté the onion in the butter until tender. • Combine ½ cup of the cheese, 1 egg and the Bisquick. Add the milk and beat until the dough is stiff. Knead it on a lightly floured board about ten times. Pat the dough into the bottom of an 8-inch square pan or pie plate. • Combine the remaining cheese and egg, mixing well. Spread over the dough in the pan and sprinkle with onions and poppy seeds. Bake at 425° for 20 minutes.

Mary Beth Gosende

DATE AND NUT BREAD   Makes 1 loaf

*"Delicious spread with cream cheese and
served with fruit salad."*

¾ cup chopped walnuts
1 cup pitted, chopped dates
1½ teaspoons baking soda
½ teaspoon salt
3 tablespoons shortening

¾ cup boiling water
2 eggs
1 teaspoon vanilla
1 cup sugar
1½ cups flour, sifted

Combine walnuts, dates, soda and salt in a mixing bowl. Add the shortening and boiling water and let stand for 20 minutes. • Beat the eggs, add the vanilla, and beat in the sugar and flour. Mix in the date and nut mixture. • Turn the dough into a greased 9 x 5 x 3 inch loaf pan and bake in a preheated 350° oven for 65 minutes or until done. • Cool in the pan for 10 minutes before removing. Cool overnight before slicing. This bread freezes well.

Dolly Hedlund

RAISIN BRAN MUFFINS   4 dozen

"Handy to mix up and store."

4 eggs
3 cups sugar
1 cup oil
1 quart buttermilk
15 ounces raisin bran cereal

5 cups flour (sift before
   measuring)
5 teaspoons baking soda
2 teaspoons salt
½ cup dark raisins

In a large bowl, beat the eggs. Add the sugar, oil, buttermilk and raisin bran cereal, mixing well after each addition. • Sift the flour again with the baking soda and salt. Stir in the egg mixture. Add ½ cup raisins. • Store the batter in a covered container in the refrigerator for up to 4 months. When ready to bake, fill desired number of greased and floured muffin tins ¾ full and bake at 400° for 15 minutes.

Amy Bagwill

BRAN N' RAISIN MOLASSES MUFFINS 1 dozen
"Very moist and light"

2 cups All Bran	1 cup sifted flour
½ cup molasses	1 teaspoon baking soda
1¼ cups milk	½ teaspoon salt
1 egg	½ cup seedless raisins

Combine All Bran, molasses and milk. Let stand until most of the moisture is absorbed. Add the egg and beat well. • Sift together the flour, baking soda and salt. Add with the raisins to the All Bran mixture, stirring only until combined. Fill greased muffin tins ⅔ full. Bake at 400° for 12–15 minutes.

Karin G. Weber

PANCAKES Makes 8 thin pancakes

1 egg	1 tablespoon flour
Yolk of 1 egg	Pinch of salt
1 teaspoon sugar	Butter for frying
1 cup light cream	

Whip all ingredients together thoroughly. Melt butter in a hot skillet and fry the pancakes, adding more butter as needed. Serve immediately.

Mrs. John A. Logan

SWEDISH "TUNNBRÖD" FLATBREAD Makes 8–10 pieces

1 cup water or milk	2½–3 cups flour
1 teaspoon salt	

Mix the milk or water with the salt and flour. Knead the dough well. Divide the dough into 8–10 pieces and roll out each as thin as possible. Dust the pieces with flour. • Cook the pieces in a skillet, using no fat, for 1½–2 minutes on each side. The bread will be crisper cooking over low heat and softer over high heat. While the bread is best eaten fresh, it can be prepared ahead and stored in the refrigerator.

Embassy of Sweden
For cooking classes to benefit
The Washington Opera

SPOON BREAD   Serves 8

*"Spoon bread was one of Mrs. Johnson's
(Lyndon's mother) delightful dishes—with
a salad (fruit or green) and meat, it makes
a perfect lunch."*

3 cups milk	Butter, the size of a walnut
3 eggs	3 level teaspoons baking powder
1 scant cup corn meal	1 level teaspoon salt

Stir corn meal into 2 cups of milk and let mixture come to a boil,
making a mush. Remove from heat and add balance of milk and well
beaten eggs. Stir in salt, baking powder and melted butter. Bake in 2-
quart greased casserole for 30 minutes at 350°.

Mrs. Lyndon B. Johnson

1897 popcorn wagon

ALICE'S CORNCAKES   Serves 4

*"The world's lightest! But be warned:
they must be eaten on the spot."*

1 cup yellow cornmeal	1 teaspoon baking soda
2 cups buttermilk	1 teaspoon salt
4 eggs, separated	Butter or bacon grease

Combine the cornmeal, buttermilk, 4 egg yolks, baking soda and salt in
a mixing bowl. • Beat the 4 egg whites until stiff and fold into the
cornmeal mixture. • Carefully spoon the batter onto a hot griddle
which has been oiled with butter or bacon grease. Cook 1–2 minutes,
turn and cook 1–2 additional minutes.

David P. Fogle

BEER-HERB ROLLS

Makes 3 dozen

2 packages dry yeast
½ cup warm water
1 12-ounce can beer
¼ cup sugar
1 tablespoon salt
¼ cup melted butter

2 eggs, lightly beaten
1 medium onion, grated
1 teaspoon sage
2 teaspoons thyme
3 teaspoons savory
6½–7 cups flour

Sprinkle yeast over the warm water and stir. Pour into a large bowl and add the beer, sugar, salt and butter. Mix well. Add eggs, onion, herbs and 6 cups of flour. Beat until smooth. Gradually add remaining flour until dough pulls away from the sides of the bowl. Turn out and knead until smooth. • Place dough in a greased bowl, cover and let rise until doubled in size. Punch down and set aside for 10–15 minutes. • Make 1½ inch rolls. Place on cookie sheets and let them rise until doubled in size. Bake at 400° for 20 minutes.

Hope Price

HERBEER BREAD

2 loaves

"Try this instead of the traditional rolls with dinner."

3 cups self-rising flour, sifted
2 tablespoons sugar
1 teaspoon baking powder
¼ teaspoon oregano

¼ teaspoon thyme
¼ teaspoon basil
1 12-ounce can beer at room
   temperature

In a large bowl sift together flour, sugar, baking powder and herbs. • Gradually add beer, beating with an electric mixer at medium speed until all lumps are gone and mixture resembles pancake batter. • Pour into two greased 8 x 4 x 2 inch loaf pans. • Bake at 375° for 40 minutes. Turn loaves upside down in pans and bake for another five minutes. Bread will be pale, not brown, when done. Cool on rack. • Slice when cold. (Note: This bread should be toasted.)

Edgar Stromberg

POPOVERS
Makes 9

"This is one of our favorite 'house dishes'—our friends know they're sure to have Popovers for one meal during a house-party."
Lady Bird Johnson

1 cup sifted flour
1 cup milk
2 eggs, beaten

¼ teaspoon salt
2 tablespoons shortening, melted

Mix and sift flour and salt. • Combine eggs, milk and shortening; gradually add to flour mixture, beating about 1 minute or until batter is smooth. • Fill greased, sizzling hot pans ¾ full and bake in very hot oven (450°) about 20 minutes. Reduce heat to moderate (350°) and continue baking for 15–20 minutes.

Mrs. Lyndon B. Johnson

FOUR-GRAIN ANADAMA BREAD
Makes 4 loaves

"This bread is at its best toasted, for breakfast or sandwiches"

3¼ cups water
5⅓ tablespoons butter
¾ cup blackstrap molasses
12–12½ cups flour
4 teaspoons salt

1⅔ cups yellow corn meal
3 packages yeast
⅔ cup dry milk powder
½ cup rolled oats
½ cup bran

Combine the water, butter and molasses in a saucepan and heat to warm only. • In a large bowl, mix 3⅓ cups flour, salt, corn meal, yeast and dry milk powder. Using an electric mixer at medium speed, beat in the warm water, butter and molasses for 2 minutes. Add ⅔ cup flour and beat 2 minutes at high speed. Gradually stir in the oats, bran and 4 more cups flour, mixing with your hands if necessary. Turn the dough out onto a floured board and knead 8–10 minutes, adding flour as necessary to prevent sticking, up to 4–4½ cups. Place dough in a greased bowl, cover with a damp cloth and let rise until doubled in bulk, about 1 hour. • Punch down the risen dough, turn out onto a floured board and divide into 4 equal portions. Mold into rounds, cover with a damp cloth and let rest 10 minutes. • Shape the dough into loaves and place in 4 greased 8 x 4 x 2 inch pans. Cover with a damp cloth and let rise until doubled in bulk, about 45 minutes. • Bake at 375° for 40 minutes, rotating pan positions on oven shelves at 10 minute intervals. Turn loaves upside down in pans and bake 10 minutes more. Cool the loaves thoroughly before slicing.

Edgar Stromberg

TINTAGEL WHOLE WHEAT BREAD
Makes 2 loaves

1½ cups very warm water
¼ cup honey
1 package dry yeast
½ cup unprocessed bran
½ cup wheat germ
2 teaspoons salt
2 eggs

⅓ cup vegetable oil
1 cup dry milk powder
2½ cups stone ground whole
 wheat flour
2½ cups unbleached flour
 plus more for kneading

Combine warm water, honey and yeast in a large bowl. Let "proof" 5–10 minutes until bubbly. Mix in the bran and wheat germ. Beat in the salt, eggs, oil and dry milk powder, mixing thoroughly. Gradually add the flour, beating vigorously with a wooden spoon. Turn the dough out on a floured surface and knead it until it forms a smooth ball. Place the dough in a well greased bowl, turning it to coat all sides with the grease. Cover with plastic wrap and let rise until doubled in bulk, 1–2 hours in a warm, draft-free place or overnight in the refrigerator.
• Punch down the dough, turn it out on a floured surface and cut it into 2 equal portions. Knead each briefly and shape into loaves. Put the loaves into 2 greased 8 x 4 inch loaf pans, cover with greased waxed paper and let rise until level with the top edge of the pans. Place the bread on the middle rack of a cold oven. Fill a shallow pan with boiling water and set this on the lowest rack. Turn oven temperature to 350° and bake the bread 40–45 minutes. The loaves should be nicely browned when done and sound hollow when tapped. Turn out on a rack to cool before storing in plastic bags in freezer or refrigerator. Serve as toast or sandwich bread. (Note: A heavy duty mixer with a dough hook can be used to mix the ingredients.)

Joan Smith

An antique table and tea things from the James Monroe Reception Room of the Department of State

NO KNEAD WHEAT BREAD   Makes 1 loaf

1 package active dry yeast
⅓ cup sugar
¼ cup water, lukewarm
½ cup milk, lukewarm

¼ pound butter, melted
1 teaspoon salt
3 eggs
3½–4 cups whole wheat flour

In a large mixing bowl, combine the yeast, sugar, and lukewarm water. Let the yeast "proof". • Combine the milk, melted butter and salt and add to the yeast mixture. Stir well and add the eggs, one at a time, beating well after each addition. Beat in the flour a little at a time until you have a stiff but workable dough. Cover and let rise until doubled in bulk. Beat the dough down, using a wooden spoon, for 1 minute, and turn into a well buttered 9-inch tube pan. Let rise again to the top of the pan. • Bake at 375°for 25–30 minutes or until bread sounds slightly hollow when tapped. Turn out on a rack and serve warm, breaking it apart with 2 forks rather than cutting it. The bread is also delicious toasted.

Gerry Nettleton

SYNERGY BREAD   Makes 2 loaves

"A light multi-grain bread"

2 tablespoons yeast
2¾ cups warm water
½ cup oil
⅓ cup honey
2 eggs
1 teaspoon salt

3–4 cups white flour
1–2 cups wheat flour
1–2 cups other grains such as
    oatmeal, corn meal or rye
⅓–½ cup whole millet seed

Mix the yeast and ½ cup warm water in a large bowl. Add the remaining ingredients and mix well. You should use 6–7 cups of flour in all, though at least ½ the total amount should be made up of the white flour. Knead the dough and let rise in a warm, draft-free place until doubled in bulk, about ½–1 hour. Divide in ½ and knead again. Turn into 2 buttered bread pans and bake at 350° about 40 minutes or until done. (Note: If desired, omit kneading the first time by adding only ½ the flours to the other ingredients and letting the resulting "mulge" rise. Then add remaining flours, divide the dough and place in the bread pans.)

Byron Swift

SOUR DOUGH RYE-WHOLE WHEAT BREAD

Makes 3 loaves

1 cup sour dough starter
1½ quarts potato water,
  lukewarm
½ cup molasses
10 cups combined rye and
  whole wheat flour

2 tablespoons salt
½ cup nutritional yeast
2 tablespoons whole
  caraway seeds
1 cup milk powder

Combine sour dough starter (recipe below) with all liquids and 6 cups of the combined flour. Mix well, cover, and let stand in a warm place for 3 hours or more. A longer time enhances sourness. • Stir. (If you wish, remove 1 cup to be used as starter for next baking. This should be covered and kept in the refrigerator.) Add the salt, yeast, caraway seeds and milk powder. Blend well and add enough of the remaining flour to make a stiff dough. • Knead the dough until it becomes elastic and no longer sticky. Shape into 3 balls and place in greased, ovenproof bowls. Set in warm place to rise 3–4 hours or until ⅓ greater in size. Bake at 350° for 1¼–1½ hours. Cool on a rack.

Sour dough starter:

½ cup rye flour
½ cup whole wheat
  flour

½ cake or ½ tablespoon
  dried yeast
1 cup lukewarm water

Soak yeast in lukewarm water to allow it to "proof". Combine all ingredients and let stand at room temperature for 2–3 days. Allow to rise and fall without stirring.

Donald Stetson Davis

WHOLE WHEAT BREAD-CUISINART

Makes 1 loaf

½ pound whole wheat flour
½ pound white flour
1 package dry yeast
½ tablespoon brown sugar

10 ounces warm water
2 tablespoons melted butter
½–1 teaspoon salt, according
  to taste

Put flour in Cuisinart bowl. Add yeast and brown sugar. Pour water over and mix a few seconds. Let rest and melt butter. Add butter and salt and let the machine knead the bread for a minute or two. Dough will form a ball. Remove and form into a loaf and place in a greased 4 x 8 x 3 inch bread pan. Let rise in a warm place until just above rim of pan. Bake at 350° for 20 minutes or until the loaf sounds hollow when tapped.

Paula Jeffries

DESSERTS

The Shrine of the Immaculate Conception

FROZEN AMARETTO SOUFFLE   Serves 12

5 large egg yolks
3 large whole eggs
⅔ cup plus 2 tablespoons
  superfine sugar

1½ ounces Amaretto
⅔ cup crumbled almond
  macaroons
1 pint heavy cream

Beat the egg yolks, whole eggs and sugar together until thick and lemon colored. • Whip heavy cream until very stiff. • Fold Amaretto and macaroons into egg mixture. Fold in the whipped heavy cream. • Make a 2 inch foil collar for a 1½ quart soufflé dish and pour in soufflé mixture. Freeze at least overnight. Place in refrigerator 2 hours before serving. Garnish with shaved chocolate.

Mrs. Sidney S. Zlotnick

APPLE MOUSSE   Serves 6

3 pounds tart apples
1 cup sugar
Rind of 1 lemon

2 sticks cinnamon
6 egg whites
3 ounces slivered almonds

Wash and quarter the apples. Cook them with the sugar, lemon rind and cinnamon sticks in a minimum of water until completely softened. Press the apples through a sieve to make a purée. • Beat the egg whites until stiff, add the apple purée and continue beating until firm in consistency. Turn into serving bowl, cover with the slivered almonds and chill 2–3 hours before serving.

Nicholas M. Salgo

BLUEBERRY PUDDING   Serves 6

1 quart blueberries
1 tablespoon lemon juice
Dash cinnamon

1 cup flour
1 cup sugar
½ cup butter

Put blueberries in a casserole and sprinkle with lemon juice and cinnamon. • With a pastry cutter, cut flour, sugar and butter together until crumbly. Place on top of the blueberries and shake casserole to combine all ingredients evenly. • Bake at 350° for 45 minutes and serve hot. Whipped cream or vanilla ice cream are suggested accompaniments.

Elizabeth Beach Rea

INSTANT BLUEBERY ICE CREAM   Serves 4–6

"This basic recipe invites imaginative variations"

1 pound package frozen
   blueberries
½ cup sugar
1 teaspoon grated orange peel

1 tablespoon or more
   Cointreau
¼ teaspoon cinnamon
1 pint half and half

Place frozen berries, sugar, peel, Cointreau and cinnamon in the bowl of a food processor or blender. Process off and on for about 30 seconds until well mixed. Gradually pour in the half and half. Blend until smooth. It will have the consistency of soft ice cream. Serve immediately. (Note: May be kept in freezer for an hour or so and stirred again. However, it will harden if made too far in advance. Frozen unsweetened strawberries or peaches may also be used.)

Mrs. Kenneth Bacon

BLUEBERRIES AND CREAM   Serves 8

2 envelopes gelatine
1 cup water
1 pint sour cream
2 tablespoons sugar

¼ teaspoon cinnamon
½ teaspoon vanilla
2 cups blueberry pie filling
8 ounces crushed pineapple

Soften the gelatine in the water in the top of a double doiler, heating until dissolved. • Pour sour cream into a mixing bowl and add ¼ cup of the softened gelatine. Add the sugar, cinnamon and vanilla, mixing well. Spoon the mixture into an oiled, 6-cup mold and cool until set. • Mix the blueberry pie filling with the pineapple and the remaining gelatine. Spoon over the molded sour cream. Chill until firm. Unmold to serve.

Mrs. Robert C. Eisele

CHOCOLATE MOUSSE

Serves 8–10

1 pound sweet chocolate
6 eggs, separated
½ pound butter, softened
Pinch salt
1–1½ cups heavy cream, whipped

Sugar to taste
Vanilla or rum to taste
⅓ cups chopped nuts or
   grated chocolate

Melt the chocolate in the top of a double boiler. Beat in the egg yolks, one at a time over low heat, beating well after each addition. Beat in the soft butter vigorously. Remove from heat. • Beat the egg whites with a pinch of salt until stiff but not dry. Fold them into the chocolate mixture thoroughly so that no white spots show. Turn into a greased 6 cup mold, bowl or individual cups. Let stand in the refrigerator overnight. • About 1 hour before serving, unmold the mousse onto a serving plate. Frost it with the whipped cream flavored with sugar and vanilla or rum. Sprinkle with nuts or grated chocolate. Chill again before serving.

Mrs. George H.W. Bush

CHRISTMAS PUDDING

Serves 12-14

1 cup flour
Pinch of salt
½ teaspoon mixed spices
1 cup bread crumbs
½ cup grated carrots
14 ounces beef suet, grated
2½ cups currants
1½ cups raisins

1 cup candied peel
2 cups sultanas
2 tablespoons ground almonds
1 cup brown sugar
3 eggs, beaten
Juice of ½ lemon
½ cup ale
½ cup brandy

Combine the flour, salt and spices in a large mixing bowl. Stir in the bread crumbs, carrots, suet, fruits, almonds and sugar. Let stand overnight. • The next day, add the well beaten eggs, lemon juice, ale and brandy. Mix well. Mixture should be soft but not too moist. Place mixture in buttered pudding bowls or crocks, cover with buttered paper and tie down with cheesecloth or cotton cloth. Set in boiling water in large pans and boil for 7 hours, maintaining water level below edge of bowls. • Serve with brandy sauce or ice cream. (Note: Will keep for 2 months in refrigerator.)

Mrs. Walter D. Innis

COLD CHOCOLATE SOUFFLE

Serves 8–10

1 envelope unflavored
  gelatine
½ cup cold water
½ cup boiling water
5 squares semi-sweet
  baking chocolate

1 cup milk
5 egg yolks
1 cup sugar
1 tablespoon vanilla
5 egg whites

Stir the gelatine into the cold water and let stand for 5 minutes. Add boiling water and stir until dissolved. • Place chocolate and milk in the top of a double boiler. Heat over boiling water, stirring occasionally, until chocolate is completely dissolved. Cool slightly. • In a mixing bowl, beat the egg yolks with the sugar until smooth and creamy. Add to chocolate mixture, over the heat, and stir well. Add dissolved gelatine and vanilla. Stir again and remove from heat. Allow to cool. • In a mixing bowl, beat the egg whites until firm but not stiff. Gently fold into chocolate mixture. Pour into serving dish and refrigerate 6–8 hours.

Garnish:

1 cup heavy cream
¼ cup sugar

1 tablespoon vanilla
Almonds, thinly sliced

Prepare garnish when ready to serve the soufflé. Beat the cream until stiff, add the sugar and vanilla. Spread the whipped cream on the soufflé in a decorative way and top with the sliced almonds.

Mrs. Edward C. Schmults

MOUSSE AU CHOCOLAT

Serves 6

4 ounces semi-sweet chocolate
4 egg yolks
4 tablespoons unsalted butter

2 tablespoons orange flavored
  liqueur
4 egg whites

Place the chocolate in a saucepan and cover with hot water. In several minutes, the chocolate will become soft but not melted. Test softness with the point of a knife. Carefully pour off the water. Add the egg yolks to the softened chocolate and beat them in with a wire whisk. Add the butter and stir over low heat until melted. Pour the mixture into a bowl and stir in the liqueur. • Beat the egg whites until stiff and fold ½ into the chocolate mixture. Add remaining whites and fold in. Pour the mousse into a serving bowl or individual cups or glasses. Chill in the refrigerator 2 hours to set. Serve cold.

Mrs. Douglas Kiker

CREME BRULEE

Serves 4–6

1 cup heavy cream
2 egg yolks
2 tablespoons sugar

Vanilla to taste
Brown sugar

Heat the heavy cream to the boiling point. • Beat the egg yolks with the sugar in a mixing bowl and gradually add the hot cream. Blend well and add vanilla to taste. • Turn the mixture into the top of a double boiler and cook over boiling water until the cream coats a spoon, taking care it does not curdle (no more than 165° on a candy thermometer). Pour into a flat ovenproof dish such as a quiche pan and refrigerate 24 hours until a crust forms. Sprinkle the entire surface evenly with brown sugar and place under a hot broiler, watching carefully, until it starts to bubble. The sugar should melt but not burn.

Mrs. Alejandro Orfila
Wife of the Secretary of The
Organization of American States

GRAND MARNIER TRIFLE

Serves 8

12 ladyfingers
⅓ cup plus 3 tablespoons
  Grand Marnier
3 tablespoons seedless raspberry
  jam
1 envelope unflavored gelatine
4 egg yolks
5 tablespoons sugar
¼ teaspoon salt
1 cup scalded milk

1 tablespoon Crème de Cassis
¼ cup orange juice
½ teaspoon vanilla
1½ cups heavy cream
¼ cup minced orange peel
4 navel oranges, peeled
  and sectioned
1   3-ounce package sliced
  almonds, lightly toasted

Separate ladyfingers, sprinkle with 3 tablespoons Grand Marnier, spread lightly with raspberry jam and sandwich them back together. Cut the ladyfingers in thirds and arrange half in the bottom of a 2-quart soufflé or glass dish. • In a small bowl sprinkle gelatine over 2 tablespoons cold water to soften. • In another bowl, beat egg yolks with sugar and salt until light and thick. Gradually pour in scalded milk, blend well and pour into a heavy saucepan. Whisk over moderate heat until thick but not boiling. Remove from heat and add gelatine, rest of Grand Marnier, Cassis, orange juice and vanilla. Whisk over a bowl of ice until it begins to set. • Whip the cream and fold into custard along with the minced orange peel. • Pour half of this custard over the ladyfingers. Cover with a layer of orange sections, then remaining ladyfingers. Pour in the rest of the custard and refrigerate several hours or overnight to set. • Just before serving, arrange remaining orange sections in a circle around the edge of the trifle and sprinkle the almonds in the center.

Mrs. Kenneth Bacon

GOETTERFREUDE

Serves 6–8

"A Black Forest treat"

3 cups fine bread crumbs
  made from 4 day old
  pumpernickel bread, crusts
  removed
¼ cup maraschino

¼ cup cherry preserves
2 tablespoons kirsch
2 cups heavy cream, whipped
¾ cup sweet black cherries,
  pitted and drained

In a mixing bowl combine the crumbs with the maraschino, the cherry preserves and the kirsch. Press a ¾-inch layer of crumb mixture on the bottom of a serving dish. Spread a layer of whipped cream over it. Continue with alternating layers of the crumb mixture and whipped cream. Cream should be in swirls on the top layer. Arrange the sweet black cherries over the cream and chill. (Note: This dessert is also very pretty layered in tall fluted glasses.)

Embassy of the Federal Republic
of Germany
For cooking classes to benefit
The Washington Opera

LUSCIOUS NO-COOK LEMON CREAM

Serves 6

1 envelope gelatine
1 cup heavy cream
3 eggs, separated
½ cup plus 3 tablespoons
  sugar
¼ cup fresh lemon juice

2 tablespoons finely grated
  lemon rind
Thin lemon slices
Whipped cream, piped
  through a pastry tube
Candied violets

In a small saucepan, sprinkle gelatine over ¼ cup cold water to soften. • Whip the cream until stiff and place in an attractive medium-sized glass serving bowl. Refrigerate. • In a mixing bowl, beat the egg whites until stiff. Gradually stir in 3 tablespoons sugar, one at a time. Beat 2–3 minutes more. • Heat the gelatine over very low heat, stirring constantly until it is dissolved. Remove from heat. • In another bowl, beat the egg yolks with ½ cup sugar until smooth and creamy. Pour in the gelatine and blend well. Add the lemon juice and grated lemon rind and mix thoroughly. • Remove the chilled whipped cream from the refrigerator and gently fold in the egg yolk mixture. When this is well blended, gently and quickly fold in the egg whites. Be careful to keep the mixture as fluffy as possible. Cover with plastic wrap and chill for at least 3 hours. • Garnish with a ring of lemon slices, rosettes of whipped cream and candied violets.

Mrs. C. G. A. Ross

Dumbarton Oaks

FROZEN LEMON TORTE

Serves 12

4 eggs, separated
1 cup sugar
1½ tablespoons grated
   lemon peel

½ cup fresh lemon juice
1½ cups heavy cream
30 lemon flavored wafer
   cookies, 2 inch diameter

Beat egg whites until stiff. Gradually beat in ¾ cup sugar, 1 tablespoon at a time, until whites form glossy peaks. With the same beater, blend egg yolks, remaining sugar, lemon peel and juice. Whip the cream until stiff. • Fold whites, yolks and cream together. • Line the bottom of a 9-inch springform pan with the cookies, then stand a row of cookies around pan, top side against the rim. Pour in the lemon mixture, smoothing the top. Cover and freeze at least 8 hours. • Remove rim of pan, cut into wedges and serve.

Mrs. William P. Clark

LEMON ROYALE   Serves 8–10

Graham Cracker Crust:

1¾ cups graham cracker crumbs
½ cup melted butter

¼ cup sugar
½ teaspoon cinnamon

Combine the four ingredients and press firmly against the bottom and sides of a 9-inch soufflé dish or a 13 x 8½ inch baking dish. Bake at 350° for 10 minutes. Cool.

Filling:

½ gallon vanilla ice cream, softened
6 tablespoons butter
Grated peel of 2 lemons
Juice of 2 lemons

⅛ teaspoon salt
1 cup sugar
2 whole eggs
2 egg yolks

Spread ½ of the softened ice cream in the cooled crust. Freeze.
• Melt the butter in a double boiler and stir in the lemon peel, lemon juice, salt and sugar. Beat whole eggs with the yolks and combine with lemon mixture. Cook over boiling water, stirring constantly, until thick and smooth. Cool. • Spread ½ the lemon filling over the frozen ice cream. Freeze. • Cover frozen lemon mixture with the remaining softened ice cream. Freeze. • Spread the rest of the lemon filling over the frozen ice cream. Freeze. • Just before serving, prepare meringue.

Meringue:

3 egg whites   6 tablespoons sugar

Preheat oven to 475°. Beat the egg whites until stiff. Gradually add the sugar. Spread over frozen dessert. Place in oven and brown lightly. Serve immediately. (Note: The frozen dessert should be prepared considerably in advance, but the meringue is best done just before serving.)

Mrs. W. Walker Lewis III

FROZEN LIME SOUFFLE

Serves 12

10 eggs, separated
½ cup lime juice
½ cup lemon juice
Grated rind of 2 lemons and
    2 limes
2 cups sugar

2 envelopes unflavored
    gelatine
½ cup medium dark rum
2 cups heavy cream, whipped
Additional whipped cream
Thin slices of lime for garnish

In a heavy pot beat the egg yolks with a hand mixer, adding sugar gradually. Add lemon and lime juices and grated rinds, and cook over medium heat until thickened. • Soak the gelatine in the rum, stir into the custard and cool. • Beat the egg whites until stiff. Fold them and the whipped cream into the custard. • Prepare a 6-cup soufflé dish with a foil collar. Oil both. Pour soufflé into dish and freeze until completely firm. Remove from freezer ½ hour before serving and garnish with a whipped cream ruffle and lime slices. (Note: Make the soufflé 1–2 days in advance for maximum flavor.)

Mrs. Robert H. Craft, Jr.

MAPLE CHARLOTTE

Serves 8

*"A favorite with European guests, for
whom maple syrup is a real treat."*

1 cup milk
1 cup maple syrup
1 envelope gelatine
¼ cup brown sugar
½ teaspoon vanilla

1 pint heavy cream
2 egg whites
1 dozen ladyfingers
¼ cup chopped walnuts

Scald the milk. Soak gelatine in 1 tablespoon maple syrup to soften then add to the milk. Blend in remaining syrup, sugar and vanilla. Cook over moderate heat for 5 minutes, stirring constantly, until gelatine is dissolved. Strain through cheesecloth and chill until partially set. • In separate bowls, whip the cream and the egg whites until stiff and fold into thickened gelatine mixture. Line a mold with ladyfingers and gently pour the mixture over them. Chill for several hours. • When ready to serve, unmold and sprinkle chopped walnuts on top.

Mrs. Guy Martin

LEMON MOUSSE WITH RASPBERRY SAUCE   Serves 6

2 envelopes unflavored gelatine   4 eggs
¼ cup cold water   1 cup sugar
⅔ cup lemon juice   1 cup heavy cream, whipped

Sprinkle gelatine on cold water to soften. Heat and stir until gelatine is completely dissolved. • Add lemon juice and chill until mixture resembles unbeaten egg whites. • Meanwhile beat eggs until foamy, adding sugar gradually. Continue beating until eggs are pale and thick. Beat in gelatine mixture. Chill slightly. • Fold in 1 cup whipped cream and turn into serving bowl. Chill until firm.

Raspberry Sauce:

1   10-ounce package frozen raspberries, thawed
1 cup heavy cream, whipped

Crush raspberries in blender or food processor. Serve with lemon mousse topped with whipped cream.

Mrs. Robert C. Eisele

ORANGES OLIVERO   Serves 4

4 oranges   1 teaspoon vanilla
1¼ cups water   Vanilla ice cream
¾ cup sugar   Fresh mint

Using a vegetable peeler, remove the orange part of the rind of each of the 4 oranges. Cut the rind into julienne strips. Boil the strips in 1 cup of the water for 10 minutes, drain them and dry them thoroughly on paper towels. • Boil the sugar in the remaining ¼ cup water until the liquid is a clear syrup. Add the dried orange peel and vanilla. Cool. • Cut the remaining white part of peel from the oranges and slice them. Remove any seeds. • To serve, place a scoop of ice cream on each of 4 dishes and surround with slices of 1 orange. Top with the candied orange rind syrup and garnish with fresh mint leaves. (Note: Any leftover syrup will keep for weeks for use on plain ice cream.)

Jerry Ryan

ORANGE CREAM

Serves 6–8

3-ounce package lemon jello
1 cup hot water
½ cup sugar

1 cup orange juice
3 tablespoons grated orange rind
1 cup heavy cream, whipped

Dissolve jello in hot water. Add sugar, orange juice and grated orange rind. Chill until just beginning to set. • Fold in whipped cream and pour into a 3 cup mold or serving bowl or divide into individual portions or molds. If molding, unmold to serve and garnish with fruit if desired.

Mrs. E. F. Bastable

ELEGANT PRUNE WHIP

Serves 6

"Light and tart, with a crunch"

1 cup cooked chopped prunes
⅓ cup brown sugar, packed
3 large egg whites
½ teaspoon salt

¼ cup chopped walnuts
1 tablespoon lemon juice
Custard sauce, see below

Combine prunes, sugar, egg whites and salt. Beat with an electric mixer until stiff enough to hold peaks. Fold in the walnuts and lemon juice. Turn into a 1-quart shallow baking dish. Set this in a pan filled with 1 inch of hot water. Bake at 325° for 40 minutes. Mixture will puff and form a thin crust. Cool, and serve with ice cream or custard sauce.

Custard sauce:

Makes 1½ cups

2 tablespoons sugar
1 teaspoon cornstarch
⅛ teaspoon salt

1¼ cups milk
3 egg yolks, beaten
1 teaspoon vanilla

Combine dry ingredients in a saucepan. Stir in the milk and heat to boiling, stirring constantly. Gradually add the hot mixture to the egg yolks, return to low heat and cook 1 minute longer, stirring constantly. Do not allow to boil. Remove from heat and add the vanilla. Serve with prune whip.

Jenne W. Jones

WINTER'S FRUIT   Serves 6

"Colorful and refreshing"

3 oranges, sliced with peel left on	Pomegranate seeds
Sugar	1 cup sour cream
6 kiwi fruit	⅓ cup dark brown sugar

Drop sliced oranges in boiling water to which has been added ⅓ cup sugar per quart. Boil 5 minutes, cool and chill. • Place chilled oranges in a serving bowl, add peeled, sliced kiwi fruit and top with pomegranate seeds. • Add dark brown sugar to the sour cream, streaking it through, not mixing thoroughly. Pass this sauce separately when serving the fruit. (Note: You might substitute blueberries, peaches and/or green grapes for the oranges.)

Mary Lynn Kotz

ORANGE SOUFFLE WITH COINTREAU   Serves 8–10

4 egg yolks	1 teaspoon grated lemon peel
2½ cups orange juice	3 tablespoons lemon juice
4 envelopes (1 ounce) gelatine	2 tablespoons Cointreau
2 cups sugar	4 medium orange sections,
Dash of salt	membranes removed
1 teaspoon grated orange peel	1 cup heavy cream, whipped

Beat the egg yolks and combine in a saucepan with 1 cup orange juice and the gelatine. Cook over medium heat, stirring constantly, until the mixture comes to a boil. Stir in the sugar, salt, peels, remaining juices and the Cointreau. Continue stirring until the sugar is dissolved. • Chill, stirring occasionally, until mixture thickens enough to form mounds. Stir in the orange sections and fold in the whipped cream. Pour into a mold and chill for 10–12 hours. • Unmold and serve.

Maurice Du Four
Ridgewells

MERRY APPLES

Serves 6

"An elegant coloratura dessert"

⅞ cup water
1 cup granulated sugar
3 tablespoons lemon juice
½ teaspoon red food coloring

6 tart, firm apples, peeled
  and cored
½ teaspoon grated nutmeg
1 teaspoon vanilla

Simmer water and sugar for 3 minutes in a shallow pan large enough to hold the apples. Stir in the lemon juice and food coloring. Continue cooking sugar syrup over low heat while preparing the apples. Add them to the syrup and cook, covered, 20 minutes, turning them occasionally. The apples should be soft but hold their shape. Place them on a serving dish and sprinkle them with nutmeg. • Reduce sugar syrup to a glaze, about 3 minutes. Add vanilla and spoon the glaze over the apples. Chill well. Serve them with Crème Anglaise.

Crème Anglaise:

3 egg yolks
⅓ cup granulated sugar
1¼ cups hot milk

2 teaspoons vanilla
1 tablespoon brandy or rum
1 tablespoon butter, softened

In a 1½ quart stainless steel or enameled saucepan, beat the egg yolks 1–2 minutes until thick. Gradually beat in the sugar. Beat in the milk very slowly, by spoonfuls. Cook over low heat, stirring constantly with a wooden spoon, about 10 minutes. Be careful not to let sauce come near a simmer or eggs will curdle. Mixture should thicken enough to coat the spoon. At this point, steam should begin to rise from the sauce. Lower heat further and stir 1 minute more. Off heat, stir in vanilla, brandy or rum and butter. Chill thoroughly. Serve with Merry Apples.

Dorothy Leavitt

The Woodrow Wilson Bridge

PAVLOVA   Serves 4–6

3 egg whites
Pinch salt
1 cup sugar
1 teaspoon flour
1 teaspoon vinegar

½ teaspoon vanilla
½ pint heavy cream, whipped
 and sweetened
Strawberries, thinly sliced
Kiwi fruit, thinly sliced

Line an 8–9 inch cake pan with greased paper. • Using an electric mixer, beat the egg whites and salt until stiff. Beat in ½ cup sugar. Lower the speed and beat in remaining sugar and flour. Stir in the vinegar and vanilla. • Spread mixture in a cake pan and bake at 300° for 1 hour. Turn upside down on a cake plate and cool. • Spread top with whipped cream and decorate with fresh strawberries and kiwi fruit.

Hope Price

QUEEN OF PUDDINGS   Serves 10–12

"Delicious hot or cold or anywhere in between!"

4 cups white bread crumbs
1½ cups sugar
1½ quarts milk
¼ pound butter
8 egg yolks, beaten

½ teaspoon vanilla
Grated rind of 1 lemon
6 tablespoons strawberry or
 raspberry preserves
8 egg whites

In a large mixing bowl, toss the bread crumbs with ½ cup sugar. Heat the milk and butter to boiling and pour over the bread crumbs. Let stand for 10 minutes. • Stir in the beaten egg yolks, vanilla and lemon rind. Pour into a well buttered 9 x 13 inch baking dish. Bake at 350° for 30 minutes or until set. • Remove pudding from oven and lower temperature to 250°. Gently spread preserves over the pudding. Beat egg whites until stiff and slowly beat in the remaining sugar. • Pile and swirl meringue over the pudding and return it to the oven until lightly browned.

Mrs. Paul F. Petrus

RASPBERRY SOUFFLE

Serves 6

5 tablespoons unsalted butter
5 tablespoons unbleached flour
1½ cups heavy cream
½ cup plus 2 tablespoons sugar
3 tablespoons Grand Marnier

5 egg yolks
5 egg whites
Salt
1 pint fresh raspberries

Butter and sugar a 2-quart soufflé mold. • In a heavy bottomed saucepan, melt the butter and whisk in the flour blending well. Add the cream, ½ cup sugar, and Grand Marnier and continue to cook, stirring with the whisk until thick and boiling. Remove from heat, whisk in the egg yolks and return to heat immediately. Blend well and set aside. • Beat the egg whites with a little salt and 2 tablespoons of sugar until soft peaks form. Whisk ¼ of the whites into the soufflé mixture and then fold in the rest. Add raspberries and gently fold entire mixture into the prepared mold, smoothing the top and flattening it toward the edges. Bake the soufflé at 450° for 15–20 minutes and serve immediately. (Note: Top soufflé if desired with whipped cream or crème anglaise.)

Anna Maria Via

FROZEN PUMPKIN DESSERT

Serves 8

1 cup graham cracker crumbs
½ cup sugar
4 tablespoons butter
½ cup pumpkin
Scant ½ cup brown sugar
½ teaspoon salt

1 teaspoon cinnamon
¼ teaspoon ginger
⅛ teaspoon ground cloves
½ gallon vanilla ice cream,
   softened

Combine the graham cracker crumbs, sugar and butter in a bowl and blend thoroughly. Sprinkle ¾ of the mixture in a 9-inch springform pan. Reserve the remaining ¼ for the topping. • Combine the remaining ingredients and mix well. Pour into the pan and sprinkle with the reserved topping. Freeze.

Mary Doremus

CREPES NORMANDES

Makes 2 dozen

Batter:

⅔ cup flour
1½ tablespoons sugar
4 eggs
Pinch salt
2 tablespoons melted butter

1¾ cups cold milk
1 tablespoon Calvados or
   Cognac
Melted butter or oil

Sift flour into a bowl, making a hole in the center. Combine sugar, eggs, salt and butter. Mix with milk and liqueur and pour into flour mixture. Blend thoroughly and refrigerate for 1 hour. • Heat a small crêpe pan and brush with butter or oil. Using 1½ tablespoons of the batter, make thin crêpes. Thin batter with milk if necessary.

Garniture Normande:

8 apples
3 tablespoons butter
¾ cup sugar

Juice of 1 lemon
¼ cup water

Peel, core and dice apples. Sauté in butter together with sugar, lemon juice and water until tender. Drop 1 tablespoon of apple mixture on each crêpe and roll up. Place crêpes side by side in ovenproof serving dish.

Sauce Sabayon:

5 egg yolks
⅓ cup sugar
1 cup white wine

1 tablespoon Calvados or
   Cognac

Place egg yolks and sugar in double boiler and beat until thick. Remove from heat and stir in the wine and liqueur. Return to heat and beat 5 minutes longer. Pour over crêpes and serve immediately.

Mrs. François de Laboulaye
Wife of the Ambassador of France

HUNGARIAN DESSERT CREPES

10–12 crêpes

Crêpes:

1 cup cold water
1 cup cold milk
4 eggs
½ teaspoon salt

4 tablespoons melted butter
2–3 tablespoons oil
2 cups sifted flour

Put liquids, eggs and salt in a blender or food processor. Add flour and melted butter. Blend well, cover, and refrigerate for at least 2 hours.
• Brush crêpe pan with oil and heat until just beginning to smoke. Pour in ¼ cup batter, tilting pan to lightly film the bottom. Cook the crêpe 1 minute, turn and cook ½ minute more. Repeat until all batter is used, stacking finished crêpes on a plate. Recipe should make 10–12 crêpes.

Sauce and Filling:

8 ounces cream cheese
4 tablespoons butter, softened
⅓ cup sugar

1 teaspoon grated lemon rind
5 tablespoons yellow raisins
1 cup heavy cream

Combine cream cheese, butter, sugar, and lemon rind. Mix in the raisins. Spread some of this mixture on each crêpe and roll up.
• Arrange the filled crêpes in a buttered baking dish, pour on the heavy cream, and bake at 350° for 10 minutes.

Mrs. Stephan M. Minikes

PEANUT BRITTLE

3 cups granulated sugar
1½ cups water
1 cup white corn syrup
3 cups raw peanuts

2 tablespoons baking soda
4 tablespoons butter
1 teaspoon vanilla

Boil sugar, water and syrup until it spins threads. Add the peanuts and stir constantly until syrup turns golden brown. Remove from heat, add remaining ingredients and continue stirring until butter melts. Pour quickly on 2 well buttered, rimmed cookie sheets. As mixture begins to harden around the edges, pull until thin.

Mrs. Jimmy Carter

RUM BALLS   Makes 5 dozen

1   12-ounce box vanilla
    wafers, crumbed
1½ cups powdered sugar
3 tablespoons cocoa

1½ cups chopped pecans
½–1 cup rum
4½ tablespoons white corn
    syrup

Combine all dry ingredients. Mix liquids together and blend into dry mixture. It will be wet and thick. • Refrigerate a minimum of 5 days, then form into balls and roll in powdered sugar. Refrigerate or freeze until needed. (Note: Rum balls can be kept for several months. The flavor improves the longer they are kept.)

Pam Burge

TARTUFI DI CIOCCOLATA (Chocolate Truffles)   10 pieces
"Makes a special holiday gift"

6 ounces semi-sweet chocolate
2 ounces unsweetened
    chocolate
4 teaspoons heavy cream

2 teaspoons rum
3 tablespoons unsalted butter
2 egg yolks, beaten
1 cup ground almonds

Melt the chocolates with the cream and rum in the top of a double boiler. Stir until smooth. Remove from heat. • Stir in butter and beaten egg yolks. Chill mixture until firm (about 3 hours). • Form mixture into small balls (truffles), and roll in ground almonds. • Store in freezer, or refrigerate, until ready to serve. This recipe is easily doubled or tripled.

Mrs. Robert C. Eisele

Cakes

The White House Christmas tree

AMARETTO CAKE

Layer 1:

½ pound unsalted butter
1 cup powdered sugar

½ pound sweet chocolate,
  melted and cooled
1 teaspoon vanilla

Cream the butter, gradually adding the sugar. Beat until light and fluffy. Add the chocolate and vanilla and mix well. • Spread on the bottom of a 9-inch ungreased springform pan. • Chill for 2 hours before adding the next layer.

Layer 2:

½ pound unsalted butter
1 cup powdered sugar

1½ cups ground, blanched
  almonds
1 tablespoon heavy cream

Cream the butter, gradually adding the sugar. Beat until light and fluffy. Add the almonds and cream and mix well. • Spread over the chocolate layer and chill.

Layer 3:

¼ pound sweet chocolate
3 tablespoons Amaretto liqueur
2 tablespoons heavy cream

Melt chocolate in the Amaretto liqueur. Add the cream and spread over the nut layer. Chill. • To serve, carefully run a knife around the pan and remove sides.

Elizabeth Luessenhop

CHESS CAKE

1 box yellow cake mix
  (ignore package directions)
4 large eggs

½ pound softened butter
1 pound powdered sugar
8 ounces cream cheese

Combine the cake mix with 2 eggs and ¼ pound butter. Pat into a greased 9 x 13 inch cake pan. • Mix the powdered sugar with the remaining 2 eggs, ¼ pound butter and the cream cheese. Pour over the batter in the pan. Bake at 350° for about 1 hour. Cake should be golden brown.

Mrs. John K. Walker, Jr.

TEDDIE'S APPLE CAKE

Serves 12

"Moist and delicious"

1½ cups vegetable oil
2 cups sugar
3 eggs
3 cups flour, sifted
1 teaspoon salt
1 teaspoon cinnamon

1 teaspoon baking soda
1 teaspoon vanilla
3 cups peeled, cored and
thickly sliced apples
1 cup chopped walnuts
1 cup raisins

Combine oil and sugar and beat. Add eggs and beat until creamy. Sift together flour, salt, cinnamon and baking soda and stir into batter. Add vanilla and fold in the apples, walnuts and raisins. Turn into a buttered and floured tube pan or Bundt pan and bake at 350° for 1 hour and 15 minutes. Cool in pan before removing.

Mrs. Alpheus W. Jessup

HUNGARIAN ALMOND CAKE

Serves 12

Cake:

6 egg yolks
½ cup sugar
4 ounces sweet chocolate,
melted

¾ cup raisins
⅔ cup ground almonds
9 egg whites

Beat the sugar into the egg yolks, add the melted chocolate and raisins, and beat in the ground almonds. • Beat the egg whites until soft peaks are formed and add them to the almond mixture. Turn into a buttered and floured 9-inch springform pan and bake at 375° for 45 minutes. Cool completely.

Cream:

3 egg yolks
½ cup powdered sugar
4 ounces sweet chocolate

6 ounces unsalted butter,
softened
1 teaspoon instant coffee
1 cup heavy cream, whipped

In the top of a double boiler, over hot but not boiling water, mix the egg yolks, sugar and melted chocolate. Let cool 5 minutes. • Off heat, gradually add the butter and instant coffee. • To assemble, cut the cake into 2 layers, spread the cream evenly on the bottom half, and top with remaining half. Sprinkle with additional powdered sugar and serve with whipped cream.

Michelle Nyirjesy

BIG YELLOW CAKE

Serves 10–12

*"You will need a dozen eggs for this unusual, very high cake
that is rich in flavor."*

8 egg yolks
8 tablespoons water
1½ cups sugar
½ teaspoon vanilla

1½ cups cake flour
12 egg whites
¾ teaspoon cream of tartar
¼ teaspoon salt

Grease and flour a tube pan and add a foil collar around its top for
additional height. • With an electric mixer beat the egg yolks in a
very large bowl, add the water, and continue beating until light,
gradually adding ¾ cup of the sugar. Add in the vanilla and flour and
set aside. • In another bowl, beat the egg whites until frothy. Add
the cream of tartar and salt. Continue beating until egg whites are
stiff, and add the remaining ¾ cup sugar. • Fold the egg whites
carefully into the yolk mixture and pour into the prepared pan.
• Bake at 325° for one hour or until done. Cool.

Yellow Frosting:

1 envelope unflavored gelatine
2 tablespoons water
4 egg yolks

½ cup sugar
¾ cup milk, scalded
1 cup heavy cream, whipped

Dissolve the gelatine in the water and set aside. • Beat the egg
yolks lightly, add the sugar and scalded milk. • Cook the yolk mix-
ture in a saucepan for 3–5 minutes until it lightly coats a spoon. Cool.
Add the gelatine and refrigerate until pudding-like in consistency.
• Combine egg mixture and whipped cream and blend until smooth.
• Spread on cooled cake.

Mrs. John S. Stump

CHOCOLATE MOUSSE CAKE

Serves 12

"Fabulous and well worth the effort"

This recipe has three parts. Both the mousse and the cake can be made a day in advance and kept in the refrigerator overnight. The chocolate cake is pressed into a bowl and filled with chocolate mousse and chilled. Thereafter, the bowl is inverted and the cake unmolded and a chocolate icing applied. The cake is served like a bombe.

Chocolate Mousse:

13½ ounces semi-sweet chocolate

2½ teaspoons unflavored gelatine

3 tablespoons Cognac

1½ cups heavy cream

3 eggs

2 egg whites

1½ tablespoons vanilla

⅛ teaspoon salt

3 tablespoons sugar

Melt the chocolate in a double boiler, slowly. In a separate bowl combine gelatine with Cognac to soften. Separate eggs and beat yolks until thick in a large saucepan. Add cream to yolks. Stir over low heat until mixture begins to thicken. Remove from heat and stir for a minute more. Add the gelatine mixture immediately to the yolk mixture and stir until the gelatine has dissolved. Add the vanilla and then the melted chocolate. • In a separate bowl, beat egg whites until foamy. Add salt and sugar. Beat egg white mixture until stiff. Fold egg white mixture into chocolate mixture. Place in a bowl, cover and chill for 5 hours.

Chocolate Cake:

½ pound unsalted butter

4 ounces unsweetened chocolate

2 cups sugar

3 eggs

1 teaspoon vanilla

½ teaspoon salt

1 cup flour

Use an 11 x 17 inch cookie sheet with an edge at least 1½ inches high. • Preheat oven to 350°. Butter the pan, cut a sheet of wax paper to fit it with 2 inches of overhang at each end and press into pan. Butter and flour the paper. Melt the chocolate and half the butter in a double boiler. Combine other half of the butter with sugar. Beat in the eggs. Add the vanilla and salt. Stir in the warm melted chocolate

Continued

mixture, then gradually add the flour. Beat well. • Spread the batter in the pan and bake for 25 minutes. Do not overcook. It should appear a bit underdone. Let cool in pan for 10 minutes. Take cake out of pan and cool on rack after removing wax paper. Cool 10 minutes more.

Completion:

15 ounces semi-sweet **Whipped cream**
   chocolate
2½ tablespoons butter

Heavily butter and flour a 6-cup bowl with a diameter of 8 inches. Line the bowl with the cake by pressing it gently against the sides and bottom. Do not be concerned if it cracks or breaks but make sure that the bowl is completely lined. Fill the cake lined bowl with mousse, pressing it into the cake and putting remaining cake on the top of the mousse to further press the mousse into the cake. Cover and chill for at least 7 hours or overnight. • After chilling thoroughly, unmold the cake by placing the serving platter on top of the bowl and inverting the bowl. Place hot towels around the bowl and carefully unmold the bombe. It may appear a bit messy at this point. • Melt the chocolate in a double boiler and pour over the bombe, applying as an icing. This will cover all the cracks in the cake and serve to seal the bombe. • Place whipped cream in a pastry tube and apply in a design around the cake on the platter to decorate it and seal the edges of the bombe. Also apply to the top in a decorative pattern. Cake may be refrigerated for 2–3 days. Remove 30 minutes before serving.

The Honorable Barbara S. Thomas

The Hope Diamond, now in the Museum of
Natural History

ORANGE-CHOCOLATE CAKE

Serves 12–14

*"This elegant cake must be prepared
a day before serving"*

Cake:

¼ pound unsalted butter,
  melted
2 eggs
2 cups sugar
2 cups sifted flour
1⅓ cups boiling water

4 ounces semi-sweet chocolate,
  melted
2 teaspoons baking powder
2 teaspoons baking soda
1 teaspoon orange extract

Combine the melted butter, eggs and sugar in a mixing bowl. Beat 2 minutes with an electric mixer. Add the flour and boiling water, a little at a time, beating well after each addition. Beat 2 minutes longer. Add remaining ingredients and beat again for 2 minutes. • Pour the batter into 2 buttered and floured 9-inch cake pans and bake at 325° for 50 minutes. Cool 10 minutes in the pans, then turn out and cool completely.

Filling:

¼ pound unsalted butter,
  softened
1 pound powdered
  sugar

8 ounces semi-sweet chocolate,
  melted
3 tablespoons orange juice
¾ teaspoon orange extract

Combine all ingredients in a mixing bowl and beat with an electric mixer until creamy and well blended.

Frosting and Assembly:

¼ pound unsalted butter,
  softened
1 pound powdered sugar
3 tablespoons orange juice

2 tablespoons freshly grated
  orange peel
½ teaspoon orange extract

Combine all ingredients in a mixing bowl and beat with an electric mixer until creamy and well blended. • Slice each cake in half to make 4 layers. Place 1 layer on a serving plate and spread with ⅓ of the filling. Repeat this procedure with 2 more cake layers. Place the last cake layer on top and chill cake until set before frosting. Store the cake, covered with foil, for 1 day in the refrigerator before serving.

Betty Taylor

CHOCOLATE MOUSSE CHEESECAKE   Serves 12

Crust:

1   8½-ounce package
    chocolate wafers
¼ pound butter, melted

Roll wafers to fine crumbs. Combine with melted butter and press onto the bottom of a 9-inch springform pan.

Filling:

12 ounces semi-sweet chocolate   1½ teaspoons vanilla
1 pound cream cheese   3 eggs, separated
¾ cup sugar   1 cup heavy cream, whipped

Melt chocolate over low heat. Set aside to cool. • Combine cream cheese, ½ cup sugar and vanilla. Stir in egg yolks and the cooled chocolate. • Beat egg whites until soft peaks form. Add ¼ cup sugar and beat until stiff. • Into the chocolate mixture, gently fold egg whites and whipped cream. Pour into pan on top of crust.

Decoration:

1 cup heavy cream, whipped
Grated chocolate

Spread whipped cream on top and decorate with grated chocolate. Freeze. (Note: Remove from freezer ½ hour before serving.)

Hope Price

CHOCOLATE ICE BOX CAKE   Serves 12–16

36 ladyfingers   8 egg yolks, beaten
8 ounces unsweetened   10 egg whites
    chocolate   1 cup heavy cream, whipped
1 cup milk   Chocolate curls, or grated
1 cup sugar   chocolate for garnish

Line the bottom of a springform pan with ladyfinger halves. • Melt the chocolate with the milk and sugar. Let cool slightly and stir in the beaten egg yolks. • Beat the egg whites until stiff but not dry. Fold them into the chocolate mixture. Pour ½ over the ladyfingers. Arrange another layer of ladyfingers on top and pour the remaining chocolate mixture over them. Refrigerate overnight. • To serve, remove the cake from the pan and place it on a serving dish. Spread whipped cream over the top and garnish with chocolate curls or grated chocolate.

Margie Davis

CHOCOLATE CHEESECAKE

Serves 10–12

Crust:

1 cup chocolate wafer crumbs ½ teaspoon cinnamon
¼ cup melted butter

Mix the crust ingredients together and press them into a 9-inch spring-form pan. Set aside and prepare the filling.

Cheesecake:

1½ pounds cream cheese,
  softened
1 cup sour cream
2 tablespoons heavy cream
1 cup sugar

3 large eggs
8 ounces semi-sweet chocolate
½ cup Bailey's Irish Cream
  or Kahlua
2 teaspoons vanilla

Beat the cream cheese and sour cream together until light and smooth. Add the heavy cream and blend well. Add the sugar, beating until fluffy. At low speed, add the eggs, one at a time, blending well after each addition. • Melt the chocolate in the top of a double boiler. Cool slightly. Gradually stir in the liqueur and add slowly to the cream cheese mixture. Stir in the vanilla. Pour this filling into the crust and bake at 325° for 50 minutes. Turn off the oven and leave the cheesecake inside with oven door ajar for 1 hour. Remove from oven, cool to room temperature and refrigerate. Chill overnight before serving.

Mrs. Melvin Gelman

CHOCOLATE DATE CAKE

Serves 8–10

1 cup chopped dates
1 teaspoon baking soda
½ cup butter
1 cup plus 4 tablespoons sugar
2 eggs

1⅔ cups flour
1 tablespoon cocoa
½ teaspoon salt
6 ounces chocolate chips
1 cup chopped nuts

Pour one cup boiling water over the dates, add the baking soda and set aside. • Cream the butter with one cup of the sugar. Beat in the eggs. • Sift together flour, cocoa and salt. • Combine all ingredients from previous steps and pour into a greased 8 x 12 inch pan. • Mix together the chocolate chips, 4 tablespoons sugar and one cup chopped nuts. Sprinkle over the cake. • Bake at 325° for 45–60 minutes.

Mrs. Edward Zorinsky
Wife of the Senator from Nebraska

CHOCOLATE CAKE WITHOUT FLOUR   Serves 10

12 ounces semi-sweet
   chocolate
½ pound butter
8 tablespoons sugar
4 eggs, separated

¾–1 cup ground almonds
   or pecans
1 tablespoon water
Nut halves for garnish

Melt 8 ounces of the chocolate with 12 tablespoons of the butter. Beat in the egg yolks, one at a time. Blend in the ground nuts. • Beat the egg whites, adding the sugar gradually. Fold into the chocolate mixture. Grease a springform pan and line it with wax paper. Pour in the batter and bake the cake at 350° for 40–50 minutes. Cool and remove cake to a serving dish. • Melt the remaining 4 ounces of chocolate with the remaining 4 tablespoons butter and 1 tablespoon water. Glaze the cooled cake with this mixture and garnish with the nut halves. Refrigerate and serve cold.

Mrs. Ernest G. Rafey

THUNDERBOLT KRAUT CHOCOLATE CAKE Serves 10–12
"Favorite of Wagnerites"

⅔ cup butter
1½ cups sugar
3 eggs
1 teaspoon vanilla
1 cup water
½ cup unsweetened cocoa
   powder

2¼ cups sifted all-purpose
   flour
1 teaspoon baking powder
1 teaspoon baking soda
¼ teaspoon salt
⅔ cups sauerkraut, rinsed,
   drained and chopped

Cream the butter and sugar. Beat in the eggs and vanilla. • Sift together the dry ingredients and add them alternately with the water to the egg mixture. Stir in the sauerkraut. Turn the mixture into 2 greased and floured 8-inch round or square pans. Bake at 350° for 30 minutes or until done. Frost as desired.

Meredith A. Gonyea

CHOCOLATE TORTE VENTANA

Serves 12–14

"Outrageously rich."

Cake:

5 eggs
1 cup sugar
1 cup butter
3 ounces semi-sweet chocolate

3 ounces unsweetened
   chocolate
¼ cup cornstarch, sifted
½ teaspoon vanilla
3 tablespoons orange liqueur

Beat the eggs and sugar over hot water in the top of a double boiler until very light and fluffy. Remove from heat. • Melt the butter and skim off the foam. Return to heat, add chocolates and melt. Stir in the vanilla and orange liqueur. • Beat the sifted cornstarch into the egg mixture at low speed to blend thoroughly. • Fold the chocolate mixture into the egg mixture, taking care not to overmix. • Spoon into a greased and floured 10-inch springform pan. Bake at 325° for 20–25 minutes. Torte will pull away from sides of pan when done but knife inserted into its center will not come out clean. Cool in pan before removing ring.

Glaze:

6½ ounces semi-sweet
   chocolate
⅓ cup heavy cream

2 tablespoons unsalted butter
Ground or chopped almonds,
   pistachios or hazelnuts

Melt the chocolate and butter with the cream. Spoon over baked torte and decorate with ground or chopped nuts. Chill completely before serving.

Marian Burros

Scene from the Cherry Blossom Festival

CHOCOLATE ALMOND CHEESECAKE   Serves 10–12

1½ cups chocolate wafer crumbs
1 cup blanched almonds, toasted
  and chopped
6 tablespoons butter, softened
1⅓ cups sugar

1½ pounds cream cheese,
  softened
4 eggs
⅓ cup heavy cream
¼ cup Amaretto
1 teaspoon vanilla

Combine the chocolate wafer crumbs, chopped almonds, butter and ⅓ cup of the sugar and press this mixture into the bottom of a buttered 9½-inch springform pan. • In a large bowl, cream the remaining 1 cup sugar and the cream cheese with an electric mixer. Beat in the eggs, one at a time, blending well after each addition. Add the heavy cream, Amaretto and vanilla and beat until the mixture is light. Pour into the prepared pan and bake at 350° for 45 minutes. Cool to room temperature before refrigerating. Chill overnight before removing from pan to serve.

Mrs. John R. Lindsay

CLEVELAND SPICE CAKE   Serves 8–10

"A nice coffee cake or dessert"

3 cups flour
2 cups sugar
½ pound butter
2 tablespoons cocoa
1 teaspoon cinnamon

2 teaspoons baking soda
1 cup chopped nuts, optional
1 cup chopped dates, optional
2 cups buttermilk

Mix the flour and sugar and cut in the butter until mixture is crumbly. Remove ½ cup of mixture and set aside for topping. Add remaining ingredients in the order given. Stir until well blended. Pour into a greased 9 x 13 inch baking dish. Sprinkle reserved crumbs evenly over the top and bake 50–60 minutes at 350°. (Note: Recipe may be halved. Use an 8 x 8 inch pan with ¼ cup crumb topping and bake 40–50 minutes.)

Mrs. Robert Ketchand

CHEESECAKE

Serves 10–12

Crust:

1½ cups graham cracker crumbs
¼ cup powdered sugar
6 tablespoons melted butter

Blend all ingredients thoroughly and press into a springform pan. Crust should reach halfway up the sides.

Bottom filling:

1 pound cream cheese
½ cup sugar

2 large eggs
¾ teaspoon vanilla

With all ingredients at room temperature, use an electric mixer to beat them together until smooth, 2–3 minutes. Pour into crust and smooth to form an even layer. Bake at 375° for 20 minutes. Cool for 15 minutes. Reset oven to 475° while preparing the top filling.

Top filling:

1 pint sour cream
¼ cup sugar
1 teaspoon vanilla

Mix all ingredients until well blended. Spread evenly and gently over the cheesecake. Bake at 475° for 10 minutes. Cake will appear thin and runny but will set as it cools. Chill 5–6 hours. When ready to serve, loosen edges and remove sides of pan.

Brigid Radford

POUND CAKE

Serves 10–12

*"This is an old Truman recipe.
I personally think it needs more butter!"*

1 pound sugar (2 cups)
1 pound flour (4 cups)
¾ pound butter

1½ teaspoons lemon extract
9 egg yolks, beaten
9 egg whites, beaten

Combine first 5 ingredients and stir until thoroughly blended. Gently fold in egg whites. Bake in a buttered and floured tube pan for 1 hour or until cake springs back when pressed. Top with a white icing and nut halves.

Mrs. Harry S. Truman

BROWN SUGAR POUND CAKE   Serves 12–16

"From the 'Today' show"

½ pound butter
½ cup shortening
5 eggs
1 pound plus 1 cup light brown
  sugar

3½ cups flour
½ teaspoon baking powder
1 cup milk

Begin with all ingredients at room temperature. • Cream together butter and shortening. Add the eggs, one at a time, creaming after each. Stir in the light brown sugar. • Sift together the flour and baking powder and add alternately with milk to the sugar mixture. • Bake in greased and floured tube pan for 1¼–1½ hours at 325°.

Frosting:

1 cup chopped pecans
¼ pound butter

1 pound powdered sugar
Milk to thin

In a heavy saucepan, brown the pecans in the butter. Let cool, then add powdered sugar. Stir in enough milk to thin the mixture to spreading consistency. Spread on top of cake, allowing it to drip down sides and center.

Willard Scott

SOUR CREAM POUND CAKE   Serves 12–16

"Authentic, old-fashioned Southern pound cake"

½ pound butter, softened
3 cups sugar
6 eggs, separated

3 cups cake flour
¼ teaspoon baking soda
1 cup sour cream

Cream butter and sugar with an electric mixer, 12–15 minutes. Add yolks, one at a time, mixing well after each addition. • Sift soda and flour, then sift 3 times more. Add flour and sour cream alternately to creamed butter mixture, (use 4 flour additions and 3 sour cream additions, starting and ending with flour). • Beat egg whites until stiff and fold into batter. Bake in a greased and floured tube pan at 300° for 1½ hours. Let stand 10–15 minutes, remove from pan and cool on a wire rack.

Mrs. Williamson S. Stuckey, Jr.

Octagon House

HARVEST TORTE

Serves 8

2 eggs
1½ cups sugar
4 tablespoons flour
2 teaspoons baking
  powder
¼ teaspoon salt

1 cup chopped pecans
1 cup apples, peeled and chopped
2 teaspoons vanilla
Whipped cream or vanilla
  ice cream

With an electric mixer, beat eggs and sugar together until very smooth. • Combine flour, baking powder and salt. Stir into egg mixture. Add nuts, apples and vanilla. Turn into a greased glass pie plate and bake at 350° for 30 minutes. Serve warm or cold with whipped cream or vanilla ice cream.

Mrs. Warwick M. Carter

HAZELNUT TORTE Serves 8

"Subtle and terrific"

Cake:

4 eggs
¾ cup sugar

2 cups hazelnuts ground, but
not pulverized

Preheat oven to 375 °. Beat egg yolks with sugar until light and creamy. Fold in nuts. Beat egg whites until firm and gently fold into mixture. Bake in a well greased 10 inch springform pan for 30–45 minutes. Turn oven off but leave cake inside with door open until cool. • Release from pan.

Topping:

1 pint heavy cream
½ teaspoon vanilla

1 teaspoon instant coffee
Nuts to decorate

Beat cream, add vanilla and instant coffee. Cover cake generously and finish with nuts to decorate. (Note: Cake will probably sink in the middle as it cools. Don't worry, the beautiful tan whipped cream will cover all errors.)

Mrs. Roger Mudd

NO-BAKE MOCHA RUMCAKE Serves 8–10

"Murder on your hips, but worth it!"

2 dozen ladyfingers
1 cup milk
1 cup rum
1 pound unsalted butter,
  softened
1 cup powdered sugar

1 tablespoon instant coffee
1 pint heavy cream, whipped
  with sugar to taste
Chopped nuts
Grated chocolate for
  decoration

Dip ladyfingers in mixture of milk and rum. Arrange a layer, pressed together, in the bottom of a greased springform pan. • Cream butter and sugar and add instant coffee. Spread ½-inch thick over ladyfingers. Add a second layer of ladyfingers and spread with another ½-inch layer of butter mixture. Repeat this procedure until the cake is of desired height, ending with the butter mixture. Chill overnight. • Whip cream with a small amount of powdered sugar to taste and spread over the top and sides of cake. Decorate with nuts and grated chocolate.

Mrs. Charles J. DiBona

ORANGE ALMOND CAKE   Serves 6

4 eggs, separated
1 cup sugar
Pinch salt
1 cup fresh bread crumbs
Juice of 3 oranges
Grated rind of 2 oranges

1 cup freshly ground almonds
1 tablespoon Curaçao
  or Grand Marnier
½–1 cup heavy cream,
  whipped

Beat the egg yolks with ¾ cup sugar and salt until pale and light.
• Combine bread crumbs, orange juice, orange rind and ¾ cup
almonds. Add to the egg yolk mixture with the liqueur. • Beat the
egg whites until stiff and fold in. Pour into a buttered 8-inch square
cake tin or springform pan and bake at 350° for 35-40 minutes. Cool
the cake in the pan, then carefully turn it out onto a serving dish.
Cover it with whipped cream and chill. • Oil a cookie sheet and
spread the remaining ¼ cup almonds on it. Boil the ¼ cup sugar in 1
tablespoon water until the sugar caramelizes. Pour over the almonds
and let stand to cool and harden. Break the hardened almond praline
with a rolling pin and garnish the cake with some of the bits. Any
remaining praline is easily stored for weeks for use on plain ice cream.

Anne Green

PRUNE CAKE   Serves 12

"A wonderful excuse to have a tea."

12 ounces pitted prunes
1 teaspoon grated lemon
  rind
2 cups flour
1 teaspoon baking powder
1 teaspoon baking soda
½ teaspoon salt
½ pound soft butter

1 cup sugar
2 eggs
1 cup sour cream or plain yogurt
1 teaspoon vanilla
⅓ cup brown sugar, packed
1 tablespoon cinnamon
½ cup chopped walnuts

Chop the prunes coarsely and add the lemon rind. • Sift together
the flour, baking powder, baking soda and salt. Remove ¼ cup and toss
with the prunes. Set them aside. • Cream the butter and sugar until
fluffy. Beat in the eggs one at a time. Beat in the flour mixture,
alternating with the sour cream and vanilla. Fold in the prunes.
• In a small bowl, combine the brown sugar, cinnamon, and
nuts. • Sprinkle half of the nut mixture into a well greased and
floured 9 inch tube pan. Add half the batter, sprinkle with remaining
nut mixture and cover with the rest of the batter. • Bake at
350° for 55 minutes. Cool the cake on a rack for 10 minutes before
removing from the pan.

Mrs. Paul F. Petrus

LANE CAKE

Serves 10–12

"A Southern favorite"

1 cup shortening
2 cups sugar
1 teaspoon salt
3 heaping cups flour
1 cup milk

2 teaspoons baking powder
6 egg whites
1 teaspoon vanilla
1 teaspoon lemon extract

Cream shortening, sugar and salt. • Sift the flour 3 times. To the creamed mixture, gradually add 2 cups flour and the milk. Add the baking powder to the last cup of flour and sift into the batter. Mix well, adding the vanilla and lemon flavoring. • Beat the egg whites until stiff and fold gently into the batter. Pour into 3 greased and floured 8-inch cake pans and bake at 375° for 12–15 minutes.

Icing:

8 egg yolks
1 cup sugar
½ cup butter
1 cup fresh grated coconut

1½ cups walnuts, coarsely
   chopped
1 cup raisins, ground
½ cup sweet wine or bourbon

Beat egg yolks well. Place in top of a double boiler. Add the sugar and butter and cook until thickened enough to coat the back of a wooden spoon. Mix the coconut, walnuts and raisins with the wine or bourbon. Add this to the yolk and sugar mixture and remove from heat. When cool, spread on cake and between layers.

Mrs. Richard T. Wright

A Metro station

SICILIAN CAKE

Serves 10–12

2 pounds ricotta cheese
1½ cups sugar
1 teaspoon vanilla
¼ cup white Crème de Cacao
¼ cup candied fruit

¼ cup tiny chocolate bits
2½ dozen ladyfingers
1 cup heavy cream, whipped,
    optional
Candied cherries for garnish

Combine the ricotta cheese, sugar, vanilla and Crème de Cacao in a mixing bowl. Beat at medium speed with an electric mixer for 10 minutes. Fold in the candied fruit and chocolate bits. • Line the sides and bottom of a 9-inch springform pan or bundt pan with ladyfingers. Pour in ⅓ of the ricotta mixture. Add another layer of ladyfingers, another ⅓ of the ricotta mixture and repeat the layers again. End with a layer of ladyfingers. Refrigerate 1–2 days before unmolding to serve. Garnish with whipped cream if desired and candied cherries.

Mrs. Delano King Boynton

SNOWBALL CAKE

Serves 8–10

"Great for a child's birthday party."

2 envelopes unflavored
    gelatine
¼ cup cold water
1 cup boiling water
1   6-ounce can frozen orange
    juice
1 cup crushed pineapple

1 cup sugar
Juice of 1 lemon
½ teaspoon salt
2 pints heavy cream
1 Angel Food cake (see note)
Shredded coconut

Soften the gelatine in the cold water, then add boiling water and stir until dissolved. • Dilute the frozen orange juice with 9 ounces of water. Add 1 cup of the juice to the gelatine along with the pineapple, sugar, lemon and salt. Mix well and chill. When mixture is partially set, stir in 1 pint heavy cream. • Roll the crust off the Angel Food cake and tear the cake into bite-sized pieces. • Line a large, round mixing bowl with wax paper. Alternate layers of cake and filling in the bowl. Chill overnight, or at least 8 hours. • 1 or 2 hours before serving, turn cake out on a cake plate. Whip the remaining pint of cream, sweetened slightly, if desired, and frost the cake. Sprinkle with coconut. (Note: It is best to use a commercially baked cake as they tend to have less crust.)

Kathleen Maxa

HUNGARIAN STRAWBERRY SPONGE CAKE   Serves 10-12

6 eggs, separated	3 pints fresh strawberries
1 cup sugar	(or more)
1½ teaspoons vanilla	½ cup powdered sugar
1 cup flour	2 cups heavy cream
½ teaspoon baking soda	2–3 tablespoons sugar

Butter and flour a round, 10-inch, false bottom cake pan. • Beat egg yolks with ⅔ cup sugar and vanilla until fluffy. Beat egg whites until soft peaks form, then add the remaining ⅓ cup sugar. Beat until stiff and fold into yolk mixture, adding the flour and baking soda. Pour batter into cake pan and bake at 350° for about 45 minutes. Cool cake in pan. Invert on a cake plate and cut into 3 layers. • Wash the strawberries and remove the hulls. Pat dry. Mash 1 pint of berries and add powdered sugar. Mix well and spread on each layer of cake. Slice the remaining berries. • Whip cream, sweetened with the sugar. Fold sliced berries into the cream and spread generously on the 3 layers. Stack the layers and use any remaining berry-cream mixture on top.

Mrs. Richard Landfield

The Library of Congress

In the Hirshhorn Sculpture Garden

UGLY DUCKLING CAKE   Serves 12–14

"Trust us . . . it grows up to a lovely, moist cake"

1 package yellow cake mix
1 package lemon pudding mix
  (not instant)
4 eggs
½ cup oil
1 17-ounce can fruit cocktail

2½ cups coconut
½ cup brown sugar
½ cup chopped pecans
½ cup sugar
½ cup evaporated milk

Combine the cake mix, pudding mix, eggs, oil, fruit cocktail and 1 cup of coconut in a mixing bowl. Beat the mixture at medium speed with an electric mixer for 4 minutes and turn it into a 9 x 13 inch baking pan. • Mix the brown sugar and pecans together and spread evenly over the batter in the pan. Bake the cake at 325° for 45 minutes. • While cake is baking, combine the sugar, evaporated milk and remaining 1½ cups coconut. Spread this topping over the baked cake while it is still warm.

Mrs. Willim E. Naylor, Jr.

STRAWBERRY TORTE   Serves 10

"Impressive-looking, delicious, and easy to prepare."

Cake:

¼ cup butter at room
   temperature
½ cup sugar
4 egg yolks
½ teaspoon vanilla
1 cup flour
2 teaspoons baking soda
4–6 tablespoons heavy cream

Meringue, Filling, and Garnish:

4 egg whites
1 cup sugar
½ teaspoon vanilla
1 pint ripe strawberries
1½ cups heavy cream
Powdered sugar

Combine all ingredients for cake and beat until smooth. (May be done in a food processor.) Spread batter in 2 greased and floured 8–9 inch false bottom cake pans. • Beat egg whites until stiff. Gradually add sugar and vanilla and spread meringue mixture over unbaked batter mixture. Bake in a preheated 300° oven for 30 minutes. Cool. • Whip the cream until very stiff. Crush 4 strawberries sweetened with sugar, and fold into the whipped cream. • To assemble, place one torte meringue side down on serving dish, cover with whipped cream filling and top with second torte, meringue side up. Dust with powdered sugar and garnish top and edge with remaining whole strawberries.

Mrs. Stephan M. Minikes

WALNUT CAKE   Serves 8

4 egg yolks
1 cup sugar
1 cup chopped walnuts
6 unsalted Uneeda biscuits,
   chopped

1 teaspoon baking powder
1 teaspoon vanilla
4 egg whites
1 cup heavy cream, whipped

Beat the egg yolks with the sugar until light and fluffy. Add the walnuts, biscuits, baking powder and vanilla and stir until well blended and stiff. • Beat the egg whites until stiff and fold gently into the yolk mixture. Pour the batter into 2 buttered cake pans. Bake at 350° for 20 minutes. Cool the cake layers. Spread the bottom layer with whipped cream, add the top cake layer and spread it with the remaining whipped cream.

Mrs. Paul F. Petrus

254

Cookies

The Victorian Bandstand

SWEDISH KNÄCKFLARN   Makes 1 dozen

"A traditional Swedish cookie"

1 cup sugar	1 cup rolled oats
½ cup light cream	1 cup white flour
¼ cup molasses	½ teaspoon baking powder
¼ pound butter	½ tablespoon vanilla sugar

Mix all ingredients well. Using a teaspoon, dot cookie dough onto a well greased and floured cookie sheet. This should yield approximately 24 cookies. Bake at 350° for 10–12 minutes.

Chocolate cream filling:

4 tablespoons butter	½ tablespoon powdered sugar
½ tablespoon cocoa powder	

Melt all ingredients together in the top of a double boiler. When the cookies have cooled, spread the filling on 1 cookie and place another on top, pressing them together gently. You will have approximately 1 dozen sandwiched cookies. (Note: A variation is to dip each single cookie in the melted chocolate to cover ½ of it, yielding 24 single cookies.)

Mrs. Charles J. DiBona

ALMOND COOKIES   Makes 13 dozen

2½ cups shortening
2 cups sugar
2 eggs
1 teaspoon almond extract

6 cups flour
1½ teaspoons baking soda
1 teaspoon salt
Red food coloring

Cream the shortening and sugar. • Add eggs, one at a time, and the almond extract. • Sift together the flour, baking soda and salt and add to moist ingredients. • Roll batter into walnut-sized balls and place on an ungreased cookie sheet. With your thumb, press each ball to make a round indentation in the center. Using a Q-tip and red food coloring, paint a line around sides of indentation. Bake at 350° for 20 minutes, until very lightly browned. (Note: The red circle is a good luck symbol of Hawaii where Mrs. Meisch spent much of her childhood.)

Mrs. Adrien Meisch
Wife of the Ambassador
of Luxembourg

CHOCOLATE CHIP COOKIES   Makes 4 dozen

"As good as money in the bank"

¾ cup brown and white sugar, mixed
¼ pound butter
1 egg
½ teaspoon vanilla

1 cup flour
1 cup Rice Krispies
½ cup chopped walnuts
6 ounces chocolate chips

Mix sugar and butter together until soft and smooth. Beat in egg and vanilla. Mix in other 4 ingredients and drop by teaspoons onto cookie sheet. • Bake in 350° oven for approximately 8 minutes. Do not overcook.

Mrs. Arthur F. Burns

GRAHAM CRACKER COOKIES   Makes 4 dozen

48 graham crackers
½ pound butter

1 cup dark brown sugar
2½ ounces chopped pecans

Lay graham crackers, sides touching, on a rimmed baking sheet. • Melt the butter over medium heat and add the sugar. Bring to a boil, stirring constantly for 1–2 minutes. • Stir in pecans and pour over graham crackers, spreading evenly to cover all of them. • Bake at 350° for 12 minutes. • Remove cookies from baking sheet immediately, place on aluminum foil and separate.

Mrs. John E. Pflieger

CRISP COCONUT COOKIES   Makes 3 dozen

½ cup butter
½ cup white sugar
½ cup brown sugar
1 egg, beaten
1 teaspoon vanilla
1 cup flour

½ teaspoon baking soda
½ teaspoon baking powder
½ teaspoon salt
1 cup crushed Rice Krispies
   or cornflakes
1 cup shredded coconut

Cream the butter and sugars. Add egg and vanilla. Stir in the flour, baking soda, baking powder and salt. Blend in the Rice Krispies and coconut. • Drop batter by teaspoons on a buttered cookie sheet. Flatten each cookie. • Bake at 325° for 10–12 minutes.

Mrs. Robert W. Oliver

FRYING PAN COOKIES   Makes about 3 dozen

¼ pound butter
1 cup sugar
2 beaten eggs
1½ cups chopped dates

1 teaspoon vanilla
3½ cups Rice Krispies
1   3½-ounce can flaked
   coconut

Melt the butter. Cool it and then add the sugar, beaten eggs, dates, and vanilla. Cook this mixture in a large skillet over medium low heat for 15 minutes, stirring constantly. Remove from heat and cool completely, preferably overnight. • In a large bowl, combine the date mixture and the Rice Krispies. Turn into 1-inch balls and roll each in the coconut. Dry the cookies for one hour before storing or freezing.

Mrs. Charles Swan Weber

KIPFEL   Makes 2-3 dozen

½ pound butter
2 cups flour
½ pound cream cheese

¼ teaspoon salt
Jam or marmalade

Cut the softened butter into small pieces and mix with the flour until well blended. Add the cream cheese and salt. Mix thoroughly. Refrigerate until dough is firm. • Roll out the dough and cut into 3-inch squares. Place a teaspoon of jam or marmalade in the center of each. Fold the corners to the center and press together. Bake at 400° until lightly browned.

Mrs. John Pflieger

MOCHA-CREAM MERINGUE COOKIES   Makes 4 dozen

3 egg whites
Pinch of salt
½ teaspoon vanilla

1 cup sugar
Powdered sugar

In the small bowl of an electric mixer, beat the egg whites until they are foamy. Add salt and beat the whites for about 30 seconds. Add the vanilla and beat for 30 seconds more. Gradually sprinkle in the sugar and beat for about 5 more minutes, until very stiff. • Grease 3 baking sheets, line with wax paper, and dust wax paper with powdered sugar. • Drop walnut-sized portions of the beaten egg white onto the baking sheets and bake at 200° for about 2 hours. • Let cool.

Filling:

¼ pound butter, softened
¾ cup powdered sugar

1½ teaspoons instant coffee
     dissolved in 1½ teaspoons
     boiling water

Mix all ingredients together. • Sandwich the meringues together with the filling.

Carla Berts

Home of Clara Barton, founder of the
American Red Cross

OATMEAL-CHOCOLATE CHIP COOKIES 7 dozen

¾ cup brown sugar
¾ cup white sugar
½ pound butter, room
  temperature
2 eggs
1½ cups flour
2 cups quick-cooking oatmeal
½ teaspoon salt

1 teaspoon baking soda
  dissolved in 1 teaspoon hot
  water
1 teaspoon vanilla
1 cup chopped walnuts
12 ounces chocolate chips
½–¾ cup coconut

Cream the butter and sugars. Add remaining ingredients and mix well. Form into small balls on cookie sheets. Bake at 350° for 10–12 minutes.

Mrs. Stephan M. Minikes

LILLY'S PEANUT BUTTER COOKIES 3 dozen

½ cup butter
½ cup white sugar
½ cup brown sugar
1 egg
½ teaspoon vanilla

¾ cup chunky peanut butter
¼ teaspoon salt
2 cups flour, sifted
½ teaspoon baking soda

Cream the butter and sugar together. Beat in the eggs, vanilla, peanut butter and salt. • Sift flour with the baking soda. Stir into the peanut butter mixture. • Form the cookie dough into small balls on greased cookie sheet and flatten with a fork. • Bake at 425° for 8 to 10 minutes.

Mrs. W. Walker Lewis, III

QUEEN LACE COOKIES 2–3 dozen (depending on size)

6 tablespoons margarine
3 tablespoons white Karo syrup
¼ tablespoon baking powder
½ cup flour

½ cup sugar
½ cup oats
1 tablespoon vanilla
2 tablespoons cream

Mix together all ingredients. Place only 3 in a row on ungreased cookie sheet. Bake in 350° oven for 5–7 minutes. Remove from sheet while still quite warm. (If they crumble, warm again.) Repeat until dough is all used. For variety, try adding chocolate chips to mix before cooking.

Renee Zlotnick Kraft

APRICOT BARS
Makes 2 dozen

1 cup dried apricots
1 cup boiling water
½ cup butter
¼ cup sugar
1⅓ cups flour
1 cup light brown sugar

2 eggs
¼ teaspoon salt
½ teaspoon baking powder
½ teaspoon vanilla
½ cup pecans

Simmer the apricots for 10 minutes in the boiling water. Drain, reserving the liquid. When the apricots have cooled, chop and set aside.
• Combine the butter, sugar and 1 cup flour and pack in a buttered 9-inch square pan. Bake at 300° for 15 minutes. • Cream the sugar with the eggs. Beat in the remaining flour, apricot cooking liquid, salt, baking powder and vanilla. Stir in the chopped apricots and pecans. Pour this mixture over the crust and bake an additional 30 minutes.

Sandra Foulis

BROWNIES
Makes 2 dozen

2 cups sugar
1 cup butter
1½ cups flour
½ teaspoon salt

4 eggs
2 teaspoons vanilla
4 squares chocolate, melted
1 cup nuts, chopped

Combine all ingredients and place in a well buttered 9 x 11 inch baking pan. Bake at 350° for 40–50 minutes.

Mrs. Harry S. Truman

SHORTBREAD
Makes about 16 pieces

"From Scotland to you"

Generous ⅓ cup butter
   (no substitutes)
Scant ¼ cup sugar

1½ cups flour
Rind of 1 lemon, grated
1 egg yolk

Cream the butter and sugar. Mix in the flour, lemon rind and egg yolk until the dough forms a ball. Pat the dough into a sheet about ½ inch thick. Prick it all over with a fork and cut it into little triangles or squares. Bake on a cookie sheet at 350° until golden brown, about 8–10 minutes.

Mrs. W. Walker Lewis III

Pies

Mount Vernon

BUTTERSCOTCH PIE   Serves 6

1 baked 9-inch pie crust   3 cups evaporated milk
1 cup brown sugar   6 tablespoons flour
3 tablespoons shortening   2 eggs, separated
4 tablespoons cream   2 tablespoons sugar

In a heavy skillet, cook brown sugar, shortening and cream until thick
and brown. The more it is browned the stronger the butterscotch
taste. • Mix together the evaporated milk, flour and egg yolks. Add
to the mixture in the skillet, stirring constantly. Cook until thick and
pour into baked pie crust. • Beat egg whites until stiff. Add sugar
and blend well. Gently place on top of pie and brown in 425° oven.
Chill. Serve pie very cold.

Vivien Woofter

KEY LIME PIE   Serves 6

1   9-inch baked pie shell or   1   15-ounce can condensed milk
    graham cracker shell   1 cup heavy cream
6 egg yolks
½ cup fresh lime juice,
    or ¼ cup fresh lemon and
    ¼ cup fresh lime juice

Combine egg yolks, lime juice and condensed milk. Beat thoroughly
and let stand a few minutes. • Pour into pie shell and refrigerate.
• Just before serving, top with whipped cream. Do not freeze.

Jenne W. Jones

KIWI TART   2   9-inch tarts

*"A versatile recipe that is easily adapted to the season
by varying the fruit and using a complementary
jam for the glaze."*

Nut Crust:

½ pound unsalted butter   1 egg, beaten
⅓ cup sugar   1 teaspoon grated lemon rind
3 cups flour   1 teaspoon vanilla
10 ounces walnuts, chopped fine

To make the crust, cream the butter and sugar with an electric mixer
or food processor. Add flour, walnuts, egg, lemon rind and vanilla. Mix
well until dough holds together and divide in half. • Lightly butter
2 9-inch flan rings and place on greased cookie sheet. Press nut crust
evenly into bottom and sides of flan casing with your fingers.
• Bake 10–12 minutes at 350°.

Filling:

½ packet unflavored gelatine   10–12 ripe kiwi fruit, peeled
3 tablespoons Cognac   and sliced crosswise about
    or Grand Marnier   ⅛ inch thick
½ cup apricot jam

Make the apricot glaze by softening the gelatine in the liqueur in a
small saucepan. Add the apricot jam and heat gently until the mixture
is smooth and clear. Cool slightly. • Brush each tart shell with the
glaze and arrange fruit slices in the shells. Brush with more glaze and
chill until ready to serve. (Note: Crust may be successfully frozen, but
do not freeze finished tart.)

Kathy Luhn

JANIE'S PEANUT ICE CREAM PIE   Serves 8

1½ cups graham cracker
  crumbs
1¼ cups sifted powdered
  sugar
6 tablespoons melted butter
1 quart vanilla ice cream,
  softened

¼–½ cup melted crunchy
  peanut butter
4 egg whites, room
  temperature
1 teaspoon vanilla
⅛ teaspoon cream of tartar

Combine the graham cracker crumbs, ¼ cup powdered sugar and melted butter. Blend thoroughly and pat into a 9-inch pie pan to form the crust. • Mix the softened ice cream and melted peanut butter and spread evenly in graham cracker crust. Freeze hard. • Just prior to serving, make a meringue topping for the pie. Begin with the egg whites at room temperature. Beat with an electric mixer until foamy. Add vanilla and cream of tartar. Continuing to beat, add 1 cup powdered sugar, a spoonful at a time, until the mixture stands in stiff peaks. Place meringue on top of frozen pie and quickly brown in a 450° oven for 5 minutes or until delicately browned. Serve immediately.

Mrs. Marvin L. Stone

PERFECT PEACH PIE   Serves 6

1 baked 9-inch pie shell
6–8 fresh peaches
1 teaspoon lemon juice
1 tablespoon sugar
1 tablespoon cornstarch
2 tablespoons butter

Topping:
¾ cup sugar
1 cup flour
¼ pound butter, softened
1 teaspoon cinnamon
1 cup heavy cream, whipped
  (optional)

Peel and slice the peaches. Place in a bowl and sprinkle with lemon juice, sugar and cornstarch. Stir gently and turn into the baked pie shell. Dot with butter. • Make a topping by mixing the sugar, flour, butter and cinnamon until crumbly. Sprinkle over the peaches. • Bake in a 400° oven for 25–30 minutes until top is browned. Serve with whipped cream, if desired.

Mrs. A. C. Nielsen

PEACH-BLUEBERRY KUCHEN

Serves 8

1 cup flour
Pinch salt
2 tablespoons sugar

¼ pound unsalted butter
1 tablespoon white vinegar

Combine all ingredients in a food processor and process until kuchen dough begins to form a ball. With your fingers, press the dough evenly into a 9-inch false bottom cake pan or springform pan and to a height of 1 inch around the sides.

Filling:

1 cup sugar
2 tablespoons flour
½ teaspoon cinnamon

1½ cups peeled, sliced peaches
2 cups blueberries, fresh or frozen

Combine the sugar, flour, cinnamon, peaches and 1 cup blueberries. Turn into prepared crust. Bake at 400° for 1 hour. Remove from oven and sprinkle remaining 1 cup blueberries over the hot pie. Cool in pan before turning out on a serving dish.

Mrs. Stephan M. Minikes

Pieces from the Freer Gallery collection

PRUNE PIE   Serves 12

"Rich and delicious. You'll wonder why
you never tried it before!"

Crust:

8 ounces cream cheese   **1 cup flour**
¼ pound butter

Cream the butter and cream cheese. Add the flour and blend well.
Chill the dough. Roll it out and fit into a 9-inch pie dish, leaving a
generous overhang as dough may shrink. Bake pie shell at 375° for
8–10 minutes.

Filling:

2 pounds pitted prunes   **Rind of both lemons and**
1½ cups sugar   **oranges, chopped**
Juice of 2 lemons   **4 cups water**
Juice of 2 oranges   **Chopped nuts**
                                     1 cup heavy cream, whipped

In a saucepan combine the prunes, sugar, lemon and orange juice and
rinds with the water. Cook until very thick, 30–40 minutes. Pour
mixture into the baked pie shell, sprinkle with the nuts. Chill. Spread
whipped cream over all and serve in small wedges as the pie is very
rich.

Mrs. Rae Viner

GEORGIA PECAN PIE   Serves 8

1 unbaked 9-inch pie shell   **¼ teaspoon salt**
3 eggs, lightly beaten   **2½ teaspoons vanilla**
¾ cup cane syrup or dark   **1 cup pecan halves**
**   corn syrup**   **3 tablespoons melted butter**
¾ cup sugar   **Vanilla ice cream**

Mix eggs and syrup well. Stir in sugar and blend thoroughly. Add salt
and vanilla and mix again. Let stand for 5 minutes. • Spread the
pecans on the bottom of the pie shell in a single layer. • Stir melted
butter into the syrup mixture and pour over the pecans. Allow pecans
to rise to the top. • Bake at 375° for 40–45 minutes or until center
is firm. Cool and serve with vanilla ice cream.

Mrs. Joseph W. Henderson, III

JOSEPH HIRSHHORN'S VINEGAR PIE Serves 5–6

2 tablespoons butter
½ cup sugar
3 tablespoons flour
1 teaspoon cinnamon
¼ teaspoon ground cloves
¼ teaspoon ground allspice

⅛ teaspoon salt
1 egg, lightly beaten
2 tablespoons vinegar
1 cup cold water
1 8-inch pie shell, baked

Cream the butter and sugar in the top of a double boiler. Add flour and seasonings and mix well. Add the egg and vinegar and gradually mix in the water. Stir this mixture over boiling water until thickened. Cool slightly and pour into the baked pie shell. • Bake in a 350° oven for 12–15 minutes.

Olga Hirshhorn

MILE HIGH STRAWBERRY PIE Serves 8

"A frozen dessert—perfect for those who must plan ahead"

1 baked 9 or 10-inch pie shell
10 ounces frozen strawberries, defrosted
¾ cup sugar
2 egg whites

1 tablespoon lemon juice
⅛ teaspoon salt
½ cup heavy cream
1 teaspoon vanilla

Combine defrosted strawberries, sugar, egg whites, lemon juice and salt in a mixing bowl. Beat the mixture at medium speed with an electric mixer until it is stiff and holds its shape. • Whip the cream, flavor it with the vanilla and fold it into the strawberry mixture. Pile this lightly into the baked pie shell and freeze at least several hours. Remove from freezer just before serving.

Carole Butler

MAYONNAISE PIE CRUST Makes 1 9-inch crust

"Excellent for chiffon pies, since the crust is very tender."

1 cup mayonnaise   1 cup sifted flour

Blend the mayonnaise with 1 tablespoon water. Add the flour, blend lightly and press into a ball. On a lightly floured board, roll out dough to fit a 9-inch pie pan. Trim and flute the edges. Prick in several places and chill for 20 minutes or longer. Bake at 425° for 10–12 minutes. (Note: This recipe is best if prepared in cool, dry conditions.)

Manuel E. Ramirez

INTERMISSION DESSERT

Serves 10–12

"George Washington would have loved this."

Pastry:

1¼ cups flour
½ cup soft butter

2 tablespoons sugar
⅓ cup chopped pecans

Combine all ingredients and press into bottom of 11 x 7 x 1½ inch pan. Bake at 400° for 20 minutes. Cool thoroughly.

Cherry topping:

1-pound can tart cherries, pitted
¾ cup cherry juice
⅔ cup sugar
3 tablespoons cornstarch

⅛ teaspoon salt
¼ teaspoon almond extract
Red food coloring

Drain cherries, reserving juice, and set aside. If necessary, add water to juice to make ¾ cup. • Combine juice, sugar, cornstarch and salt in saucepan. Cook, stirring constantly, until thick. Remove from heat and add almond extract and coloring. • Cool slightly and fold in cherries. Let stand until cool.

Cheese filling:

11 ounces cream cheese
1 cup powdered sugar
2 tablespoons milk
1 cup chopped pecans

1 teaspoon vanilla
2 tablespoons sugar
1 cup heavy cream, whipped

Beat together cream cheese, powdered sugar and milk until smooth. Spread over pastry. • Sprinkle pecans over cheese mixture. • Fold vanilla and sugar into whipped cream and spoon over pecans. • Pour cooled cherry topping over all and spread evenly. • Refrigerate at least 8 hours before cutting and serving.

Linnea Bucher

BEVERAGES

Mary Todd Lincoln's dress and tea service
in the Museum of History and Technology

COFFEE PUNCH
Makes 30 cups

"Good for a morning coffee"

1 cup boiling water
1 cup instant coffee
1 cup sugar
5 cups milk

1 quart ginger ale
½ cup Crême de Cocoa or
  to taste
1 quart vanilla ice cream, soft

Combine first 3 ingredients to form a coffee base. Chill. • When ready to serve, pour the coffee base into a punch bowl and add the milk, ginger ale and liqueur. Spoon in the softened ice cream and serve.

Donna Claflin

LE THE GLACE
Serves 8

*"This is a perfect summer drink, even if you cannot
enjoy it in a beautiful embassy garden."*

1 pot strong tea
Juice of 4–6 lemons
Rind of 1 lemon
Rind of orange

1 cucumber, sliced and peeled
Large sprig mint
4 ounces sugar
1½ pints ginger beer

Use Indian or China tea, or a mixture of both, depending on your taste. We use Twinings' Earl Grey. Carefully make about 2 pints of tea. Use 1 teaspoon tea per person, heat the pot first, and be sure the water is boiling when you pour it into the heated pot. • Put the lemon juice (I use 6 lemons), lemon and orange rinds, cucumber slices and rind, mint and sugar in a jug. Try to cut the rinds and peel all in one piece, like a snake; they are best that way. Pour over the hot tea and stir. When cold, add the ginger beer and keep in refrigerator until ready to serve. Serve iced in glasses. (Note: You can alter the recipe according to your taste, using orange and lemon slices, cherries, more or less sugar, but the above recipe is the one we prefer.)

*Lady Henderson
Wife of the Ambassador of
Great Britain*

RUM ICED TEA   Makes 1 large pitcher

"Perfect for a summer luncheon"

1 pot strong tea, such as
   Constant Comment
1 bottle Tom Collins mix

3 jiggers rum
Orange slices

Steep 1 pot of strong tea, cool until moderate in temperature, and pour into a large pitcher. Fill pitcher to ½ full with ice and add the Tom Collins mix and rum. Serve the tea with slices of oranges.

Jane Roberts DeGraff

LEMON POSSET   Serves 4–6

1 pint crème fraîche or
   2 cups heavy cream plus
   2 teaspoons buttermilk
   heated to lukewarm and
   allowed to stand at room
   temperature overnight

Juice and grated rind of
   2 lemons
½ cup dry white wine
Sugar to taste
3 egg whites

Place the crème fraîche in a mixing bowl with the grated lemon rind. Beat until stiff. Stir in the lemon juice and white wine. Add sugar to taste. • Beat the egg whites until they form peaks, then fold them into the whipped cream mixture. Serve in a punch bowl or individual glasses.

Mrs. Sander Vanocur

BELLINI   About 8 drinks

Fresh peaches
Water

Asti Spumante

Drop peaches in boiling water for 1 minute to loosen skin. Peel, pit and purée in a blender or food processor. (You will need about 1 cup peach purée for each bottle of Asti Spumante.) • In each fluted champagne glass place 2 tablespoons peach purée and fill with very cold Asti Spumante. Stir and serve. (Note: If peaches are puréed ahead, cover with lemon juice.)

Mrs. Robert H. Craft, Jr.

APPLE BRANDY PUNCH   Serves 25–30

"Be careful!"

1 pint good Jamaican rum	1 dozen large baked apples
1 gallon apple brandy or whiskey	2 nutmegs, grated ½ teaspoon allspice
1 gallon hot water, well sweetened	½ teaspoon ground cloves Pinch of mace

Mix all ingredients. Let stand 3–4 days. Serve from a punch bowl.

Mrs. Richard E. Shands

PEPPER VODKA   1 bottle

"Served with a smoked salmon appetizer,
this will liven the deadest party!"

1 bottle vodka, any brand	Several stalks fresh dill
2–3 slices hot peppers	Lemon peel, cut in long coils

In a bottle of vodka, place 2–3 slices hot pepper, several stalks of dill and several long thin coils of lemon peel. Allow to stand a minimum of 3 weeks before serving. It will keep indefinitely. Place the vodka bottle in the freezer at least 5–6 hours before serving time as vodka should be served extremely cold. (Note: For an elegant presentation, place the bottle in a slightly wider container, such as an empty 2-pound coffee can, that is as high as the bottom of the bottle neck. Fill the container with water, put in flowers and greenery and freeze. Unmold, place in a shallow silver bowl to collect the drips and serve.)

Mrs. Robert H. Craft, Jr.

KATE'S OLD GEORGETOWN EGGNOG   Serves 12–14

"Must be tested as you go along"

2 cups brandy	12 eggs
1 cup Jamaican rum	¾ cup sugar
½ cup rye whiskey	2 quarts half and half
½ cup dry sherry	

Mix the liquors and allow to settle. • Separate the eggs. In a large mixing bowl, beat yolks lightly and add the sugar. Whisking constantly, slowly add the liquor and then the half and half. Beat the egg whites until stiff and gently fold into the eggnog. Cover and store in refrigerator for several days before serving.

Mrs. Richard E. Shands

SWEDISH JULGLÖGG   Serves many

"This is a traditional cold weather drink, served in
Sweden around the Christmas holidays. Be careful!"

1 gallon apple juice	1½ cups blanched almonds, peeled
1½ cups sugar	
12 whole cloves	1½–2 cups seedless raisins
6 whole cardamons	Peel of ½ orange, cut in strips
6 sticks cinnamon	
½ teaspoon ground ginger	1 gallon red wine
1 slice fresh ginger (optional)	1 liter Aquavit

In a large pot, heat ½ the apple juice, the sugar, all spices, almonds, raisins and orange peel. Bring to a boil and immediately reduce heat. Let simmer for at least 1 hour. Add remaining apple juice. Let stand until ready to serve. • Add wine and heat again. Do not boil! Pour into a large punch bowl and add Aquavit. Ladle into cups to serve.

Mrs. Charles J. DiBona

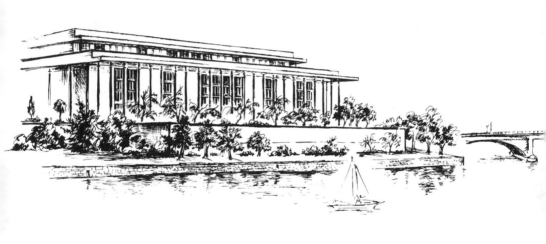

The Kennedy Center, home of The Washington Opera

Index

DESSERTS

Cakes

Cookies

EGGS AND CHEESE

FISH AND SEAFOOD

Fish

Seafood

MEAT

PASTA AND RICE

The Washington Cookbook
P.O. Box 40897   Washington, D.C. 20016

Please send _____ copies of The Washington Cookbook at $8.50 each $ _____

Postage and handling $1.50 per copy _____

Tax (Washington, D.C. residents only) .51 per copy _____

Total enclosed $ _____

Make check or money order payable to The Washington Cookbook and enclose with order.

To: (Please print)

Name _____

Address _____

City _____ State _____ Zip _____

All profits from the sale of these books will go to The Washington Opera

. . . .

The Washington Cookbook
P.O. Box 40897   Washington, D.C. 20016

Please send _____ copies of The Washington Cookbook at $8.50 each $ _____

Postage and handling $1.50 per copy _____

Tax (Washington, D.C. residents only) .51 per copy _____

Total enclosed $ _____

Make check or money order payable to The Washington Cookbook and enclose with order.

To: (Please print)

Name _____

Address _____

City _____ State _____ Zip _____

All profits from the sale of these books will go to The Washington Opera

. . . .

The Washington Cookbook
P.O. Box 40897   Washington, D.C. 20016

Please send _____ copies of The Washington Cookbook at $8.50 each $ _____

Postage and handling $1.50 per copy _____

Tax (Washington, D.C. residents only) .51 per copy _____

Total enclosed $ _____

Make check or money order payable to The Washington Cookbook and enclose with order.

To: (Please print)

Name _____

Address _____

City _____ State _____ Zip _____

All profits from the sale of these books will go to The Washington Opera

The Washington Cookbook
P.O. Box 40897   Washington, D.C. 20016

Please send _____ copies of The Washington Cookbook at $8.50 each $ _____

Postage and handling $1.50 per copy _____

Tax (Washington, D.C. residents only) .51 per copy _____

Total enclosed $ _____

Make check or money order payable to The Washington Cookbook and enclose with order.

To: (Please print)

Name _____

Address _____

City _____ State _____ Zip _____

All profits from the sale of these books will go to The Washington Opera

- -

The Washington Cookbook
P.O. Box 40897   Washington, D.C. 20016

Please send _____ copies of The Washington Cookbook at $8.50 each $ _____

Postage and handling $1.50 per copy _____

Tax (Washington, D.C. residents only) .51 per copy _____

Total enclosed $ _____

Make check or money order payable to The Washington Cookbook and enclose with order.

To: (Please print)

Name _____

Address _____

City _____ State _____ Zip _____

All profits from the sale of these books will go to The Washington Opera

- -

The Washington Cookbook
P.O. Box 40897   Washington, D.C. 20016

Please send _____ copies of The Washington Cookbook at $8.50 each $ _____

Postage and handling $1.50 per copy _____

Tax (Washington, D.C. residents only) .51 per copy _____

Total enclosed $ _____

Make check or money order payable to The Washington Cookbook and enclose with order.

To: (Please print)

Name _____

Address _____

City _____ State _____ Zip _____

All profits from the sale of these books will go to The Washington Opera